Guide to Mammals of the Plains States

Guide to Mammals of the Plains States

J. Knox Jones, Jr.

David M. Armstrong

Jerry R. Choate

University of Nebraska Press

LINCOLN AND LONDON

The paper in this book meets the guidelines for permanence and durability
of the Committee on Production Guidelines for Book Longevity of the
Council on Library Resources.

Library of Congress Cataloging in Publication Data

Jones, J. Knox.
    Guide to mammals of the Plains States.

    Includes index.
    I. Armstrong, David Michael, 1944–   . II. Choate,
Jerry R. III. Title.
QL719.G73J66   1985   599.0978   84-21012
ISBN 0-8032-2562-8 (alk. paper)
ISBN 0-8032-7557-9 (pbk.)

Contents

Figures

Maps

Acknowledgments

We are grateful to a number of colleagues and students for assisting in the preparation of this guidebook. Most important, we should mention Laura Armstrong, Vera Ramirez, and Ted Warm of the University of Colorado; Janice Unrein of Fort Hays State University; and Jean Cokendolpher, Marijane R. Davis, Betty Johnson, Mary Ann Seaman, and Carole J. Young of Texas Tech University for their work in typing the manuscript and preparing illustrations. Also, we thank Ronald K. Chesser and Robert Owen of Texas Tech University for reviewing the distribution maps for mammals in Oklahoma.

A number of individuals and several corporations generously provided photographs of mammals. We thank them collectively here; credits appear in individual figure legends. Especially helpful were Ronn Altig of Mississippi State University, Robert J. Baker of Texas Tech University, Roger W. Barbour of the University of Kentucky, Donald F. Hoffmeister of the University of Illinois, Robert S. Hoffmann and Robert R. Patterson of the University of Kansas, Thomas H. Kunz of Boston University, Floyd E. Potter, Jr., of the Texas Parks and Wildlife Department, Daniel Q. Thompson of the U.S. Fish and Wildlife Service, and John L. Tveten of Baytown, Texas.

Last, we thank our families and our three institutions for at least tolerating us while work on the book was in progress.

Introduction

The Great Plains region was termed the "Great American Desert" by early pioneers from Europe who crossed it—a sea of grass stretching from the well-watered forests of the East to the mountains of the West. Persons who crossed or settled this vast region where East meets West endured environmental hardships that previously were unknown to them or their kin. These same environmental conditions, over the millennia, shaped the adaptations of the native fauna and flora of the Great Plains. How one class of the fauna—the Mammalia—has responded to the rigorous environment of the plains region is the focus of this guidebook.

Although our coverage deliberately is limited to five states—North Dakota, South Dakota, Nebraska, Kansas, and Oklahoma—the potential usefulness of this guidebook is much wider. Mammalian species seldom respect political boundaries. As noted in the description of patterns of mammalian distribution, many of the species of the plains states range well beyond the region treated. Therefore, this guidebook should apply with little exceptions to most of the mammalian fauna of the broad region extending from the Canadian Prairie Provinces southward to northern Mexico and from the Rocky Mountains eastward to the Mississippi River and beyond.

In preparing this book, we tried to take into account all relevant literature published through the end of 1983 (a few entries dated 1984 also are included). Some important references are cited at the end of each species account. Additionally, we took notice of major faunal publications and checklists relating to the five-state region covered here and adjacent states, as follows: Jones et al. (1983) for the Dakotas and Nebraska; Bailey (1927) and Wiehe and Cassel (1978) for North Dakota; Choate and Jones (1982) for South Dakota; Swenk (1908), Jones (1964), and Jones and Choate (1980) for Nebraska; Cockrum (1952), Hall (1955), and Bee et al. (1981) for Kansas; Blair (1939) for Oklahoma; Hazard (1982) for Minnesota; Bowles (1975) for Iowa; Schwartz and Schwartz (1981) for Missouri; Sealander (1979) for Arkansas; Davis

(1974) and Schmidly (1983) for Texas; Findley et al. (1975) for New Mexico; Armstrong (1972) for Colorado; Long (1965) for Wyoming; and Hoffmann and Pattie (1968) for Montana. No comparable publications dealing with the Prairie Provinces of Canada are available, but Beck's (1958) list of Saskatchewan mammals and Soper's (1961) treatment of those in Manitoba proved useful as did Banfield's (1974) *The Mammals of Canada* and the two volumes by Hall (1981) on North America as a whole.

Organization of This Book

Our aim in preparing this guidebook was to provide, among other things, concise accounts of all species of mammals occurring (or that occurred within historic times) in the plains states of North Dakota, South Dakota, Nebraska, Kansas, and Oklahoma. Each species account is limited to one page. Thus it was necessary to select carefully the information presented for each kind of mammal, and still be as complete and accurate as possible, within the space allowed, in covering the biology of each. Knowledgeable readers will sympathize with our having to decide what available data to include and what to exclude from the accounts, particularly for well-studied species. With three exceptions, all resulting from recently published studies, scientific and vernacular names of species follow Jones et al. (1982).

After the introductory sections, there is a checklist, organized by order and family, of the 138 native species of mammals (excluding man) and eight introduced species found in the five-state region, and a key to orders. The following chapters are grouped by mammalian order, with brief introductory remarks and keys preceding the accounts of species (arranged in the same fashion as in the checklist) in each order. In two instances (Rodentia and Carnivora), keys are broken down by family because of the large number of included taxa.

The keys are provided to assist users of this guidebook in identifying mammals of the plains states to a particular species. They consist of pairs of contrasting statements, termed couplets, numbered on the left with the same Arabic numeral (one of which bears a prime sign). Characters of a specimen in hand should best fit one or the other of the statements in a couplet, beginning at the top of the key. At the right of each statement is the number of the couplet to which the user is directed next or the name of the species or group to which the specimen belongs. By carefully selecting characteristics used in progressive couplets of a key, it is possible to provide means of identifying all included taxa.

Characters used in keys are those of adult mammals, although many may also apply to immature individuals. When keying out specimens, you should also consult descriptions of individual species and distribution maps.

Technical terms used in the keys and the species accounts are described in the Glossary. A few, however, will be difficult for the novice to comprehend because they are, by necessity, known primarily to specialists. A millimeter rule or perhaps calipers calibrated in millimeters will be needed to appreciate some key characters, as will a hand lens or low-power binocular microscope. Dental formulae are used in keys and occasionally in the text. The statement "incisors 2/1," for example, means there are two incisors in each half of the upper jaw and one in each half of the lower jaw (see also the Glossary).

No account of the order Primates is included, for its single representative in the plains states, our own species, *Homo sapiens,* is at once too familiar to warrant description and too complex to permit it. One should not, however, lose sight of the fact that humans have been an integral and profoundly influential part of the mammalian fauna of the Great Plains for at least 13,000 years. The overall pattern of the environment of the plains states—drainage, landforms, soils, plant communities, animal communities—bears the indelible stamp of human presence.

For each native species, the information is divided into five categories: Distribution, Description, Habits and Habitat, Reproduction, and Suggested References.

Distribution. A statement of the general (or former) distribution of the mammal and an indication of its range or status in the plains states is given. The distribution of all species (except those introduced to the region and a few that have been extirpated in the wild) is mapped; except as indicated, the historically documented range is shown.

In preparing maps, we consulted primarily Jones et al. (1983) on the Dakotas and Nebraska, Bee et al. (1981) on Kansas, and Hall (1981) on North America as a whole. No up-to-date treatment of mammals in Oklahoma is available, although one is in preparation. To augment scattered published records, we consulted persons knowledgeable of the distribution of mammals in that state.

Description. The general characters of each species, such as size and coloration, along with important distinguishing features or comparisons with closely related taxa, are indicated in telegraphic style. Ranges of measurements for typical adults (thus not necessarily the absolute extremes), usually based on specimens from the plains region, are given in millimeters in conventional sequence: total length, length of tail, length of hind foot, and length of ear (from notch). Length of ear is excluded for insectivores and some pocket gophers, because their ears are small; length of forearm is included for bats. Ranges of weights are given in grams for smaller species and in pounds for larger mammals. Photographs were available for all but two species.

Habits and Habitat. An overall impression of local environments preferred or tolerated by each mammal and its general habits are indicated. Space limitations precluded inclusion of the same kinds of information for all species; thus, an indication of some special aspects of biology—such as molt, longevity, parasites, and predators—may be given for only one or a few species as an example representative of all those in a genus or family.

Reproduction. This section normally includes information on time of breeding, gestation period, and litter size. Occasionally, other data (such as length of lactation of females, duration in time of the family group, size of neonates, and development of young) are also given.

Suggested References. Important published references that appeared before the end of 1983 are listed for each species. Citations are purposely kept to a minimum, no more than five and frequently only one or two. The references and the literature cited therein will lead the interested student to additional sources of information on a particular species. For this purpose, we routinely cited available numbers of the series *Mammalian Species,* published by the American Society of Mammalogists. These are concise but complete accounts of the biology of individual species, including in most cases a lengthy bibliography.

Following the species accounts of native mammals is a short chapter on introduced species and those that occur natively near the borders of the plains states, a glossary of terms used by mammalogists (adapted from Jones et al., 1983), a list of literature cited, and an index to scientific and vernacular names.

Environments of the Plains States

The misconception is widespread that the plains states are a region of monotonous landscapes. It is true that the region encompasses vast tracts of nearly featureless plains, and that huge areas of native ecosystems have been plowed to produce the grains that make the North American plains the "breadbasket of the world." To really understand the environment of an area dominated by grasses and grainfields, however, you must look beyond the rule to the exceptions: ribbons of forest along rivers, prairie wetlands, woodlands perched atop escarpments, sandhills, isolated mountains, mesas, canyons, and cliffs. These breaks in the uniformity of the plains lend a rich pattern to the landscape and provide a rich opportunity for wildlife to flourish.

The environmental pattern of any region represents the sum of interactions of earth and life over time. Living and nonliving systems interacting in a particular place, involving the flow of energy and the exchange of materials, are termed ecosystems. The pattern of ecosystems—native and man-made—reflects patterns in the physical environment (landforms, geology, drainage, climate, soils) and the response of organisms (plants, animals, microbes) to environmental opportunity over time. Let us briefly examine patterns in the physical environment, the biotic environment, and their interactions.

Physiography and Drainage Patterns

Patterns of drainage are important to patterns of mammalian distribution. River systems provide well-watered corridors for mesic-adapted vegetation (and associated fauna) in otherwise dry regions. River valleys pose barriers to the distribution of upland species, and the elevated areas between valleys, in turn, pose barriers to lowland species. Thus, broad patterns of mammalian distribution are likely to show relationships with hydrographic patterns.

Most master streams of the plains states are tributaries of the Mississippi system, and most head in the Rocky Mountains. Therefore, the predominant drainage pattern is from west to east. The majority of the area of the plains states is drained by the Missouri River. The Missouri heads in the mountains of Montana, courses diagonally across the Dakotas, and forms the eastern boundary of Nebraska. On its route across the plains states it receives the waters of myriad tributaries. Tributaries from the west are long, flowing in sinuous channels across the Great Plains, carrying mountain water toward the sea: the Yellowstone, Little Missouri, Cheyenne, White, Niobrara, North Platte, South Platte, Republican, and Kansas rivers. These names have the ring of poetry and adventure; they were the routes of westward exploration and settlement. By pronounced contrast, tributaries of the Missouri from the east are short, flowing as they do off the Missouri Coteau, the line of hills running diagonally across North Dakota into South Dakota. Exceptions to the rule are the James River and the Big Sioux, which drain parts of the eastern Dakotas east of the Missouri Coteau.

The Arkansas River heads in the Rockies of Colorado. It meanders across southwestern Kansas and Oklahoma, where it receives such major tributaries as the Cimarron (which heads in the Raton Section of northern New Mexico and adjacent Colorado) and the Canadian (which heads in the mountains of New Mexico).

The plains states are bounded on the north and the south by two great rivers with the same name. On the north is the Red River, which, gathering the waters of eastern North Dakota, flows northward, eventually to Hudson Bay. This is the only region of the plains states that does not drain to the Gulf of Mexico. Southern Oklahoma is drained by another Red River, the river that forms the sinuous southern boundary of the state. This southern Red River heads on the Llano Estacado of Texas and merges with the Mississippi in Louisiana.

Over the centuries, the rivers of the plains states have helped to shape the course of human history. Over millennia they have, likewise, helped to shape the evolution of the mammalian fauna. Drainage patterns interact with geologic structures to form physiographic patterns. Water courses and bodies of standing water obviously influence the regional and local distribution of vegetation. The importance of drainage to mammalian distribution becomes clear in subsequent sections of this introduction.

Physiography is the study of landforms, the topography of a region. The plains states encompass major parts of one great physiographic division—the Interior Plains—and minor parts of two others—the Interior Highlands and the Atlantic Plains. Physiographic units of the five-state region are indicated on map 1. Some topographic features of note that are used frequently in this book to describe ranges of mammalian species are shown on map 2.

The Interior Plains Division is subdivisible in the plains states (sometimes with difficulty) into two provinces—the Central Lowland Province and the Great Plains Province. The Central Lowlands Province includes the eastern third of the Dakotas, the eastern quarter of Nebraska, the eastern half of Kansas, and most of Oklahoma. This is a region of flat to rolling terrain drained by broad, flat rivers that head mostly outside the province.

The northern part of the Central Lowlands Province was covered by glaciers in at least four successive episodes over the past two million years, in the Pleistocene epoch or Ice Age. (See Glossary under *geologic time.*) This glaciated area, the Western Lake Section, is relatively flat and marked by lakes, the largest of which is Devils Lake, North Dakota. The lakes are remnants of much larger Pleistocene bodies of water, one of which was once continuous with the present-day lakes Manitoba and Winnipeg.

The Turtle Mountains, along the North Dakota–Manitoba boundary, are an outlying remnant of a formerly more extensive Missouri Plateau. Rising more than a thousand feet above the surrounding plain, these hills are an island of forest habitat in a sea of agriculture, and they are important to the richness of the mammalian species in the plains states, as are the Pembina Hills farther east. To the south, in eastern Nebraska and northeastern Kansas, lie the Dissected Till Plains. (Till is material left behind as glaciers recede.) Tributaries of the Missouri and Kansas rivers have carved the till plains into an area of high relief.

Still farther south, in southeastern Kansas and in Oklahoma, lie the Osage Plains. This area was not glaciated and shows gentler relief than the till plains. It is drained by the Arkansas and Red rivers. In southern Oklahoma, two smaller uplifts rise above the Osage Plains, adding ecological diversity—the Wichita Mountains and the Arbuckle Mountains.

To the west of the Central Lowlands lie the Great Plains, the other province of the Interior Plains Division. The boundary between the Central Lowlands and the Great Plains is marked in the Dakotas by the Missouri Coteau, a long ridge of low hills. This is a moraine representing the southwesternmost extent of Pleistocene ice.

The Great Plains are more complicated than one might suspect at first. The northern portion is the Missouri Plateau, comprising the western Dakotas. The northern part of the region was glaciated; the southern part was not. The Unglaciated Missouri Plateau is widely eroded into badlands, the most famous of which were carved by the White and Cheyenne rivers in South Dakota and the Little Missouri in North Dakota. Between the Missouri Plateau and the High Plains farther south lies an escarpment, the Pine Ridge, so named because it is clothed with ponderosa pine. This and analogous features elsewhere on the plains (Slim Buttes, Wildcat Hills) add topographic diversity and ecological interest to the region.

One of earth's largest flat regions is the High Plains, which stretch from western Nebraska to West Texas, including western Kansas and most of the Oklahoma Panhandle. This flat landscape resulted from level layers of outwash derived from the Rocky Mountains to the west, long undisturbed by most of the forces that change the earth's crust. The only relief in the area is due to cutting by streams, but the region is dry, so such cutting is confined mostly to the eastern edge of the High Plains. Through-flowing streams from the west lie in broad flood plains.

The northern part of the High Plains does not appear to be flat because overlying it is the largest dune system in North America—the Nebraska Sandhills—a feature of Pleistocene age that is still only partially stabilized. The Sandhills are a beautiful, distinctive, and well-preserved region, the exposed water table supporting a vast system of wetlands interspersed with immense hills covered with grass, sagebrush, and soapweed.

The highest elevations in the plains states are reached in the Black Hills of South Dakota. The Black Hills are an elliptical dome some 60 miles wide and 125 miles long, rising 4,000 feet above the Missouri Plateau. They were formed by a core of Precambrian rock some 600 million years old that was pushed up through thousands of feet of younger sediments. The younger sedimentary rocks were stood on end and have weathered, leaving the metamorphic core surrounded by concentric rings of progressively younger sedimentary formations. The montane island of the Black Hills provides habitat for a rich ecosystem that has faunal affinities both with the Rocky Mountains to the west and the boreal forest to the northeast. In addition, large caverns dissolved in the limestones of the area provide habitat for a diverse bat fauna.

In central Kansas and adjacent small areas of Nebraska and Oklahoma, is a region referred to as the Plains Border. Here, headward cutting is pushing the boundary of the High Plains westward. The Plains Border is a region of physiographic transition between the Central Lowlands and the High Plains. It is an area of significant ecological transition as well.

In Tertiary times, volcanism near the Southern Rockies produced flows of lava that capped soft Great Plains sediments, thus protecting them from erosion. The result is the Raton Section, a distinctive mesa area in northeastern

A. Central Lowlands
   1. Western Lake Section
   2. Dissected Till Plains
   3. Osage Plains
B. Great Plains
   1. Glaciated Missouri Plateau
   2. Unglaciated Missouri Plateau
   3. Black Hills
   4. High Plains
   5. Plains Border
   6. Raton Section
C. Interior Highlands
   1. Ozark Plateau
   2. Ouachita Mountains
D. Coastal Plain

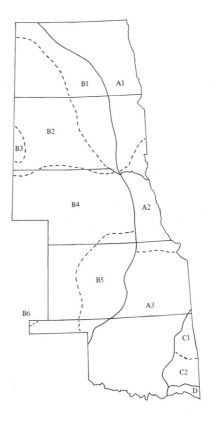

Map 1. Approximate boundaries of physiographic regions of the plains states (modified after Fenneman 1931 and 1938, and subsequent sources).

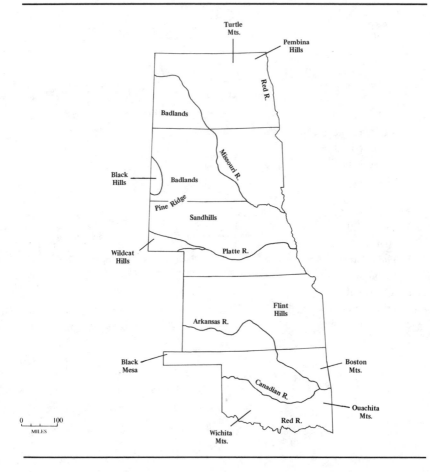

Map 2. Major topographic features of the plains states.

New Mexico and adjacent Colorado that also encompasses the northwestern corner of the Oklahoma Panhandle, the Black Mesa. The Raton Section supports a distinctive biotic community, including eight mammalian species that occur nowhere else in the plains states.

The Interior Highlands Division is a small fraction of the area of the plains states, but the region—consisting of two mountain provinces and the intervening Arkansas Valley—adds a great deal of ecological interest. In southeastern Oklahoma lie the Ouachita Mountains. This area is typified by low mountains and intervening valleys, remnants of a much grander mountain range related to the Appalachians. The mountains were built of Paleozoic rocks in late Mesozoic time, and through the Cenozoic era have been much eroded. They appear today as hills a few hundred feet above valley floors.

To the north of the Ouachita Mountains is the western end of the Ozark Plateau, which encompasses part of northeastern Oklahoma. In particular, the Ozarks of Oklahoma are the west end of the Boston Mountains. In this dissected region, ridges are 500 to 1,000 feet above valleys and the result is an area of topographic interest and rich ecological contrast. Like that of the Ouachita Mountains to the south, formation of the Boston Mountains was related to the evolution of the Appalachians.

Extreme southeastern Oklahoma lies in the Coastal Plain Province of the Atlantic Plains Division. South of the Ouachita and Arbuckle mountains and east of the Edwards Escarpment, this small area is important to the ecological complexity of the plains states, for it has the lowest elevations, highest rainfall, and mildest temperatures in the region. The Oklahoma segment of the Coastal Plain includes the floodplain of the Red River and the adjacent Grand Prairie.

Topography underlies drainage and the geologic foundations provide the parent material for soils. Because soils interact with vegetation, it comes as no surprise that landforms and general ecological patterns are strongly related.

Climate

A single word describes the climate of the plains states—variable. Whoever named it the "temperate zone" did not live in the plains states; the climate is not only intemperate, it is unpredictable. The extremes are due to the generally high elevation of the area. The elevation averages more than 2,000 feet and ranges from 287 feet in southeastern Oklahoma to well above 5,000 feet in western South Dakota and Nebraska. The maximum elevation of 7,242 feet is atop Harney Peak in the Black Hills. In addition, the plains states are distant from the ocean and hence from the ameliorating effects of moist maritime wind systems. These two factors—elevation and distance from the sea—combine to produce a continental climate, with pronounced seasonal and daily fluctuations in temperature and moisture, and climatic unpredictability from one year to the next. Continentality increases from southeast to northwest across the plains states.

One major factor of climate is precipitation. This varies widely but in an orderly manner across the plains states. The highest mean annual precipitation (56 inches) is in extreme southeastern Oklahoma; the lowest mean annual precipitation (as low as 13 inches) is in the western Dakotas. Between those extremes, isohyets (lines connecting points of equal rainfall) have a general north-south orientation, with the mean annual precipitation decreasing four to eight inches per hundred miles westward. Over much of the plains states, most precipitation comes as rain during the warmer months, often in the form of torrential thunderstorms.

As might be expected, temperatures decrease from south to north across the plains region. Mean July temperatures are in the 70s over the northern and central plains, and in the 80s over most of Kansas and Oklahoma. Mean January temperatures are zoned more finely; grading from 40 to 50°F in southern Oklahoma, to 10 to 20°F over most of North Dakota, and to a low mean between 0 and 10°F in the extreme northeastern part of the region.

The usual daily range of temperatures tends to be greater in the drier western part of the region than in the more humid east, because atmospheric water vapor is a temperature buffer. Because of lower humidity, the western part of the region is also sunnier. The 20-inch isohyet—which runs in a generally south-southwesterly direction from the southeastern corner of North Dakota to the eastern edge of the Oklahoma Panhandle—roughly marks the transition from the humid farming country of the Middle West to the more arid ranching country of the West. Thus, climatic patterns underlie ecological and cultural patterns in the landscape.

Soils

Soils integrate the effects of climate, vegetation, and geologic parent material to form a pronounced pattern in the landscape. You might think of the mosaic of soils as a pattern of opportunity. Humans have responded to that opportunity with a variety of agricultural enterprises. The rich, heavy soils of eastern North Dakota produce potatoes; the black loams of Nebraska produce corn; the brown soils of central Kansas produce wheat; the Sandhills of Nebraska produce grass and, indirectly, beef. Similarly, soils present diverse opportunities to wild mammals. Plains pocket gophers prefer deep loams, northern pocket gophers occupy rocky soils, and chestnut-faced pocket gophers live in clay soils. Kangaroo rats, plains pocket mice, and spotted ground squirrels inhabit dune sand. Eastern moles burrow in loams. Plains harvest mice prefer rocky pasturelands. Given the preferences of particular mammals for particular soil types, the pattern of soils partially underlies patterns of mammalian distribution and abundance.

The eastern Dakotas, eastern Nebraska, and central Kansas are characterized by chernozem soils (from the Russian for "black soil"), the deep, dark soils that develop under tall-grass prairie. Farther west, soils are paler in color. Chestnut soils developed under mixed-grass prairie and brown soils (in extreme western Kansas and the Oklahoma Panhandle) developed under true short-grass prairie. Podzols develop under forests. A true podzol, which develops in a cool, humid climate, is found on the Turtle Mountains, along the North Dakota–Manitoba boundary. Podzols also developed on the mountains and plateaus of eastern Oklahoma, but these are reddish to yellowish soils, not the dark podzols of the north. Planosols have developed extensively under grassland or forest on uplands in south-central Nebraska and adjacent parts of Kansas, and in southeastern Kansas and adjacent areas in Oklahoma. Such soils are neither as friable nor as fertile as true prairie soils; the surface is strongly leached of nutrients and a hardpan typically is present.

In south-central Oklahoma, a distinctive type of soil occurs, termed rendzina. Such soils are grayish brown to black, overlaid with yellowish calcareous materials. They developed under either grassland or deciduous forest. Soils elsewhere in Oklahoma and southwestern Kansas are reddish chestnut soils, similar to chestnut soils farther north but developed under grasses and shrubs in a warmer climate. Like chestnut soils generally, these reddish soils show a distinct hardpan of lime.

At various places in the five-state region, the land is sufficiently unstable that mature soils with distinctive horizons (zones or layers) never develop. The largest such area is the Nebraska Sandhills, marked by undifferentiated dune sand. Large areas of western South Dakota are covered with undeveloped clays weathered from shale. Parts of the Oklahoma Panhandle, the Black Hills, the Badlands, and the Wichita and Arbuckle mountains are sufficiently rugged that soils are poorly developed. Furthermore, the floodplains of master streams of the region have soils that are poorly developed because such ecosystems are subject to periodic flooding. Such alluvial soils may be rich in nutrients, but they do not exhibit the zones typical of mature soils.

Ecosystems

Life and earth interact on a global scale in the ecosphere (the ecosphere is the sum of all processes linking living organisms with each other and with their nonliving environment). On a regional scale the ecosphere is divisible into a variety of kinds of ecosystems, or volumes of environment, including living organisms (the biotic community) and their abiotic (nonliving) resources. Living and nonliving components of ecosystems interact to exchange materials. Most ecosystems are powered by the energy of the sun.

In an aerial view of the plains states, patterns in the living landscape are striking. The most obvious component is the mosaic of vegetation (map 3), which is patterned because the physical environment (climate and geologic substrate) is also patterned. Vegetation, climate, and geologic parent material interact to form a pattern of soils. Animals (including humans) interact with vegetation and soils to complicate the pattern further. Some understanding of the complex patterns in the living environment is essential to understanding the distribution and abundance of mammalian species.

Broadly speaking, categorized by the dominant plants, the ecosystems of the plains states are of two sorts: grasslands (dominated by herbaceous plants), and shrublands, forests, and woodlands (dominated by woody plants). These basic types of ecosystems are by no means mutually exclusive—they overlap, interdigitate, and blend together. They are distinctive enough, however, to lend pattern to the landscape, and each provides habitat for a rather distinctive group of mammalian species.

Within each of these broad ecosystems are a variety of distinctive biotic communities. Some, like the short-grass prairies, are vast areas; others, such as piñon-juniper woodlands, are of restricted occurrence in the plains states. Whatever their extent, these biotic communities add environmental diversity to the region and thereby increase ecological opportunity for the mammalian fauna.

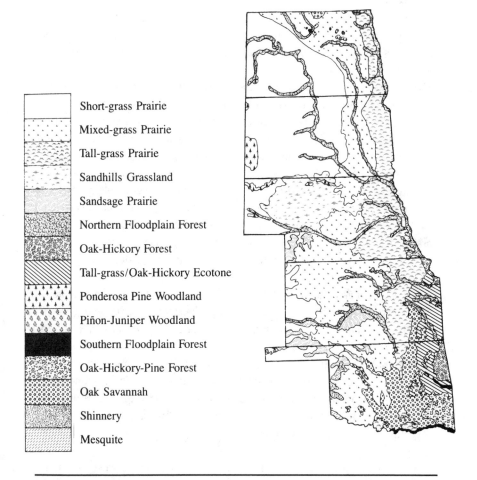

Short-grass Prairie

Mixed-grass Prairie

Tall-grass Prairie

Sandhills Grassland

Sandsage Prairie

Northern Floodplain Forest

Oak-Hickory Forest

Tall-grass/Oak-Hickory Ecotone

Ponderosa Pine Woodland

Piñon-Juniper Woodland

Southern Floodplain Forest

Oak-Hickory-Pine Forest

Oak Savannah

Shinnery

Mesquite

Map 3. Vegetation of the plains states (after U.S. Forest Service, 1978).

Grasslands

The predominant vegetation over most of the five-state region is grass. Native grasslands have been widely altered by humans. We shall consider the fauna of man-made habitats shortly. For now, let us consider native ecosystems, bearing in mind that some of these ecosystems persist only as remnants, incapable of supporting the entire mammalian fauna once characteristic of them.

Short-grass Prairie. Native grasslands in the western parts of the plains states consist mostly of short-grass species. Shoots of such grasses are low in stature but have extensive root systems. In the south, species that exhibit these adaptations to arid conditions include sod-formers such as buffalograss (*Buchloë dactyloides*) and some of the gramas (*Bouteloua*). In the north, bunchgrasses such as needlegrass (*Stipa comata*), and sod-forming species such as western wheatgrass (*Agropyron smithii*), predominate. Heavy grazing in both areas favors the spread of prickly pear (*Opuntia*) and small soapweed (*Yucca glauca*). Mammals characteristic of short-grass rangeland include the black-tailed prairie dog, thirteen-lined ground squirrel, silky pocket mouse, plains pocket mouse, swift fox, black-footed ferret, pronghorn, and bison.

Tall-grass Prairie. Native grasslands in the eastern part of the plains states are dominated by tall grasses, especially big bluestem (*Andropogon gerardii*), switchgrass (*Panicum virgatum*), and Indiangrass (*Sorghastrum nutans*). Mammalian species typical of the tall-grass prairie include the least shrew, eastern mole, Franklin's ground squirrel, plains pocket gopher, western harvest mouse, prairie vole, and—in the southern part of the region—hispid cotton rat. Bison and wapiti (American elk) once grazed these prairies, many of which are now plowed and given over to row crops, including corn, sorghum, soybeans, and potatoes.

Mixed-grass Prairie. Between the short-grass prairie in the west and the tall-grass prairie in the east is a zone in which the predominant vegetation is a mixture of tall-grass and short-grass species. Tall-grass varieties, such as big bluestem, ordinarily occur in mesic lowlands, whereas short-grass species, such as blue grama (*Bouteloua gracilis*), occur on level uplands. Species of intermediate stature, including little bluestem (*Schizachyrium scoparium*) and sideoats grama (*Bouteloua curtipendula*) occupy hillsides and depressions. The distribution of tall-grass species contracts in dry years and expands in wet years. The species of mammals dependent on features of habitat afforded by tall-grass or short-grass species also fluctuate in distribution from year to year. Heavy grazing converts mixed-grass prairie to short-grass prairie.

Mammals typical of the mixed-grass prairie include the hispid pocket mouse and the badger. Species more abundant on short-grass and tall-grass prairies also inhabit the region.

Sandhills Grassland. The vast Sandhills of central and western Nebraska are clothed with bluestem (*Andropogon*) and sandreed (*Calamovilfa*). The water table is exposed between the hills, creating myriad wetlands. Uplands provide the habitat for several species typical of mixed-grass prairie; species such as the plains pocket mouse and Ord's kangaroo rat seem to be in their optimal habitat in the Sandhills. Wetlands in the Sandhills provide an abundant habitat for such species as the meadow vole and the muskrat.

Sandsage Prairie. On sandy hills in southwestern Nebraska, south-central Kansas, and western Oklahoma, a distinctive grassland characterized by sand sagebrush (*Artemisia filifolia*) and little bluestem (*Schizachyrium scoparium*) occurs. The eastern mole reaches its western limits in such regions, and the least shrew, spotted ground squirrel, and northern grasshopper mouse are especially common there.

Prairie Wetlands. Pond margins, marshes, and potholes occur locally across the plains states. Often they are dominated by tall grasses, sedges (*Carex*), rushes (*Scirpus*), and cattails (*Typha*). Many native wetlands have been drained, but others have been created around gravel pits, irrigation works, and other impoundments. Mammals typical of prairie wetlands include the masked shrew, meadow vole, muskrat, southern bog lemming, meadow jumping mouse, and mink.

Forests, Woodlands, and Shrublands

Wooded ecosystems cover less than 10 percent of the area of the plains states, and in the western half of the region no more than 1 or 2 percent, but the importance of such ecosystems to the overall diversity of mammals is great. Wooded ecosystems appear to be more widespread than they are in fact because many towns and cities across the plains are densely wooded. In addition, shelterbelts about farmsteads have increased the acreage of woodland. Still, wooded country is the exception to the rule on the Great Plains.

Woodlands of the plains states are of several kinds. Some are of local extent, being more widespread in areas to the east or west adjacent to the five-state region.

Northern Floodplain Forest. This type of forest, the most frequently occurring kind of woodland on the plains, is dominated by cottonwoods (*Populus*), willows (*Salix*), and, to the east, elms (*Ulmus*). There may be a rich undergrowth of shrubs. This is a riparian community (occurring along watercourses across the plains); it is more widespread and more continuous than it was a century ago, because floods and prairie fires have been controlled and irrigated plantings in towns and cities (most of which are along riparian corridors) and farm shelterbelts augment the forest. Floodplain forest, however, still covers less than 5 percent of the area of the plains states. A productive corridor of moist shelter threading through the prairie, riparian forest greatly enriches the ecological opportunity for mammals, supporting such species as the opossum, eastern cottontail, fox squirrel, white-footed mouse, eastern woodrat, raccoon, red fox, and white-tailed deer.

In northern North Dakota on the Turtle Mountains, the Killdeer Mountains, and the Pembina Hills, riparian woodland supports some elements of the Great Lakes forest, especially paper birch (*Betula papyrifera*) and aspen (*Populus tremuloides*). Some mammalian species (the arctic shrew, marten, snowshoe hare, moose, and formerly the fisher, wolverine, and caribou) are more or less restricted in the plains states to that area. In addition, these forested uplands share with the Black Hills the least chipmunk, red squirrel, northern flying squirrel, and southern red-backed vole.

Oak-Hickory Forest. In the eastern parts of Nebraska, Kansas, and Oklahoma occurs a forest typical of the Ohio and Mississippi valleys to the east, an oak-hickory (*Quercus-Carya*) forest. Often this forest covers steep hillsides, with riparian forest in the valleys and prairie grassland (or agricultural ecosystems) on gentle hillsides and hilltops. This is the habitat of the eastern chipmunk, gray squirrel, southern flying squirrel, and woodland vole, in addition to many species typical of riparian forest.

Ponderosa Pine Woodland. Ponderosa pine (*Pinus ponderosa*) occurs on the Black Hills of South Dakota; on buttes and escarpments of badlands along the Little Missouri, Cheyenne, and White rivers; and in Nebraska on the Pine Ridge and the Wildcat Hills, and along the Niobrara River. The undergrowth includes wheatgrass, blue grama, and needlegrass. In some of the higher parts of the Black Hills, especially on north-facing slopes, isolated stands of aspen, lodgepole pine (*Pinus contorta*), and white spruce (*Picea glauca*) can be found. Mammals of this community that occur on the Black Hills include the Nuttall's cottontail, yellow-bellied marmot, red squirrel, long-tailed vole, southern red-backed vole, least chipmunk, bushy-tailed woodrat, and (until recently) bighorn sheep. The latter three species are known from other scarp (steep cliffs) woodlands in the western Dakotas and Nebraska, but only the bighorn sheep occurred along the Niobrara.

Piñon-Juniper Woodland. This community type, so widespread in the southwestern United States, occurs in the plains states only at the northwestern tip of the Oklahoma Panhandle. There it provides the only habitat in the five-state region suitable for such species as the Mexican woodrat, piñon mouse, rock mouse, Colorado chipmunk, and rock squirrel.

Southern Floodplain Forest. This is the typical ecosystem of the lower Mississippi Valley. Southern floodplain forest occurs in the five-state region only along the Arkansas and Red rivers in eastern Oklahoma. The forest is dominated by oaks and black gum or tupelo (*Nyssa aquatica*); the wettest areas also include baldcypress (*Taxodium distichium*). There is a profuse undergrowth of herbs, shrubs, and vines. The southern floodplain forest provides habitat for a wide variety of mammals, and the swamp rabbit, cotton mouse, and golden mouse are restricted in the plains states to this and similar ecosystems.

Oak-Hickory-Pine Forest. In southeastern Oklahoma, there is a forest of oak, hickory, and pine typical of uplands of the Gulf Coast states. This ecosystem is rich in mammalian species, and a number of taxa with southeastern affinities (the swamp rabbit, cotton mouse, southeastern myotis, social myotis, Rafinesque's big-eared bat, and red wolf) reach their northern and western limits here and in the adjacent floodplain forests. Openings in the forest are the habitat of Baird's pocket gopher, the marsh rice rat, and the eastern harvest mouse.

Oak Savanna. Savannas are grasslands interspersed with trees; they tend to have some ecological characteristics of both woodlands and grasslands. Uplands rising from the plains of central and eastern North Dakota support a savanna of oak and big bluestem. This area is inhabited by some woodland mammals as well as grassland species. Savannas are examples of ecotones, areas of overlap between adjacent ecosystems. Ecotones often show higher species diversity and greater productivity than ecosystems on either side. Another oak savanna in eastern Oklahoma and adjacent Kansas is composed of post oak (*Quercus stellata*), blackjack oak (*Q. marilandica*), and big bluestem prairie, the so-called Cross Timbers. Occurring on dissected terrain, this is habitat for the eastern woodrat, opossum, striped skunk, and Texas mouse, as well as a variety of grassland species, such as the prairie vole.

Shinnery. Savannas and shrublands of shinnery oak (*Quercus mohriana*) mixed with little bluestem occur along the Canadian River drainage of western Oklahoma. This is the habitat of mammals such as the black-tailed jackrabbit, spotted ground squirrel, plains harvest mouse, northern grasshopper mouse, and southern plains woodrat.

Mesquite. In southwestern Oklahoma, there is an ecosystem that is quite widespread in adjacent Texas, a shrubland of mesquite (*Prosopis julifora*). This ecosystem supports a variety of drought-adapted mammals, including many of the species of the adjacent shinnery shrublands.

Replacement Ecosystems

Ecosystems are pieces of environment, with living things and their nonliving resources interacting in cycles of materials and exchanges of energy. Under that definition, cornfields are ecosystems and so are abandoned city lots, pastures, and highway rights-of-way. Such habitats represent for native wildlife the leftovers of civilization. Some species can tolerate man-made habitats and some cannot.

In the most disturbed sites one expects primarily introduced species such as house mice and Norway rats, which are Eurasian invaders on the plains, living on the waste of industrial civilization but for the most part unable to move into native ecosystems. Several generalized native mammals, however, such as deer mice, thrive in such areas. A wide variety of native species prosper in suburban areas and around farmsteads. Representative species include the opossum, big brown bat, deer mouse, fox squirrel, woodchuck, coyote, raccoon, striped skunk, and white-tailed deer.

Overgrazed rangeland is a favored habitat of the black-tailed prairie dog and the thirteen-lined ground squirrel. The deer mouse and hispid pocket mouse live in irrigated corn, the plains pocket gopher in hayfields, harvest mice and pocket mice in wheat, the hispid cotton rat in sunflowers, and the eastern mole and thirteen-lined ground squirrel in cemeteries, lawns, and golf courses.

In short, some species have adapted fairly well to the presence of humans on the plains, but others have not. The bison and the gray wolf went early and so did the grizzly bear, bighorn sheep, and wapiti. The black-footed ferret was nudged toward extinction as prairie dogs were poisoned to make room for wheat and cattle. Native mammals of the woodlands and the mixed-grass prairie are in rather good shape. Vast tracts of their habitat remain unbroken in the plains states and adjacent areas. Species of the tall-grass prairie, for example, Franklin's ground squirrel, however, have not fared so well, and neither have species dependent on clean water (such as the river otter) or those that require freedom from human persecution (such as the gray wolf and the red wolf).

The mammals of the plains states today represent a piece of an integrated, functioning, symbiotic fauna that once existed in the region. Through a little conscious effort and considerable good luck, that remaining piece is a major portion of the fauna. Its continuing persistence, however, is in some doubt. The rich fauna of the plains states depends on a rich mosaic of native habitats. Preservation of that mosaic is in our hands. To future generations we owe the tenacious grip of thoughtful management.

Patterns of Mammalian Distribution

We have looked at a variety of patterns in the landscape of the plains states: patterns of landforms and climate, vegetation and soils. From the standpoint of mammals—both human and nonhuman—these patterns represent a mosaic of opportunity. We have also seen how particular environmental features favor particular species (further details of habitat are provided in the accounts of individual species below). Now look briefly at the overall pattern made by the mammalian fauna itself.

The distributions of mammalian species are shown throughout this handbook in a series of maps. Glance at some of those maps. You will note that all but a few species reach limits somewhere in the plains states. They reach a point where environmental conditions (biotic or abiotic or some combination) no longer meet their needs. Only 18 species (13 percent of the native fauna) find no broad distributional limit in the plains region. Of those, several (the black bear, mountain lion, wapiti, and bison) are large, wide-ranging species that have been extirpated, or nearly so, from the plains since the advent of permanent settlement. Others are (or were) broadly distributed but narrowly restricted in habitat (the silver-haired bat, hoary bat, beaver, muskrat, red fox, mink, river otter, and raccoon). Thus, only about six mammalian species even come close to being present throughout the five-state region: the big brown bat, coyote, long-tailed weasel, striped skunk, bobcat, and white-tailed deer. Even those species are not truly ubiquitous. None of them lives in areas without cover or in areas of open water, and all thus reach local limits.

Why are there such limits of habitation? Why do nearly 90 percent of native mammals occupy less than the whole five-state region? The answer lies in the genetic makeup of each individual mammal. The cellular nuclei contain the genetic codes (giant molecules of DNA) that provide instructions on how to make a living—how and what to eat, how to utilize cover and avoid perils both living and physical, how to communicate, how and when to reproduce. That information sets limits to distribution (even those species that know no limits in the plains states meet limits elsewhere).

Where a species limit occurs, it inscribes in a sense a line on the landscape, although the position of the limit may change over time. Marginal individuals may die and the limit may contract a bit; dispersing young move the limit out a little. Changing climate may shift resources, the base of opportunity, and the species will shift apace. Despite these changes, however, the distributional limit of a species may be described as a line on a map.

Leafing through a series of distribution maps, you can see that limits do not occur at random; they seem to form a pattern. This pattern becomes more obvious when a number of limits are combined on a single map, as in map 4. That map shows, superimposed, the distributional limits of the 120 native mammalian species that reach limits in the plains states.

At first glance, map 4 may seem to have no more pattern than a plate of spaghetti, but take a longer look. It is true that a number of limits fall with little pattern across the central plains, but if you dissect them carefully, you can learn a great deal about history and ecology. The most pronounced patterns are those about the edges of the map. Many species have, in a sense, only peripheral distribution in the plains states, but they add greatly to species richness. For example, in northeastern North Dakota, several members of the fauna of the boreal coniferous forest reach limits together in the Turtle Mountains and the Pembina Hills. Among them are such species as the marten, fisher, and caribou. A bit more widespread, but still confined to the northeastern part of the region are the arctic shrew, pygmy shrew, water shrew, snowshoe hare, western jumping mouse, ermine, and moose.

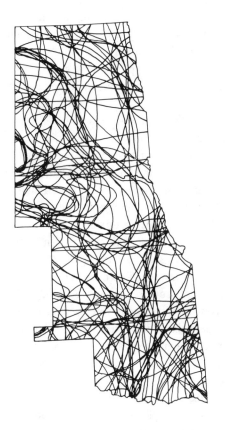

0 _____ 100
MILES

Map 4. Distributional patterns of plains mammals (see text).

The Black Hills of western South Dakota have a fauna more reminiscent of that of the Central Rocky Mountains to the west, and thus distinctive from that of the Great Plains generally. Species restricted in the plains states to the Black Hills are the yellow-bellied marmot and the long-tailed vole. In addition, the northern flying squirrel, red squirrel, and southern red-backed vole are shared with the Turtle Mountains and adjacent areas of North Dakota but are absent from the intervening plains. The wolverine formerly followed the same pattern, and so did the lynx, although these two species once ranged also through open country.

Occasionally the Great Plains are marked by escarpments, canyons, and other broken country. Wherever that happens, a few species will seize the opportunity of the unique habitat, adding their limits to the overall pattern of the landscape. For example, the bushy-tailed woodrat, least chipmunk, long-legged myotis, and fringed myotis occur eastward on the Pine Ridge of northwestern Nebraska and in the badlands of the western Dakotas, and the bighorn sheep once did. Along the steep bluffs above the Niobrara River in northern Nebraska an outlying, relict population of eastern woodrats occurs.

The most distinctive of such patterns is the Black Mesa of Oklahoma. The physiography of the northwestern tip of the Oklahoma Panhandle is unique in the plains states. Its lava-covered mesas are continuous into southern Colorado and northern New Mexico, and the area's characteristic southwestern fauna is also found nowhere else in the plains region. That fauna includes the Yuma myotis, Colorado chipmunk, rock squirrel, rock mouse, piñon mouse, white-throated woodrat, Mexican woodrat, and western spotted skunk. The chestnut-faced pocket gopher almost shares the same pattern, but it also occurs at the base of the mesas and farther east in the Panhandle, as well as in southwestern Kansas. (This pocket gopher is one of a number of species in the region with a range that appears to be changing rapidly at the present time.) The big free-tailed bat also occurs in this area but may not be a permanent resident.

Some species occur in the plains states only in the southwest—in western Oklahoma and, to a lesser extent, southwestern Kansas. This is a topographically diverse area including the Wichita Mountains and the Gypsum Hills. A number of species of the southern plains reach limits there: the cave myotis, western pipistrelle, pallid bat, Texas kangaroo rat, and southern plains woodrat. Townsend's big-eared bat partially shares this pattern, but it also occurs in the Black Hills region and in the Ozarks.

In eastern Oklahoma, there are two general landscapes seen nowhere else in the plains states. They are the Ozark and Ouachita highlands and the intervening Arkansas and Red river valleys. The highlands and lowlands each provide access to the plains states for species of mammalian faunas that have distributions centered elsewhere. On the highlands are such species as the gray myotis, social myotis, and Rafinesque's big-eared bat; the Texas mouse shares the pattern also. The lowlands are even richer in distinctive taxa—the southern short-tailed shrew, southeastern myotis, Seminole bat, swamp rabbit, Baird's pocket gopher, marsh rice rat, cotton mouse, eastern and fulvous harvest mice, golden mouse, and red wolf. A few of these species occur northward into southeastern Kansas.

The distinctiveness of the southeastern part of the region is accentuated by the conspicuous absence of mammalian species that are widespread over the plains states generally: the eastern mole, small-footed myotis, thirteen-lined ground squirrel, plains pocket gopher, deer mouse, gray wolf, badger, mule deer, and pronghorn.

The rivers of the plains states provide corridors of habitat on the Great Plains for a number of mammalian species poorly suited to open country. Often these riparian corridors are narrow. In some places they have been disturbed, their continuity interrupted by grazing, fire, or water projects. In other places, they have been augmented by human activities and supplemented by shelterbelts and urban plantings. Species restricted to riparian corridors in the western part of the region frequently are more generally distributed in the east. Where mammalian species of deciduous forest reach limits, those limits lend a pattern to the landscape that, however subtle, is important to our understanding of the environments of the Great Plains. Among such species are the beaver, Keen's myotis, red bat, eastern cottontail, gray squirrel, fox squirrel, red bat, white-footed mouse, eastern woodrat, gray fox, and river otter.

Species that are more closely restricted to eastern forest habitats and that do not follow riparian corridors westward are the eastern chipmunk and the woodchuck, and in the southern part of the region, the eastern pipistrelle, evening bat, southern flying squirrel, and pine vole.

Wetlands are also associated mainly with riparian corridors. Such situations, like deciduous forest, have been much modified since permanent settlement in the plains states, but they still provide habitats that greatly enrich the fauna of the region. Species of wetlands include the masked shrew, meadow vole, meadow jumping mouse, southern bog lemming, and muskrat. Wetlands and deciduous forest both are occupied by such species as the red fox, raccoon, mink, and eastern spotted skunk.

We have noted how islands and peninsulas of suitable habitat have provided, over time, resources for a wide variety of species that have a principal range elsewhere—to the north, east, southeast, southwest, or west of the plains states. There remain, however, a number of species typical of the Great Plains proper. And even in the limits of those species there are patterns. A few mammals range widely throughout the Great Plains: the thirteen-lined ground squirrel, plains pocket gopher, western harvest mouse, deer mouse, northern grasshopper mouse, prairie vole, swift fox, pronghorn, and bison, for example. Beyond this group of generally distributed plains species, some mammals meet east-west limits and others reach north-south limits. Species widespread across the Great Plains but limited to the southern part of the region are the least shrew, Elliot's short-tailed shrew, eastern mole, nine-banded armadillo, Brazilian free-tailed bat, black-tailed jackrabbit, spotted ground squirrel, hispid cotton rat, and ringtail. The desert shrew occurs only in Oklahoma.

The white-ankled mouse has one of the most restricted ranges of mammals of the plains states, occurring only in extreme southern Oklahoma (Love County). By contrast, species limited to the northern part of the region are the northern short-tailed shrew, white-tailed jackrabbit, Richardson's ground squirrel, olive-backed pocket mouse, and least weasel. Widespread across the central plains but reaching both northern and southern (or southeastern) limits are the plains pocket mouse, hispid pocket mouse, and plains harvest mouse.

Only one species is strictly limited to the tall-grass and mixed-grass prairie—Franklin's ground squirrel. A greater number of species are limited to the short-grass and mixed-grass prairie of the western part of the region—the desert cottontail, black-tailed prairie dog, silky pocket mouse, Ord's kangaroo rat, and black-footed ferret.

The distributional patterns of mammals in the plains states are the product of a dynamic environmental history that continues to unfold. Most living species of mammals evolved during Pleistocene times. Although the Pleistocene is popularly termed the Ice Age, there was not one ice age, but several. Between episodes of glaciation were periods that were as warm or warmer than the present. As glaciers advanced onto the northern plains, faunas moved southward, each species compelled to retreat at its own rate. As the glaciers retreated, faunas rebounded, moving into newly reopened landscapes and evolving new symbiotic relationships.

The distributional patterns seen today usually provide clues only to the most recent of the major glacial advances (the Wisconsin) and its retreat. Evidence of earlier patterns was almost obliterated by the dramatic environmental changes accompanying the most recent glaciation. As climates ameliorated with the retreat of the glaciers, some species were left behind as relicts. Among them were the boreal and montane species of the Black Hills, for example. Further warming has allowed access to the region by mammals of southern affinities, species from both the Mexican Plateau and the Gulf Coast. This dynamic faunal evolution continues, influenced increasingly by human industrial civilization. One of the great biological challenges of our time is to understand this magnificent evolutionary drama and to preserve it as an ongoing phenomenon for future generations of humans and the other native mammals of the plains states.

Introduction to Class Mammalia

Mammals are vertebrate animals characterized by the presence of hair. Female mammals have mammary glands that produce milk to nourish their young. Beyond these two fundamental features and those common to higher vertebrates generally, the diversity of major mammalian groups is more striking than their similarity. Mammals have evolved to assume important roles in virtually all of the ecosystems of the earth—on land, in fresh and salt water, and in the air. They occur on all continents, in all oceans, and on all but the most remote oceanic islands. Mammals move about by running, walking, burrowing, climbing, swimming, and flying. They range in size from tiny shrews and bats that weigh little more than a penny to the blue whale, which at 150 tons is the largest animal ever known. One or another species of mammal is specialized to feed upon virtually every conceivable kind of food. No other group of living vertebrates approaches the Mammalia in diversity of body plans and ecological roles.

Mammals first evolved from reptiles in Triassic times, some 200 million years ago. For the first 130 million years of their history, mammals diversified in the shadow of the ruling reptiles, that great group of vertebrates that included those popularly known as dinosaurs. During that long apprenticeship, mammals perfected a suite of adaptations that were to become the basis for remarkable success. At the end of the Cretaceous period, the ruling reptiles slipped from overwhelming dominance to nearly complete extinction, ending the Age of Reptiles (Mesozoic era) and inaugurating the Age of Mammals (Cenozoic era).

Among the adaptations that mark the mammalian grade of organization are these anatomical, physiological, and behavioral traits: a coat of insulating hair and the oil-secreting sebaceous glands that lubricate and protect it; endothermy (warm-bloodedness); sweat glands to produce moisture that allows evaporative cooling; production of live young except in the monotremes (the duck-billed platypus and echidnas) after some period of internal development; mammary glands (derived from sweat glands) that produce the milk that provides young mammals with a nutritional head start; a four-chambered heart that allows complete separation of oxygen-rich and oxygen-poor blood and thus supports activity regardless of most environmental conditions; non-nucleated red blood cells in the form of biconcave discs; a complex dentition in which teeth are borne in sockets and the toothrow is differentiated to allow the efficient processing of food; and an advanced brain that allows the processing and integration of information and the most complex, individually variable behavior of any animal group. These adaptations, embellished by natural selection in variable environments over the past 70 million years, have assured the success of mammals in the diverse landscapes of the plains states, as elsewhere.

There are more than 4,000 species of Recent mammals, arranged in about 1,000 genera and 135 families. Living species are divisible into some 21 orders, of which eight (excluding Primates) are native to the plains states.

Mammals are fascinating in their own right. Most humans find it intriguing to know more of the habits and adaptations of their wild kin. Beyond that, mammals have a great cultural importance to humans. Our dependence on domestic mammals for food, fiber, companionship, and (formerly) transportation and motive power is too familiar to need elaboration. Our culture is influenced as well, however, by native mammals. On the negative side, wild mammals are important carriers of diseases that afflict humans and other domestic animals; they also compete with us for the productivity of fields, rangelands, and forests. On a more positive note, the controlled harvest of native mammals for food, fur, and sport is a multimillion-dollar industry in the plains states. Exploitation of the mammalian resource—especially bison—was the economic base for most of the native American tribes of the Great Plains. Similarly, the search for mammals—especially beaver—provided the impetus for the earliest European exploration of the region. Finally, the diverse mammalian fauna of the plains states is essential to the integrity of native ecosystems, and that integrity is, in turn, essential to the quality of human life.

Checklist of Mammals of the Plains States and Guide to Species Accounts

The following checklist of wild mammals occurring in the Dakotas, Nebraska, Kansas, and Oklahoma is provided as a ready reference to the 138 native and eight introduced species (marked with an asterisk here and in the keys that follow) treated in this guidebook. Page references to species accounts are given. Orders, families, and genera are listed in currently accepted phylogenetic sequence, but species within each genus are listed alphabetically, as they are in the text.

Key to Orders of Mammals of the Plains States

1. First toe on hind foot thumblike, apposable; marsupium present in
   females; incisors 5/4 .... Marsupialia
1'. First toe on hind foot not thumblike or apposable; marsupium absent;
   incisors never more than 3/3 2
2. Forelimbs modified for flight .... Chiroptera
2'. Forelimbs not modified for flight 3
3. Cheekteeth peglike, lacking enamel; dorsum covered by bony
   carapace .... Edentata
3'. Cheekteeth not peglike, bearing enamel; dorsum covered with fur 4
4. Upper incisors absent; feet provided with hooves .... Artiodactyla
4'. Upper incisors present; feet provided with claws 5
5. Toothrows continuous (no conspicuous diastema); canines present 6
5'. Toothrows having conspicuous diastema between incisors and
   cheekteeth; canines absent 7
6. Canines approximately equal in size to adjacent teeth; size
   small .... Insectivora
6'. Canines conspicuously larger than adjacent teeth; size medium
   to large .... Carnivora
7. Ears of approximately same length as (or longer than) tail;
   incisors 2/1 .... Lagomorpha
7'. Ears much shorter than tail; incisors 1/1 .... Rodentia

Order Marsupialia

Marsupials are one of the oldest orders of living mammals, with a history in the fossil record dating back some 130 million years. They are also one of the most primitive. Marsupials differ from placental mammals in many ways including: young are not nearly so well developed at birth; females have a bifid reproductive tract and males have a bifurcate penis; females of most species have a pouch (marsupium) in which the young develop after birth; males have a scrotum anterior to the penis; upper and lower incisors are never of equal number; cheekteeth consist primitively of three premolars and four molars (the reverse of the primitive formula in placentals).

Marsupials occur naturally in Recent times only in the Australian region and in the temperate and tropical parts of the Americas. They are represented in the New World by only three living families, two limited to western South America and the other, the family Didelphidae, occurring from southern Canada to Argentina. In all, about 200 modern species are recognized.

Some authorities have recently elevated Marsupialia to supraordinal rank and have recognized several distinct orders in that grouping. Because there is yet no consensus in the literature as to the probable correct classification, we continue to recognize Marsupialia at the ordinal level.

Didelphis virginiana / Virginia Opossum

Distribution. The Virginia opossum occurs over much of eastern North America from southern Canada southward to Nicaragua. It is found throughout most of the five-state region, northward to the eastern part of North Dakota. See map 5.

Description. About the size of a house cat; snout pointed; legs short; ears naked; tail long, scaly, scantily haired. Dorsum grayish, underparts somewhat paler. Total length, 640–830 mm; tail, 250–380 mm; hind foot, 60–75 mm; ear, 45–52 mm; weight normally 5–8 lb but may be 13 lb or more. See figure 1.

Habits and Habitat. The opossum lives primarily in wooded areas, especially along streams and rivers, but it is not uncommon in more open habitats. Dens are located in such places as hollow logs and trees, brush piles, rock crevices, and abandoned burrow systems. This hardy animal seemingly can sustain a variety of injuries and still survive; evidence of previously broken bones is not uncommon in preserved skeletal material, and in northern populations the distal parts of the ears and tail sometimes are lost as a result of frostbite.

D. virginiana eats a wide variety of foods. Important items include carrion, corn, insects and other invertebrates, fruits, small vertebrates, and eggs. This species rarely lives longer than two years in the wild. Estimates of home range vary from about 10 acres to more than 100 acres.

Opossums are eaten in some places by humans and are also preyed upon by large raptors and by many carnivores. Young animals are particularly susceptible to predation. After they leave the pouch (about day 70), until they are weaned, the young accompany the female by clinging to her back or sides and later by running along beside her.

Reproduction. Most females bear two litters annually, one in mid-winter and another in late spring; the second litter usually is slightly larger than the first. The small, naked young are born only 13 days after mating and make their way with little maternal assistance to the distinctive pouch (marsupium) of the female, which contains the mammae. Counts of pouch young usually number between six and nine, but extremes of one to 13 have been reported.

Suggested References. Gardner (1973, 1982); Hazard (1982); Jones et al. (1983); McManus (1974).

Figure 1. Virginia opossum, *Didelphis virginiana* (L. C. Watkins).

Figure 2. Arctic shrew, *Sorex arcticus* (E. C. Birney).

Figure 3. Masked shrew, *Sorex cinereus* (Valan Photos, photograph by M. Bourque).

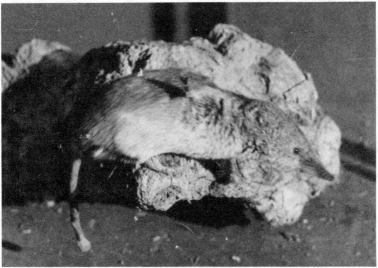

Figure 4. Pygmy shrew, *Sorex hoyi* (Photo Researchers, photograph by S. Dalton).

Figure 5. Merriam's shrew, *Sorex merriami* (D. F. Williams).

Figure 6. Dwarf shrew, *Sorex nanus* (D. L. Pattie). Note paper match for size comparison.

Figure 7. Water shrew, *Sorex palustris* (Animals Animals, Stouffer Productions).

Order Insectivora

Insectivores are the most primitive placental mammals and are representative of the stock from which other placentals evolved. They occur on all major land areas except Australia, Greenland, Antarctica, and southern South America. Living representatives constitute at least seven families, about 70 genera, and approximately 400 species. Only two families, Talpidae (moles) and Soricidae (shrews), occur on the North American mainland.

Most insectivores have a well-developed W-shaped pattern of cusps on the molars. Most eat insects, as the name implies, but many also take other kinds of invertebrates, such as earthworms and centipedes, and some other animal and plant material.

Key to Insectivores / Shrews and Moles

1. Front feet more than twice as broad as hind feet, possessing stout claws; zygomatic arches and auditory bullae present . . . . *Scalopus aquaticus*
1'. Front feet less than twice as broad as hind feet, possessing delicate claws; zygomatic arches absent; tympana ringlike, lacking auditory bullae 2
2. Tail less than 40 percent of length of head and body; three, four, or five unicuspid teeth in each upper jaw; if five unicuspids (only four visible in side view), then condylobasal length more than 20 mm and cranial breadth more than 11 mm 3
2'. Tail more than 40 percent length of head and body; five unicuspid teeth in each upper jaw (three to five visible in side view); condylobasal length rarely 20 mm or more (usually less than 19); cranial breadth less than 11 mm (usually less than 10) 7

3.   Dorsal color brownish to pale gray; three or four unicuspid teeth in
     each upper jaw 4
3′. Dorsal color dark gray to blackish; five unicuspid teeth in each upper
     jaw (only four usually visible in side view) 5
4.   Dorsal color silvery gray to brownish gray; three unicuspid teeth in
     each upper jaw . . . . *Notiosorex crawfordi*
4′. Dorsal color dark brownish; four unicuspid teeth in each upper jaw
     (sometimes only three clearly visible in side view) . . . *Cryptotis parva*
5.   Total length usually 125 mm or more; length of hind foot usually 16
     mm or more; occurring southward approximately to Platte River in
     Nebraska (see map 9) . . . . *Blarina brevicauda*
5′. Total length usually less than 120 mm; length of hind foot usually less
     than 16mm; occurring in southern Nebraska, Kansas, and much of
     Oklahoma (see map 9) 6
6.   Total length more than 100 mm; occurring from southern Nebraska to
     Oklahoma except southeastern part (see map 9) . . . *Blarina hylophaga*
6′. Total length less than 100 mm; occurring only in southeastern
     Oklahoma (see map 9) . . . . *Blarina carolinensis*
7.   Length of hind foot usually 10 mm or less; third unicuspid in upper
     jaw compressed anteroposteriorly, disklike; usually only three upper
     unicuspids visible in side view . . . . *Sorex hoyi*
7′. Length of hind foot usually 10 mm or more; third unicuspid in upper
     jaw not disklike; at least four (sometimes all five) upper unicuspids
     visible in side view 8
8.   Pelage dark grayish to blackish dorsally; hind foot more than 18 mm,
     fringed with stiff hairs; condylobasal length more
     than 19.5 mm . . . . *Sorex palustris*
8′. Pelage brownish to grayish dorsally; hind foot less than 18 mm, not
     fringed with stiff hairs; condylobasal length 19.5 mm or less 9
9.   Third unicuspid in upper jaw smaller than fourth; condylobasal length
     14.5 mm or less . . . . *Sorex nanus*
9′. Third unicuspid in upper jaw as large as, or larger than, fourth;
     condylobasal length 14.6 mm or more 10
10. Pelage distinctly tricolored (dark brown middorsally, distinctly paler on
     flanks; grayish ventrally); total length more than 100 mm; condylobasal
     length more than 17.5 mm . . . . *Sorex arcticus*
10′. Pelage not distinctly tricolored; total length less than 100 mm;
     condylobasal length less than 17.5 mm 11

11. Pelage pale brownish gray to grayish dorsally; whitish ventrally;
     maxillary breadth more than 4.6 mm; first upper incisors lacking
     medial accessory cusps .... *Sorex merriami*
11'. Pelage dark brown to grayish brown dorsally, pale brownish or grayish
     ventrally; maxillary breadth less than 4.6 mm; first upper incisors
     having accessory cusps .... *Sorex cinereus*

Sorex arcticus / Arctic Shrew

Distribution. The geographic range of this shrew extends from the north-central United States northward into Canada and Alaska and probably through much of Siberia. On the northern plains, the species occurs in northern and eastern North Dakota and adjacent northeastern South Dakota. See map 6.

Description. One of the larger members of the genus *Sorex* in this region; resembles *S. cinereus* but is larger both externally and cranially. Pelage distinctly tricolored in winter, dark brown dorsally, pale brown laterally, grayish ventrally; color of adults in summer pelage and young animals less noticeably tricolored. Total length, 108–117 mm; tail, 38–42 mm; hind foot, 13–14 mm; weight 7–11 g. See figure 2.

Habits and Habitat. Within its range in the plains states, the arctic shrew occurs in lowland areas of marsh grasses, mixed forbs, cattails, and willows, usually in moist valleys and along the shores of lakes. These shrews usually are nocturnal but may be found active at any time. The home range frequently is less than an acre; in one study in Wisconsin, the population density was 3.5 per acre on a 5.7-acre plot. Field studies have indicated that few individuals live beyond 15 months in the wild. Molt takes place twice a year in adults, in spring and again in autumn.

The diet of this shrew consists of moth larvae, grasshoppers, larval and adult click beetles, caterpillars, larval and adult sawflies, aquatic insects, and other invertebrates. Probably a few small vertebrates are also consumed. Earthworms, hamburger, mealworms, fly larvae, grasshoppers, and parts of dead rodents are recorded as having been eaten by captives.

Raptors feed on arctic shrews, as do some species of mustelids. Most other carnivores avoid them. Because of their food habits, these animals generally benefit the interests of humans, as do other shrews.

Reproduction. The breeding season extends from late winter through most of the summer. Young born early in the year sometimes breed toward the end of the breeding season but normally do not do so until the year after their birth. Litters vary in size from four to 10 but average about six.

Suggested References. Baird, Timm, and Nordquist (1983); Hazard (1982); Jackson (1928, 1961); van Zyll de Jong (1983).

Sorex cinereus / Masked Shrew

Distribution. This shrew occurs throughout much of the northern half of North America and in eastern Siberia. In the plains states, it is found southward to north-central Kansas and is sometimes regarded as a distinct species (*S. haydenii*). See map 7.

Description. A medium-sized member of the genus. Summer pelage dark brownish dorsally, paler brownish on sides, grayish white ventrally, resulting in slightly tricolored appearance; dorsum somewhat paler in winter, usually grayish brown. Total length, 85–98 mm; tail, 34–38 mm; hind foot, 11–13 mm; weight, 3–5 g. See figure 3.

Habits and Habitat. This species prefers moist or damp surroundings in forests and in marshes, grassy bogs, and other riparian environments. It is found, however, in a wider variety of habitats than many of its near relatives, including some that are relatively dry. These animals may be active at any time of day or night but are mainly nocturnal. Populations normally range from one to 10 shrews per acre; the home range is small, usually no more than an acre and a half.

Foods include a variety of invertebrates such as beetles, flies, moths, ants, bees, grasshoppers, crickets, centipedes, worms, spiders, mollusks, sowbugs, and some small vertebrates. Minute amounts of vegetable matter also are eaten and these shrews, like many others, can be taken in traps baited with rolled oats. Vision is somewhat restricted but important to the animal as is the sense of smell; hearing probably is acute in certain sound ranges, some above the range perceptible to humans. Molt in adults takes place between April and June and again in early autumn.

Nests are spherical, four to five inches in diameter, constructed from soft vegetation. They are found in stumps or logs, under rocks, and in similar situations. Burrows of other small mammals often are used but *S. cinereus* occasionally constructs burrows of its own.

Reproduction. The masked shrew breeds from April to October in the plains states. Adult females bear two or three litters a year; young-of-the-year sometimes breed by late summer. A litter of four to 10 young is born after a gestation period of 19 to 22 days.

Suggested References. Jackson (1928, 1961); van Zyll de Jong (1976, 1980, 1983).

Sorex hoyi / Pygmy Shrew

Distribution. Pygmy shrews are restricted in distribution to boreal and north temperate North America. In the five-state region, this species is known only from the eastern Dakotas. See map 8.

Description. Resembles *S. cinereus* externally but slightly smaller and with relatively shorter tail; easily distinguished from all other *Sorex* by dental differences used in key. Pelage reddish brown to grayish brown dorsally; sides paler than back; hairs of venter blackish at the base, tipped with gray or white. Total length, 75–95 mm; tail, 27–34 mm; hind foot, 9–11 mm; weight averaging about 3 g. See figure 4.

Habits and Habitat. Little is known of habitat selection by this shrew in the plains region. One taken in southeastern South Dakota was trapped in a cattail-rush community along the edge of a slough. In montane areas to the west, this species favors moist sphagnum bogs but also occurs in forested areas, meadows, and even disturbed vegetational communities near human habitation. There is some evidence that *S. hoyi* inhabits drier areas as summer progresses. Like many other shrews, it is most easily captured in pitfalls.

Examination of stomach contents from wild-taken specimens revealed butterfly larvae, larval and adult beetles and flies, other insects, earthworms, snails, and slugs. In captivity these shrews have eaten mice, other shrews, raw fish, annelids, grasshoppers, beetles, and flies. They hoard food when it is available in abundance.

Not much is known about the intraspecific relationships of *S. hoyi*. It is generally thought to occur in low densities but this may be a result of inadequate census methods. Pygmy shrews are good climbers and can run rapidly when disturbed. They burrow in soft substrates, making tunnels not much larger than those made by large earthworms. Networks of their tiny burrow systems can be found under fallen logs, around tree roots, and under old stumps. Spring molt probably occurs typically in April or early May and autumnal molt from early October to early November.

Reproduction. Unlike most other soricids, females evidently bear but one litter annually. Lactating and pregnant females have been taken from June through August. Three to eight young per litter have been reported.

Suggested References. Diersing (1980); Long (1974); van Zyll de Jong (1983).

Sorex merriami / Merriam's Shrew

Distribution. Merriam's shrew occurs from the northern plains westward to Oregon and Washington and southward to Arizona and New Mexico. In the plains region it is known only from one specimen from northwestern Nebraska and a questionable record from western North Dakota. See map 8.

Description. Size medium and color pale among species of *Sorex.* Upper parts ash-gray tinged with buff; sides and venter whitish to pale buff; feet and underside of tail white, tail buff above. Total length, 90–101 mm; tail, 32–39 mm; hind foot, 11–13 mm; weight, 4–7 g. See figure 5.

Habits and Habitat. Little is known of the ecology of this species in the northeastern part of its range. The specimen from Nebraska was taken along with *Sorex cinereus* in a moist meadow adjacent to a semiarid area of sage and grasses. In several western states, Merriam's shrew appears to be most common in areas of sagebrush and bunchgrasses, frequently in association with the sagebrush vole, *Lemmiscus curtatus,* the runways of which are used by the shrew. Analysis of stomach contents of specimens from Washington revealed the presence of caterpillars, larval and adult beetles, cave crickets, and spiders.

Owls are the only known predators of *S. merriami,* and owl pellets are a potential source of specimens of this and other insectivores. Pitfalls have proved to be effective traps. Known parasites include fleas, cestodes, and trematodes.

Vernal molt in adults, which occurs in April, first appears in nearly symmetrical patches on the dorsum. The autumnal molt in October or early November seems to begin on the posterior part of the back and progresses anteriorly and laterally. Summer pelage is reputedly longer and more brownish than winter pelage; hairs on the feet and tail do not change color seasonally. Flank glands of males are most evident during the breeding season. These glands probably produce the strong musky odor of these animals, which may attract other individuals.

Reproduction. The breeding season is known to extend from mid-March to at least early July in Washington. Females that carried five, six, and seven fetuses have been reported.

Suggested References. Armstrong and Jones (1971); Diersing and Hoffmeister (1977); Jones et al. (1983).

0 ____ 100
MILES

Map 5. *(Left).* Distribution of the Virginia opossum, *Didelphis virginiana.*

Map 6. *(Right).* Distribution of the arctic shrew, *Sorex arcticus* (1); the water shrew, *Sorex palustris* (dot); and the eastern mole, *Scalopus aquaticus* (2).

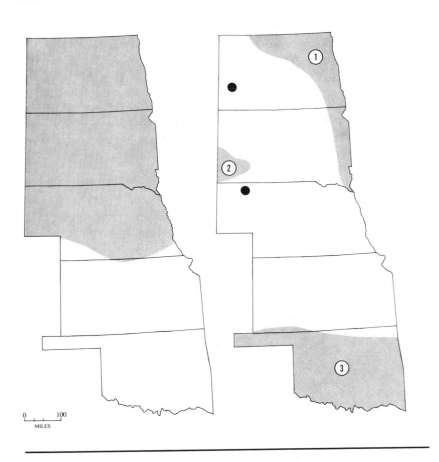

Map 7. *(Left).* Distribution of the masked shrew, *Sorex cinereus.*

Map 8. *(Right).* Distribution of the pygmy shrew, *Sorex hoyi* (1); the dwarf shrew, *Sorex nanus* (2); Merriam's shrew, *Sorex merriami* (dots); and the desert shrew, *Notiosorex crawfordi* (3).

Sorex nanus / Dwarf Shrew

Distribution. This species occurs mainly in subalpine and alpine habitats in parts of the intermontane West of the United States. In the five-state region, it is known only from southwestern and west-central South Dakota (Cottonwood, Custer, Fall River, and Pennington counties). See map 8.

Description. Smallest shrew in the plains states. Brownish dorsally, sometimes olive-brown; smoke-gray ventrally; tail indistinctly bicolored. Total length, 85–94 mm; tail, 36–45 mm; hind foot, 10–11 mm; weight averaging about 2.5 g. See figure 6.

Habits and Habitat. Dwarf shrews are often taken in relatively arid places compared with other members of the genus, and their ecological distribution seems to be more or less independent of availability of surface water and moist substrates. They were thought for many years to be inhabitants primarily of montane rockslides, but some specimens have recently been taken from short-grass prairie habitats in South Dakota and at relatively low altitudes in several other western states. These animals are seldom taken in conventional traps but have been caught in good numbers in pitfalls made from large cans. Short ground-level fences leading to the pitfalls are recommended. The easternmost records from South Dakota were specimens captured in cans placed in roadside ditches where vegetative cover consisted of grasses, clover, and clumps of sage.

Insects, soft-bodied spiders, and possibly other invertebrates make up the diet of this species, but much remains to be learned about its biology. Captive individuals have been observed to cache extra food. Insofar as the meager data now available reveal, populations of *S. nanus* are stable throughout the year. There is no other information at hand, however, on demographic characteristics. One specimen from South Dakota was found in the regurgitated pellet of a barn owl.

Reproduction. Judging from limited data, breeding in alpine populations probably begins in late June and early July; possibly it commences earlier in shrews inhabiting lower elevations. Most females evidently bear two litters annually. Fetus counts of six to eight have been recorded. There is no evidence that young shrews reproduce in their first summer of life.

Suggested References. Hoffmann and Owen (1980); Jones et al. (1983).

Sorex palustris / Water Shrew

Distribution. This shrew occurs in the northeastern and north-central United States, in montane areas in the western part of the country, and in southern Canada and Alaska. On the plains, it is known only from four specimens taken many years ago in northeastern South Dakota; it will possibly be found northward in the Red River Valley of North Dakota. See map 6.

Description. Largest species of genus *Sorex* in the region. Tail nearly as long as head and body; hind feet large, fringed with stiff, whitish hairs to aid in aquatic locomotion. Pelage soft and dense; dorsum black to brownish, sometimes with greenish to purple iridescence; venter silver-white to smoke-gray; tail distinctly bicolored. Total length, 138–164 mm; tail, 63–72 mm; hind foot, 19–20 mm; weight, 12–20 g. See figure 7.

Habits and Habitat. Water shrews live in grassy and shrubby areas along the banks of streams, ponds, and lakes, and around potholes in bogs or forests. They are primarily nocturnal, with peak periods of activity several hours after sundown and the hour before sunrise. They are also secretive, frequently remaining out of sight under overhanging banks or in debris and heavy vegetation. These animals are excellent swimmers and divers and also move well along the bottom of streams and pools; they are also reportedly capable of running on the surface of water for short distances, aided by small bubbles adhering to the fringes of their hind feet. Their pelage is resistant to saturation with water.

Nearly half the diet consists of aquatic insects. Other foods include planaria, annelids, spiders, small fish and other vertebrates, and some vegetable matter. Enemies of *S. palustris* include raptors, mustelid carnivores, and snakes. There is but one maturational molt, from the thin juvenile coat to the adult pelage of season. Mature animals molt twice annually, in spring and again in late summer.

Reproduction. Water shrews breed from late winter through early autumn. Adult females have two or three litters annually; those born early in the breeding season may bear young later in the same year. Five to eight (most frequently six) young make up the normal litter.

Suggested References. Conaway (1952); Jackson (1928, 1961); Sorenson (1962); van Zyll de Jong (1983).

Blarina brevicauda / Northern Short-tailed Shrew

Distribution. This shrew inhabits the northeastern and north-central United States and southeastern Canada. On the plains it occurs in the eastern parts of the Dakotas and is found west along tributaries of the Missouri River to the 101st meridian in Nebraska, south to the south-central part of that state. See map 9.

Description. A robust shrew with a short tail; largest species of *Blarina*. Coloration grayish to grayish black, darker on the dorsum than on the belly. Total length, 124–141 mm; tail, 23–31 mm; hind foot, 16–18 mm; weight, 20–30 g. See figure 8.

Habits and Habitat. This species inhabits woodlands, grasslands, and brushy or weedy fencerows, and is common in some areas. In the western part of its range in the Dakotas and Nebraska, it is more or less restricted to riparian habitats.

This short-legged animal moves about with apparent rapidity but little actual speed, keeping the tail elevated as in other shrews. The front feet are relatively broad and powerful. Burrows and tunnels are at two levels—a few inches below the surface and down to about 20 inches below ground; the two levels are joined at irregular intervals. Nests also are of two types, a breeding nest and a much smaller resting nest. Both are constructed of readily available vegetative material formed into a hollow ball four to eight inches in diameter.

Individuals are active both day and night but seek subdued light during daytime periods. Populations vary from two to 50 per acre. Home ranges of males may range to four and a half acres. Foods are the same as for other shrews but may include more earthworms and vegetable material. There are two pelages annually in adults. Longevity rarely exceeds two years.

Reproduction. Breeding commences in late winter and litters, born after a gestation of 21 to 22 days, are brought forth in early April. There is little reproduction in midsummer, but another peak occurs in early autumn. Young animals may breed later in the year of their birth. Litter size ranges from four to 10, averaging between six and seven.

Suggested References. Dapson (1968); Jones et al. (1983); Pearson (1944, 1945).

Blarina carolinensis / Southern Short-tailed Shrew

Distribution. This short-tailed shrew occurs throughout much of the southeastern United States westward to eastern Texas. In the states treated in this book, it is known only from the southeastern part of Oklahoma. See map 9.

Description. Smallest of short-tailed shrews; measurements not overlapping (or only barely so) those of the larger *Blarina hylophaga* (see below); color as described for *B. brevicauda.* Total length, 72–95 mm; tail, 13–22 mm; hind foot, 10–14 mm; weight averaging about 9 g. See figure 9.

Notes. Until just a few years ago, *Blarina carolinensis* was thought to be the same species as *B. brevicauda.* Only after sophisticated study of morphological features and chromosomal characteristics was it determined that there were three rather than one species in this genus. For this reason, differences in habitat requirements, habits, and reproductive biology, if any, from *B. brevicauda* are unknown. The three currently recognized species are thought to have mutually exclusive geographic ranges (see map 9).

Suggested References. Davis (1974); George, Choate, and Genoways (1981); George et al. (1982); Lowery (1974); Schmidly (1983).

Blarina hylophaga / Elliot's Short-tailed Shrew

Distribution. This species evidently occurs from southern Nebraska and southwestern Iowa southward to northeastern Louisiana and probably parts of northern Texas. See map 9.

Description. A medium-sized species of *Blarina,* smaller than *B. brevicauda* but larger than *B. carolinensis;* color as described for *B. brevicauda.* Total length, 103–121 mm; tail, 19–25 mm; hind foot, 13–16 mm; weight, 13–16 g. Not figured.

Notes. The discussion under *Blarina carolinensis* above applies also to *B. hylophaga,* which has only recently been recognized as distinct from that species.

Suggested References. Bee et al. (1981); George, Choate, and Genoways (1981); George et al. (1982); Moncrief, Choate, and Genoways (1982).

Map 9. *(Left).* Distribution of the northern short-tailed shrew, *Blarina brevicauda* (1); the southern short-tailed shrew, *Blarina carolinensis* (2); and Elliot's short-tailed shrew, *Blarina hylophaga* (3).

Map 10. *(Right).* Distribution of the least shrew, *Cryptotis parva*.

Cryptotis parva / Least Shrew

Distribution. The least shrew occurs from southernmost Ontario, Canada, southward throughout the eastern United States (westward to eastern Colorado) to Panama. The species ranges over much of the southern part of the five-state region, north to central South Dakota. See map 10.

Description. A small shrew, as the name implies, with a short tail. Pelage dark brown dorsally and dark gray ventrally in winter, paler in summer. Total length, 70–86 mm; tail, 15–18 mm; hind foot, 10–11 mm; weight 4–6 g. See figure 10.

Habits and Habitats. Least shrews frequently are found in open habitats such as upland prairies, meadows, weedy fields, and grassy roadsides. In much of the western part of the region, they may be more or less restricted to river valleys. *C. parva* may be common locally, and it is known to be gregarious in some situations, 25 to 30 individuals inhabiting the same nest. Nests are usually constructed of shredded vegetation and built in surface depressions or under rocks, logs, or other ground cover.

These shrews are active both day and night but probably more so during periods of darkness. They move about in rapid bursts of speed, constantly twitching their sensitive noses. Runways of rodents are used both on and beneath the surface, but least shrews also make their own burrows in soft soil or under ground litter.

The diet consists mostly of invertebrates such as insects, earthworms, snails, and slugs; small vertebrates and vegetable matter are sometimes eaten. Owls regularly catch least shrews, and hawks, snakes, and carnivores also prey on them. Chiggers, fleas, and mites are known ectoparasites.

Reproduction. The breeding season probably extends from March to October in the five-state region, and adult females usually bear two or three litters a year. Females born early in the year may themselves breed before the end of the season, because they become reproductively active at three months of age. The number of young per litter ranges from two to seven but is usually four to six. Gestation lasts 21 to 23 days and, as in other shrews, the young are born helpless and virtually naked.

Suggested References. Jones et al. (1983); Mumford and Whitaker (1982); Whitaker (1974).

Notiosorex crawfordi / Desert Shrew

Distribution. This species is known from the American Southwest (north to southern Colorado) southward to central Mexico, including Baja California. In the five plains states, it is known only from Oklahoma but may be found also in southern Kansas. See map 8.

Description. A small shrew with a silvery gray to brownish gray dorsum and a slightly paler venter. Tail relatively short, less than a third of the total length, well haired and indistinctly bicolored. Superficially, *N. crawfordi* most closely resembles *Cryptotis parva* but has two fewer teeth (28 as opposed to 30) and the anterior teeth both above and below are only lightly pigmented. Total length, 77–98 mm; tail, 22–32 mm; hind foot, 9–13 mm; weight usually 3–6 g. See figure 11.

Habits and Habitat. The desert shrew has been taken in a fairly wide range of ecological situations but seems to prefer semidesert scrub habitats. This species uses a variety of cover—logs, brush piles, rubbish, and the like—but it evidently favors woodrat houses. In a study in southwestern Oklahoma, 10 shrews were collected from such houses located in "mesquite, mixed-grass, prickly pear cactus ranchlands." Like other shrews, *N. crawfordi* is difficult to capture in conventional traps, but large cans buried level with the ground have proved to be an effective means of collecting these animals. Inspecting holes dug for fence posts or telephone poles, and, of course, tearing apart woodrat houses have also produced these shrews.

The nest is a ball from 40 or 50 to 150 mm in diameter and is built from fine grass, feathers, leaves, and other soft materials. These shrews apparently do not shred the nesting materials but use those of appropriate size that are readily available.

Captive animals have been known to eat a variety of foods, but invertebrates such as insects and centipedes probably make up most of the diet in the wild. Owls are known predators.

Reproduction. The reproductive season apparently extends through the warm months of the year, at least from April through November. It is not known for certain that females are polyestrous, but probably they are. The known range of young per litter is three to five.

Suggested References. Armstrong and Jones (1972).

Scalopus aquaticus / Eastern Mole

Distribution. This species is found in the eastern and central United States, barely reaching southern Canada and northern Mexico. In the plains states, it occurs through most of the southern part of the region, northward to southern South Dakota. See map 6.

Description. Largest insectivore in the five-state region, and the only one adapted for fossorial life. Coloration lead-gray to dark brownish in the east, silver-gray in the west; many individuals have a yellowish orange patch in the pectoral region. See figure 12.

Moles on the eastern plains are larger than those to the west, and males are larger than females on the average. Total length, 136–185 mm; tail, 19–38 mm; hind foot, 19–25 mm; weight, 50–100 g.

Habits and Habitats. Moles spend most of their lives underground. They construct two types of tunnels—those for foraging, which are only an inch or so below the surface and result in the ridges so familiar to gardeners and lawn keepers, and permanent tunnels, six to 10 inches deep. The nest is located in one of the permanent tunnels. When tunnels are damaged, moles burrow under the damaged area and heave up the floor of the old burrow. Mounds of dirt are thrown out on the surface when deep tunnels are excavated. Because feeder tunnels leading to the surface are vertical, the mounds are nearly circular, in contrast to the semicircular mounds of pocket gophers.

The diet is comprised mostly of earthworms and insects, but other invertebrates and some vegetable material are also consumed. Molt occurs twice annually, in spring and autumn. The winter coat is longer and thicker than that of summer. Local distribution is limited by soil moisture and, in the western part of the region, moles are primarily confined to stream and lake borders, lawns, golf courses, and other mesic environments. Raptors and carnivores occasionally prey on moles, but flooding may be the greatest cause of mortality.

Reproduction. Females produce a single litter annually, in March or April, after a gestation period of about six weeks. Four is the usual number of young per litter, but the known range is two to five. Neonates weigh about 5 grams.

Suggested References. Jones et al. (1983); Yates and Schmidly (1978).

Figure 8. Northern short-tailed shrew, *Blarina brevicauda* (E. C. Birney).

Figure 9. Southern short-tailed shrew, *Blarina carolinensis* (R. Altig).

Figure 10. Least shrew, *Cryptotis parva* (T. H. Kunz).

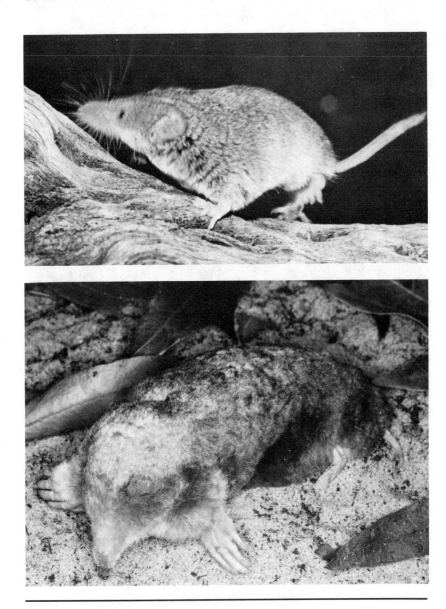

Figure 11. Desert shrew, *Notiosorex crawfordi* (R. J. Baker).

Figure 12. Eastern mole, *Scalopus aquaticus* (J. L. Tveten).

Figure 13. Southeastern myotis, *Myotis austroriparius* (B. J. Hayward).

Figure 14. Long-eared myotis, *Myotis evotis* (T. H. Kunz).

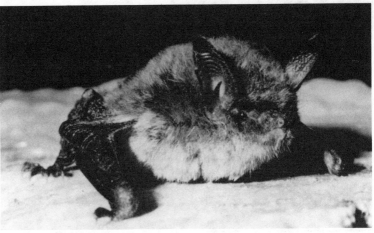

Figure 15. Gray myotis, *Myotis grisescens* (R. W. Barbour).

Figure 16. Keen's myotis, *Myotis keenii* (T. H. Kunz).

Figure 17. Small-footed myotis, *Myotis leibii* (M. D. Tuttle).

Figure 18. Little brown myotis, *Myotis lucifugus* (T. H. Kunz).

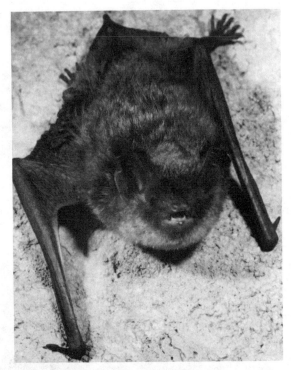

Figure 19. Social myotis, *Myotis sodalis* (R. W. Barbour).

Figure 20. Fringed myotis, *Myotis thysanodes* (R. W. Barbour).

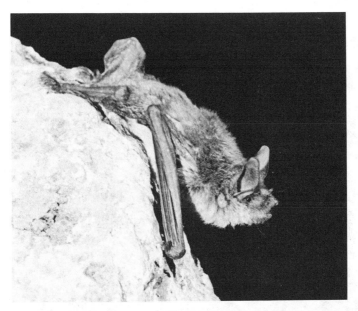

Figure 21. Cave myotis, *Myotis velifer* (R. J. Baker).

Figure 22. Long-legged myotis, *Myotis volans* (R. W. Barbour).

Figure 23. Yuma myotis, *Myotis yumanensis* (R. W. Barbour).

Order Chiroptera

Bats are the only mammals that can truly fly. They are almost worldwide in distribution, absent only from cold latitudes and some oceanic islands. Chiropterans are separated into two great suborders, only one of which (Microchiroptera) occurs in the New World. Modern representatives are placed in 17 families, of which only two, Vespertilionidae and Molossidae, occur in the plains region. About 170 genera and 900 species are recognized among Recent representatives of the order.

All bats in the plains states are insectivorous. Some occurring elsewhere feed on fruit, nectar, fish, and even small terrestrial vertebrates, and members of one group (vampire bats) lap the blood of mammals and birds. The number of teeth varies from 20 to 38, but the range is 28 to 38 in species found in the plains region.

The teeth of all species treated in this guidebook are not much modified from the primitive condition found in the Insectivora, the W-shaped occlusal pattern of the molars being especially evident. The flying surface of bats consists of the wing (patagium) and the interfemoral membrane (uropatagium), double-layered extensions of the body skin that encompass the forelimbs, hind limbs (except the feet), and, in all species of this region, most or all of the tail. The wing is supported by elongate bones of the hand and fingers, excepting the first finger (thumb), which is small, clawed, and free of the membrane.

Bats are able fliers, and some species annually migrate many miles, quitting the plains during the cold months when their insect food is scarce or nonexistent. Other kinds of bats hibernate over the colder parts of the year. At least a few individuals of many species may live a surprisingly long time, 20 years or more.

Key to Chiropterans / Bats

1. Tail extending conspicuously beyond posterior border of uropatagium
    (tail membrane); anterior border of ear with six to eight horny
    excrescences; lower incisors bifid 2
1'. Tail not extending conspicuously (5 mm at most), if at all, beyond
    posterior border of uropatagium; anterior border of ear relatively
    smooth; lower incisors trifid 3
2. Size large, forearm 55 mm or more; ears joined at base, extending well
    beyond nose when laid forward; greatest length of skull more than 21
    mm . . . . *Tadarida macrotis*
2'. Size medium, forearm less than 50 mm; ears not joined at base,
    extending little if any beyond nose when laid forward; greatest length
    of skull less than 19 mm . . . . *Tadarida brasiliensis*
3. Single pair of upper incisors; total number of teeth 28–32 4
3'. Two pair of upper incisors; total number of teeth 32–38 8
4. Upper surface of uropatagium essentially naked; one pair of upper
    premolars (total of 28–30 teeth) 5
4'. Upper surface of uropatagium thickly furred throughout; two pair of
    upper premolars (total of 32 teeth) 6
5. Color dark brown; forearm 40 mm or less; three pair of lower incisors
    (total of 30 teeth) . . . . *Nycticeius humeralis*
5'. Color pale; forearm more than 45 mm; two pair of lower incisors (total
    of 28 teeth) . . . . *Antrozous pallidus*
6. Dorsal pelage "frosted" (dark brownish tipped with grayish white);
    forearm more than 45 mm; greatest length of skull more than
    17.5 mm . . . . *Lasiurus cinereus*
6'. Dorsal pelage rich mahogany to chestnut; forearm less than 45 mm;
    greatest length of skull less than 14.5 mm 7
7. Dorsum reddish orange to chestnut; lacrimal ridge or shelf well
    developed . . . . *Lasiurus borealis*
7'. Dorsum rich mahogany, hairs sometimes white tipped; lacrimal ridge
    poorly developed . . . . *Lasiurus seminolus*
8. Dorsal pelage blackish frosted with white or, if not, ear tremendously
    enlarged (usually 30 mm or more in length from notch); premolars 2/3
    (total of 36 teeth) 9
8'. Dorsal pelage not blackish frosted with white (dark brown through
    reddish brown to yellowish); ear not noticeably enlarged (23 mm or

less in length from notch); premolars 1/2, 2/2, or 3/3 (total of 32, 34, or 38 teeth) 11

9. Upper surface of uropatagium furred proximally from a third to half its length; dorsal pelage blackish frosted with white; ear from notch less than 15 mm .... *Lasionycteris noctivagans*

9'. Upper surface of uropatagium only thinly furred at base; dorsal pelage pale brownish; ear from notch 27 mm or more 10

10. Hairs on hind feet projecting beyond toes; underparts nearly white; dorsal pelage gray and distinctly bicolored; first upper incisor bicuspid .... *Plecotus rafinesquii*

10'. Hairs on hind feet not projecting beyond toes; underparts brownish; dorsal pelage brownish, not distinctly bicolored; first upper incisor unicuspid .... *Plecotus townsendii*

11. Upper surface of uropatagium furred proximally, sometimes thinly, for a third to half its length; two pair of upper premolars (total of 34 teeth)... 12

11'. Upper surface of uropatagium only thinly furred at base; one or three pair of upper premolars (total of 32 or 38 teeth) 13

12. Dorsal color usually pale yellowish, membranes dark; calcar keeled; skull more or less flat in dorsal profile .... *Pipistrellus hesperus*

12'. Dorsal color usually brownish to reddish brown, membranes pale; calcar not keeled; skull concave in dorsal profile *Pipistrellus subflavus*

13. Total length usually more than 110 mm (average about 120); greatest length of skull more than 18 mm; one pair of upper premolars (total of 32 teeth) .... *Eptesicus fuscus*

13'. Total length usually less than 110 mm; greatest length of skull less than 18 mm; three pair of upper premolars (total of 38 teeth) 14

14. Pelage woolly in appearance and relatively thin; forearm more than 40 mm (usually more than 42) 15

14'. Pelage thick, not woolly in appearance (except somewhat in *Myotis austroriparius*); forearm 43 mm or less (usually less than 40) 16

15. Dorsal pelage dark grayish to grayish brown; greatest length of skull usually less than 16.5 mm; wing attached to foot at ankle .... *Myotis grisescens*

15'. Dorsal pelage pale brownish; greatest length of skull usually more than 16.5 mm; wing attached to foot at base of toe .... *Myotis velifer*

16. Ear long, usually 18 mm or more from notch; greatest length of skull more than 15.7 mm; breadth across upper molars usually 6.0 mm or more 17

16'. Ear short or of moderate length, usually 17 mm or less from notch; greatest length of skull less than 15.7 mm; breadth across upper molars usually less than 6.0 mm 18

17. Posterior border of uropatagium with conspicuous fringe of hairs; forearm rarely less than 39 mm; ear smaller in direct comparison, usually 18–20 mm from notch . . . . *Myotis thysanodes*

17'. Posterior border of uropatagium not conspicuously fringed with hairs; forearm rarely more than 39 mm; ear larger in direct comparison, usually 20–22 mm from notch . . . . *Myotis evotis*

18. Membranes dark brownish to blackish, contrasting noticeably with color of pelage, distinct dark facial mask; forearm usually less than 33 mm; hind foot small, usually 8 mm or less . . . . *Myotis leibii*

18'. Membranes brownish, not contrasting noticeably with color of pelage, no distinct facial mask; forearm usually more than 33 mm; hind foot usually 9 mm or more 19

19. Calcar keeled; underside of wing furred outward to level of elbow; ear short, usually 11–13 mm from notch . . . . *Myotis volans*

19'. Calcar not keeled or only slightly so (*M. sodalis*); underside of wing not furred to level of elbow; ear of moderate length, usually 13 mm or more from notch 20

20. Ear relatively long, usually 16–17 mm from notch; tragus long and pointed at tip . . . . *Myotis keenii*

20'. Ear of moderate length from notch, usually 13–15 mm; tragus moderate in length, not distinctly pointed at tip 21

21. Braincase low, rising only gradually from rostrum; hairs on hind foot not extending beyond toes . . . . *Myotis sodalis*

21'. Braincase higher, rising moderately to abruptly from rostrum; hairs on hind foot extending beyond toes 22

22. Braincase rising moderately from rostrum; dorsal pelage distinctly glossy in appearance . . . . *Myotis lucifugus*

22'. Braincase rising abruptly from rostrum; dorsal pelage dull to woolly, not glossy 23

23. Dorsal color dull, pale tan to brown; greatest length of skull normally less than 14 mm; occurring in plains states only in western Oklahoma Panhandle . . . . *Myotis yumanensis*

23'. Dorsal color grayish to russet, somewhat woolly; greatest length of skull usually more than 14 mm; occurring in plains states only in southeastern Oklahoma . . . . *Myotis austroriparius*

Myotis austroriparius / Southeastern Myotis

Distribution. The southeastern myotis occurs, as the name implies, in the southeastern United States. It reaches its northern distributional limits in the southern parts of Illinois and Indiana, and ranges barely into the plains states in southeastern Oklahoma. See map 11.

Description. A medium-sized myotis with a globular braincase. Dorsal color grayish to russet, even orangish prior to molt in late summer, and somewhat woolly in appearance; venter tan to whitish. Total length, 80–95 mm; tail, 35–45 mm; hind foot, 7–11 mm; ear, 14–15 mm; forearm, 36–41 mm; weight, 4–9 g. See figure 13.

Habits and Habitat. This species hibernates principally in caves in the northern part of its range but may not hibernate in the Deep South, where groups take up winter residence in places such as crevices between timbers of bridges, storm sewers, culverts, buildings, and tree hollows. Maternity colonies, sometimes containing thousands of bats, are formed in late winter or spring depending on latitude, most often in caves. In hibernation, tightly packed clusters of 50 to 100 or more bats have been reported, although some individuals, usually males, hibernate singly wedged into small holes or crevices in caves. Wintering grounds or hibernation sites are in the same general vicinity as summer haunts. Homing ability does not seem to be as well developed as in some other species.

This bat is said to be closely associated with water. It emerges when darkness falls, later than most species of myotis, and usually forages but a few feet above the surface of streams or ponds. The flight pattern has been described as "low, rapid and stable," compared to that of other small bats.

Mites, chiggers, and both winged and wingless batflies are conspicuous ectoparasites. Known predators include several species of snakes, which inhabit caves frequented by *M. austroriparius,* carnivores, and owls.

Reproduction. Time of mating in this species is not certainly known but may be in autumn, prior to hibernation, or, at least in Florida, in spring. Most females produce twins, a circumstance unique among American myotis, which are born in late April or May. Neonates are relatively small and poorly developed at birth.

Suggested References. Barbour and Davis (1969); LaVal (1970); Lowery (1974); Mumford and Whitaker (1982).

Myotis evotis / Long-eared Myotis

Distribution. This long-eared bat ranges over much of temperate western North America—from southern Canada southward to the highlands of Arizona, New Mexico, and southern California. In the five-state region, it is known only from western North Dakota and northwestern South Dakota. See map 11.

Description. A relatively large myotis with the longest ears of any American member of the genus. Fur long and glossy. Dorsum pale yellowish brown, contrasting noticeably with dark membranes; venter pale yellowish. Most closely resembles *M. thysanodes,* but slightly smaller, ears longer, and lacks conspicuous fringe of hairs on border of uropatagium. Total length, 87–100 mm; tail, 34–45 mm; hind foot, 8–11 mm; ear, 19–22 mm; forearm, 37–40 mm; weight, 5.5–8 g. See figure 14.

Habits and Habitat. Although the long-eared myotis is not an uncommon bat over much of its known geographic range, less is known of its biology than that of most other American members of the genus. This species evidently favors wooded areas, principally coniferous or oak forests, near rocky bluffs or canyons. It has been reported to use sheds, cabins, caves, mines, sinkholes, and rock fissures as daytime roosting places; individuals are likely to secrete themselves under the loose bark of trees as well. Caves and mines are used for night roosting and probably also serve as the principal sites for hibernation. These bats emerge at late dusk or after nightfall to forage among trees or over water. In the Dakotas, several other species of myotis, big brown bats, hoary bats, and silver-haired bats frequent the same foraging areas as *M. evotis.*

Females apparently form small maternity colonies, but not much is known of reproductive behavior. As in other temperate bats, there is a single molt annually, which takes place in July and August. Stomach contents of three specimens from southeastern Montana included the remains of beetles, dragonflies, leafhoppers, midges, moths, and muscoid flies.

Reproduction. Pregnant females (each with a single fetus) have been taken in South Dakota from late May to mid-June, and as late as early July elsewhere. Breeding presumably takes place mostly prior to entry into torpor in late summer or early autumn.

Suggested References. Barbour and Davis (1969); Jones et al. (1983).

Myotis grisescens / Gray Myotis

Distribution. The gray myotis has a restricted range in the United States, known only from the states of Alabama, Arkansas, Florida, Illinois, Indiana, Kansas, Kentucky, Missouri, North Carolina, Oklahoma, and Tennessee. In the region covered by this guidebook, it occurs only in eastern Oklahoma and extreme southeastern Kansas. See map 15.

Description. A relatively large myotis, smaller only than *M. velifer* of the species occurring in the plains states. Dorsal pelage grayish brown, relatively sparse and woolly in appearance; venter slightly paler. Wing membrane attached to ankle rather than at base of toe as in other *Myotis*. Total length, 88–107 mm; tail, 32–47 mm; hind foot, 9–13 mm; ear, 12–16 mm; forearm, 40–45 mm; weight 8–16 g. See figure 15.

Habits and Habitat. This species is found almost exclusively in caves, although man-made tunnels and storm sewers occasionally are occupied. No reports from mines are on record. This is a migratory bat in that individuals rarely overwinter in the same retreats used in summer. For example, of the 2,000 to 3,000 *M. grisescens* that inhabit a storm sewer in Pittsburg, Kansas, from March or April to October or November, fewer than 50 remain all winter. The others evidently move to winter quarters in caves about 100 miles east in southern Missouri.

The best-known maternity colonies are in large caves, usually those containing streams, and may number 100,000 or more individuals. These colonies disband when movement begins to winter quarters in autumn, although there is some evidence that these bats travel in flocks when migrating. Preferred hibernacula are deep caves; some, because of their previous inaccessibility, were undiscovered for many years.

Populations of the gray myotis have been declining in recent years, a source of great concern to conservationists and mammalogists. Human activity is probably the principal cause of the decline, through environmental disturbance, direct vandalism in colonies, and possibly use of insecticides.

Reproduction. As in other hibernating species, mating takes place mostly in autumn prior to entry into winter torpor. Sperm is stored over the winter in the female. The single young is born in June.

Suggested References. Mumford and Whitaker (1982); Tuttle (1975, 1976*a*, 1976*b*, 1979); Tuttle and Stevenson (1977).

Myotis keenii / Keen's Myotis

Distribution. Keen's myotis occurs throughout southeastern Canada and much of the eastern United States westward to British Columbia in the north and the plains states in the south. A disjunct population in western British Columbia and Washington may represent a separate species. In the five-state region, *M. keenii* is found from North Dakota southward to eastern Oklahoma. An isolated population occupies the Black Hills. See map 13.

Description. A medium-sized myotis with relatively long ears. Resembles *M. lucifugus* but color slightly paler and ears longer. Differs from *M. evotis* and *M. thysanodes* in being smaller, generally darker in color, and having shorter ears. Dorsum dull brown, venter pale grayish brown. Total length, 82–99 mm; tail, 34–43 mm; hind foot, 8–10 mm; ear, 16–18 mm; forearm, 31–36 mm; weight, 5–9 g. See figure 16.

Habits and Habitat. This bat is evidently less gregarious than many other species of myotis and thus is less well known. Foraging begins about dusk and continues intermittently through the night, with a second period of activity just before dawn. This is a bat of wooded areas—both deciduous and coniferous forests. In one study, *M. keenii* was found to forage principally over forested hillsides, frequenting areas just above shrub height under forest canopy. Temporary night roosts may be utilized, but this bat seeks more permanent shelter by day in caves or man-made structures such as mines and abandoned buildings, behind the loose bark of trees, and in similar retreats. Individual *M. keenii* occasionally are found roosting with bats of other species. Females form small maternity colonies of up to 30 or so individuals.

In hibernation, these bats usually are found in caves or mines, individually or in small clusters. Moist, cool sites where there is little air movement seem to be preferred. The hibernation period is not well known but probably extends from September or early October to April or May.

Annual molt takes place in adults in July and August. The known longevity revealed by banding studies is 18.5 years.

Reproduction. Most breeding takes place in autumn prior to hibernation. A single offspring is born in June or July. Lactating females have been taken on the Black Hills as late as mid-August.

Suggested References. Fitch and Shump (1979); Mumford and Whitaker (1982).

Myotis leibii / Small-footed Myotis

Distribution. This species has a fairly broad but curious distribution. In western North America, it occurs from southern Canada southward to central Mexico, and from the Pacific states eastward to the Great Plains. In the East, *M. leibii* is found from New England and southeastern Canada to the Ozarks. The two segments of the range do not meet. In the plains states, this bat occurs from southwestern North Dakota to western Oklahoma, and also in eastern Oklahoma. See map 12.

Description. A handsome bat; smallest member of genus *Myotis* in region. Dorsal pelage long and glossy, pale yellowish brown to golden brown and contrasting markedly with blackish membranes, ears, and face mask; venter paler, sometimes almost white. Calcar keeled. Total length, 80–89 mm; tail, 34–44 mm; hind foot, 7–9 mm; ear, 13–15 mm; forearm, 30–33 mm; weight, 3.5–6 g. See figure 17.

Habits and Habitat. This is a saxicolous species. Its distribution thus is closely associated with rocky habitats and is discontinuous over much of the plains region. It is common on the Black Hills, in the adjacent Badlands of South Dakota, and on the Pine Ridge of Nebraska. In Kansas, it is known only from four western counties, and in Oklahoma only from Black Mesa, the Wichita Mountains, and the Ouachita Mountains in the southeast.

These bats begin to forage rather early in the evening, coursing along cliffs, ledges, and deciduous riparian growth, and over streams and ponds. Night roosts in summer usually are in caves, mines, and man-made structures, and under overhanging rocks. Daytime retreats are in buildings, behind bark on trees, in rocky cracks and crevices, in holes in banks and hillsides, and even in abandoned swallow nests and under rocks on the ground.

Females and their young normally roost alone by day, but small maternity colonies have been reported. Hibernation takes place mostly in caves and abandoned mines, where individuals or small groups are frequently wedged into cracks or crevices.

Reproduction. Females bear one offspring (one report of apparent twins is on record) in late June or early July. Volant young have been taken in South Dakota as early as the last week of July.

Suggested References. Barbour and Davis (1969); Jones et al. (1983); Robbins et al. (1977).

Myotis lucifugus / Little Brown Myotis

Distribution. This species occupies a broad range in North America, from Alaska and Labrador south to northern and perhaps central Mexico. In the five states, it occurs over much of North Dakota, in eastern and western South Dakota, in eastern and northwestern Nebraska, in eastern and central Kansas, and in eastern Oklahoma. See map 14.

Description. Medium in size for the genus. Dorsal pelage sleek and glossy, often with metallic coppery sheen, dark brown (east) to buffy brown (west); venter paler than dorsum, sometimes slightly grayish. Ears and membranes brownish. Total length, 83–100 mm; tail, 33–42 mm; hind foot, 9–12 mm; ear, 13–16 mm; forearm, 34–40 mm; weight usually 5.5–8.5 g. See figure 18.

Habits and Habitat. This is one of the best known American bats because it is widespread (common in many areas) and frequently inhabits man-made structures. Maternity colonies, numbering up to more than 1,000 individuals, form in spring and early summer. These frequently are in warm buildings, but they are also found in caves, crevices, hollow trees, and similar retreats. Males and barren females roost in a variety of sites in the warm months. All roosts are in the vicinity of available water.

Hibernation takes place from September or early October to April or May, depending on latitude. In late summer and early autumn, swarms of *M. lucifugus* have been reported around potential hibernating sites, which usually are in caves and mines. When torpid, the bats frequently hang singly or in small groups, or wedge themselves into cracks or crevices, but clusters also have been reported. Sites selected have high humidity and vary from a few degrees above freezing to about 60°F.

The little brown myotis begins to forage at late dusk, frequently following set patterns night after night. Preferred foraging areas are over water, along the borders of woods and riparian growth, and in nearby open areas. The known record of longevity in this species is slightly more than 30 years.

Reproduction. Parturition dates vary with latitude, but most young probably are born from late May to late June. The single neonate (twins are rare) weighs 1.5 to 2 grams at birth and can fly in about three weeks.

Suggested References. Fenton and Barclay (1980).

Myotis sodalis / Social Myotis

Distribution. The social myotis occurs throughout much of the eastern United States, from New Hampshire and Vermont south to northern Florida, and westward to the eastern edge of the plains region. In this region, it is known only from eastern Oklahoma, but it may be found in eastern Kansas and southeastern Nebraska as well. See map 16.

Description. Medium-sized, dark-colored myotis. Pelage fine and fluffy, but dull, not glossy, in appearance. Dorsal color usually dark pinkish gray to blackish brown, the individual hairs tricolored; venter slightly paler. Calcar slightly keeled; hairs on hind foot short and inconspicuous. Total length, 77–95 mm; tail, 35–43 mm; hind foot, 7–10 mm; ear, 13–16 mm; forearm, 34–41 mm; weight usually 5–8 g. See figure 19.

Habits and Habitat. The greatest concentrations of this bat, at least in winter, seem to be in southern Indiana, Kentucky, and the Missouri Ozarks, where tight clusters of hibernating *M. sodalis* occur in caves. In summer, females form maternity colonies; those thus far reported have been found in hollows of trees and behind loose bark. Males evidently disperse into small groups in the warm months, seeking nighttime shelter principally in caves and mines.

Swarming takes place around hibernating sites, both upon departure in spring and arrival in autumn. Males enter hibernation later than females, in October or early November, but quit winter quarters later in the spring. Individuals of both sexes may be active from time to time over winter within a hibernaculum. Known longevity in this species is about 14 years.

Like other myotis, this bat forages in the evening and at night, frequently over or near water, in search of its flying insect prey. In a study in Indiana, individual *M. sodalis* foraged from a few meters above the ground to as high as about 100 feet "near the foliage of riparian and floodplain trees."

Reproduction. Mating takes place mostly in autumn, about the time that winter quarters are occupied, but copulation has been observed in winter months and even in spring, prior to the time these bats leave hibernacula. Scant available data suggest that females produce only one young, from June to early July.

Suggested References. Mumford and Whitaker (1982); Thomson (1982).

Myotis thysanodes / Fringed Myotis

Distribution. This fringe-tailed species is found from British Columbia southward to southern Mexico. The easternmost segment of the distribution in the United States, possibly isolated from the main range of the species to the west, is on the Black Hills and in adjacent areas of western South Dakota and Nebraska. See map 11.

Description. Size medium among long-eared members of *Myotis* in North America. Dorsum pale brownish to pale buff, contrasting with blackish brown ears and membranes; venter somewhat paler than above. Fringe of pale hairs extending beyond posterior border of uropatagium. Total length, 90–96 mm; tail, 40–44 mm; hind foot, 10–11 mm; ear, 18–21 mm; forearm, 39–44 mm; weight, 5.5–8.5 g. See figure 20.

Habits and Habitat. This is a bat of montane habitats throughout much of its range. It is found in wooded areas of the Black Hills, and on the Pine Ridge and Wildcat Hills of the Nebraska Panhandle, but it is also known from the treeless Badlands of South Dakota. *M. thysanodes* is often observed at dusk coursing over rivers, streams, or standing water. It commonly utilizes buildings as day roosting sites but also frequents caves and abandoned mines, especially at night. Individuals occasionally cluster with those of other species while roosting by day, and females form nursery colonies that may number several hundred mothers and young.

This bat hibernates from September to April or early May in this region, usually in caves or mines but possibly in other retreats as well. As in many species of *Myotis,* local migrations between summer habitats and winter hibernacula are known.

Molt, usually noticeable as new hairs protrude through the old pelage over both dorsum and venter, takes place in July and early August. Longevity is not well documented in this species, but one banded female lived at least 11 years.

Reproduction. A single young is born in late June or early July; gestation after implantation is thought to last 50 or 60 days. Lactating females have been collected well into August. Neonates are pinkish and hairless, measuring about 50 mm in total length. Young bats can fly by about day 20.

Suggested References. Jones et al. (1983); O'Farrell and Studier (1980); Turner (1974).

Myotis velifer / Cave Myotis

Distribution. This bat is known from the southwestern and south-central United States southward through most of Mexico to Honduras. In the plains states, it is found in southern Kansas and western Oklahoma (except the Panhandle). See map 15.

Description. Largest myotis treated in this book. Dorsum buffy brown, pelage woolly and relatively thin; venter pale grayish brown. Total length, 97–115 mm; tail, 41–49 mm; hind foot, 10–13 mm; ear, 15–17 mm; forearm, 41–47 mm; weight, 9–16 g or more. See figure 21.

Habits and Habitat. This myotis, as its name implies, seeks caves as preferred roosting sites, frequently in company in summer with the Brazilian free-tailed bat, but mines and buildings are also used. Cool caves are favored hibernacula in winter. In our area, *M. velifer* occurs only in the gypsum cave region of western Oklahoma and adjacent Kansas, where it is found throughout the year.

After emergence at dusk, most bats fly more or less directly to a source of water to drink. Feeding usually takes place at heights of six to 30 feet above the ground, around trees, along canyons, and over floodplains. Bats foraging in relatively open areas prefer to fly near whatever vegetation may be available.

The sexes hibernate together, but females form maternity colonies in spring, some of which may total 5,000 or more bats. Males spend the summer months in small groups in a variety of shelters, but not far distant from the nurseries in at least Kansas and Oklahoma. Known longevity is six years, but these bats probably live at least twice that long.

Foraging behavior usually results in two nightly periods of activity, a major period soon after sunset and another, less intense, before sunrise. The home cave usually serves as the night roost between foraging periods. Beetles and moths are the most common items in the diet.

Reproduction. Females bear a single offspring annually in June or early July. Most mating takes place in autumn, prior to entry into hibernation, but copulating pairs have been observed in winter as well. Young bats grow rapidly and begin to forage on their own between three and four weeks of age.

Suggested References. Fitch, Shump, and Shump (1981); Hayward (1970); Kunz (1973, 1974*b*).

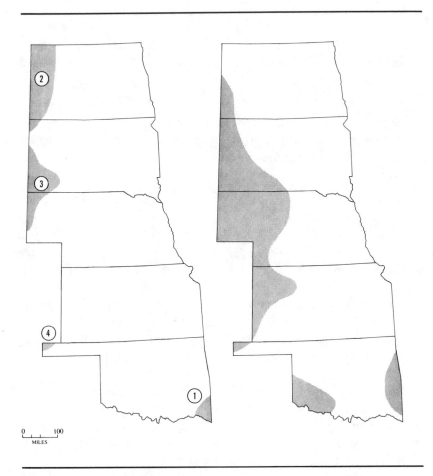

Map 11. *(Left).* Distribution of the southeastern myotis, *Myotis austroriparius* (1); the long-eared myotis, *Myotis evotis* (2); the fringed myotis, *Myotis thysanodes* (3); and the Yuma myotis, *Myotis yumanensis* (4).

Map 12. *(Right).* Distribution of the small-footed myotis, *Myotis leibii*.

Map 13. *(Left).* Distribution of Keen's myotis, *Myotis keenii.*

Map 14. *(Right).* Distribution of the little brown myotis, *Myotis lucifugus.*

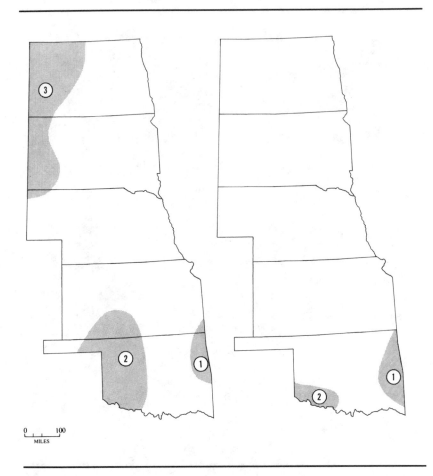

0 ___ 100
MILES

Map 15. *(Left).* Distribution of the gray myotis, *Myotis grisescens* (1); the cave myotis, *Myotis velifer* (2); and the long-legged myotis, *Myotis volans* (3).

Map 16. *(Right).* Distribution of the social myotis, *Myotis sodalis* (1), and the western pipistrelle, *Pipistrellus hesperus* (2).

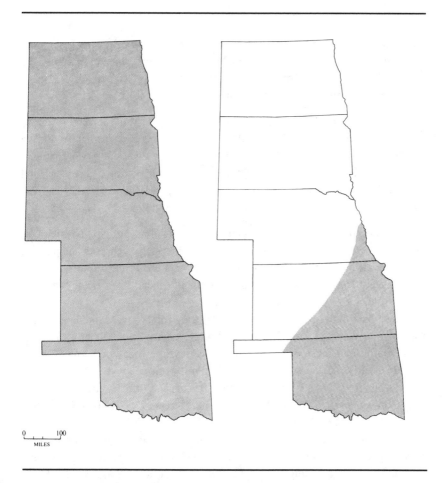

0 ⌊___⌋ 100
MILES

Map 17. *(Left).* Distribution of the silver-haired bat, *Lasionycteris noctivagans.*

Map 18. *(Right).* Distribution of the eastern pipistrelle, *Pipistrellus subflavus.*

Myotis volans / Long-legged Myotis

Distribution. This is a species of western North America, ranging from northern British Columbia to central Mexico. It reaches the eastern limits of distribution on the northern plains, occurring in the western parts of the Dakotas and northwestern Nebraska. See map 15.

Description. A medium-sized myotis with short ears. Wing furred on ventral surface to level of elbow. Dorsal pelage relatively long and soft, smoke brown to chocolate brown, tips of individual hairs slightly burnished; venter smoke brown to dull yellowish, washed with buff. Calcar distinctly keeled. Total length, 87–104 mm; tail, 35–46 mm; hind foot, 8–10 mm; ear, 12–14 mm; forearm, 37–41 mm; weight usually 6–9 g. See figure 22.

Habits and Habitat. The long-legged myotis inhabits principally open forested lands, such as the Pine Ridge area of northwestern Nebraska and parts of the Black Hills, but it is common also in the badlands of the western Dakotas and adjacent Nebraska. It is common throughout much of its range, yet relatively little is known of its natural history.

These bats may be seen first at dusk as they forage over woodland meadows or watercourses. Abandoned buildings, caves, fissures, hollow trees, mine shafts, and loose bark are utilized as daytime roosts in summer. Individuals usually roost singly except for maternity colonies, which may number several hundred females. In hibernation in caves or mines, these bats hang singly on walls or from ceilings of the winter retreat or wedge themselves into cracks and crevices.

The annual molt begins in mid- to late June and is completed in July, except that, as in other bats, it may be delayed in lactating females. A variety of small insects including moths, beetles, midges, and several kinds of flies have been found in stomachs of specimens from southeastern Montana.

Reproduction. Parturition usually occurs about a month or month and a half later in the plains states than farther west; the single offspring is born from mid-July to mid-August, later than in most other bats. Volant young have been taken as early as 20 July in South Dakota, however, perhaps indicating an unusually long and variable reproductive season.

Suggested References. Barbour and Davis (1969); Jones et al. (1983); Turner (1974); Warner and Czaplewski (1984).

Myotis yumanensis / Yuma Myotis

Distribution. This species is distributed in western North America from British Columbia south to central Mexico. In the five-state region, it is known only from the westernmost county in the Oklahoma Panhandle. See map 11.

Description. Smaller than average of bats of the genus *Myotis.* Dorsal coloration pale tan to brownish, pelage shorter and less glossy than that of *M. lucifugus;* underparts whitish to buff. Total length, 78–89 mm; tail, 34–40 mm; hind foot, 8–11 mm; ear, 12–16 mm; forearm, 32–38 mm; weight (specimens from Nevada), 4–7.5 g. See figure 23.

Habits and Habitat. This species is closely associated with well-watered habitats. Individuals have been noted to emerge early in the evening (although a report on habits in western Oklahoma indicated *M. yumanensis* did not leave daytime retreats "until darkness is almost complete"), frequently to forage over waterways, no more than a foot or so above the surface. These bats, like other insectivorous chiropterans, are efficient feeders and have been reported to seek night roosts no more than half an hour after dusk with stomachs filled. After feeding for a few minutes, they drink water by skimming it from the surface of ponds and streams, as do many other bats.

Maternity colonies, formed by females in April, are usually located in man-made structures such as barns, bridges, and church belfries, but they are also known from caves and mines. Bats in such nurseries frequently react to disturbance by relocating the colony, even after young have been born. Adult male bats of this genus as well as many others usually do not associate with maternity colonies and live solitarily in the warm months, scattered in buildings and other suitable retreats or even swallow nests. Although *M. yumanensis* presumably hibernates in winter, virtually nothing has been published about this.

In New Mexico, *M. yumanensis* has been described as a characteristic inhabitant of riparian communities in desert, grassland, and woodland at elevations of from 4,000 to 7,000 feet.

Reproduction. Females of this species bear a single offspring. Dates of parturition vary from late May to early July depending on locality.

Suggested References. Barbour and Davis (1969); Glass and Ward (1959); Harris and Findley (1962).

Lasionycteris noctivagans / Silver-haired Bat

Distribution. The silver-haired bat is found throughout most of temperate North America, from southern Alaska and Canada south to northern Mexico. In the five-state region, it may occur anywhere as a migrant. As a resident, it is known from the Black Hills but probably occurs elsewhere in the Dakotas and Nebraska. See map 17.

Description. A striking bat with distinctive coloration. Dorsal pelage long and blackish brown, frosted with silvery white; underparts slightly paler and less frosted; membranes blackish brown. Ears short, rounded, and naked; uropatagium furred dorsally on basal half. Total length, 91–108 mm; tail, 38–45 mm; hind foot, 7–10 mm; ear, 12–17 mm; forearm, 38–43 mm; weight, 8.5–12.5 g. See figure 24.

Habits and Habitat. This species has been characterized as a late flier, but there are other reports that it begins to forage at dusk. A marked bimodality in individual nocturnal activity apparently is common in some areas, evidently depending on the presence of certain other species of bats. Favored foraging grounds on the Black Hills are grassy valleys with standing water between forested hillsides. The flight pattern is slow and leisurely.

Individuals roost singly by day, principally under bark and in hollows of trees. Other roosts reported include buildings, woodpecker holes, bird nests, and dense canopy. Migrants have been found in outbuildings and in piles of boards, bricks, and the like. Torpid bats are known from caves, buildings, mines, rock crevices, hollow trees, and from beneath loose bark.

L. noctivagans occurs in the plains states from March or April to September or October, migrating southward in early autumn and northward again in spring. Some individuals evidently spend the winter in the southern states and northern Mexico, whereas others apparently hibernate at middle latitudes, possibly including the southern part of this region.

L. noctivagans is an opportunistic feeder, taking a variety of available insects. It is parasitized externally by mites, batflies, fleas, and bat bugs; and internally by cestodes, nematodes, and trematodes.

Reproduction. Mating takes place in autumn, and the young, usually twins, are born in June or early July. Gestation lasts 50 to 60 days. Neonates are pink with dark membranes, hairless, and weigh about 2 grams.

Suggested References. Kunz (1982).

Pipistrellus hesperus / Western Pipistrelle

Distribution. The center of the distribution of the western pipistrelle is the southwestern United States and adjacent Mexico, although it extends as far north as Oregon and Washington. In the five-state region, this species is known only from southwestern Oklahoma but almost certainly will be found also on the Black Mesa in the western Oklahoma Panhandle. See map 16.

Description. Smallest bat in the plains region. Color throughout usually pale yellowish; membranes dark, contrasting with pelage. Calcar keeled. Dorsum of uropatagium thinly furred on basal third. Total length, 70–83 mm; tail, 25–36 mm; hind foot, 5–7 mm; ear, 11–13 mm; forearm, 29–33 mm; weight, 3–5.5 g. Males average slightly smaller than females. See figure 25.

Habits and Habitat. This species is closely associated with rocky canyons, cliffs, and outcroppings, which provide the cracks and crevices used as daytime retreats. Thus the vernacular name "canyon bat" is sometimes used. A source of free water, such as that provided by cattle tanks, streams, and ponds, is critical to *P. hesperus,* and, because it is not a strong flier, roosting sites are not far distant from water.

These pipistrelles hibernate, but not much is known of their hibernacula; evidently caves, mines, and deep rock crevices are used for this purpose. In warm months, individuals leave daytime roosts relatively early, at dusk, to drink and forage for small insects. A variety of flies, bugs, and beetles is eaten as well as leafhoppers, flying ants, wasps, and gnats. Maximum activity is from dusk to an hour or so after sunset. Night roosts probably are in bushes, trees, and on rock faces or under overhanging rocks. These bats have been observed flying abroad, even drinking, in full daylight. Little is known of the life span of this species.

Reproduction. As in the eastern pipistrelle, females of *P. hesperus* normally have two young. These are born in late June or early July. Young reach adult size and become volant about a month after birth. Spermatozoa are stored by females after copulation in autumn and fertilization of the eggs takes place in spring. The gestation period has been estimated to be about 40 days.

Suggested References. Findley and Traut (1970); Glass and Morse (1959); Hayward and Cross (1979).

Pipistrellus subflavus / Eastern Pipistrelle

Distribution. This bat occurs over much of eastern North America, from southeastern Canada to Honduras. In the five-state region, it is found in southeastern Nebraska, eastern and central Kansas, and most of Oklahoma. Its range barely overlaps that of *P. hesperus.* See map 18.

Description. One of the smaller bats in the five states. Dorsal pelage varies from yellowish brown to grayish brown; venter somewhat paler; membranes generally darker than dorsum. Dorsal third of uropatagium furred. Calcar not keeled. Total length, 75–90 mm; tail, 33–41 mm; hind foot, 8–10 mm; ear, 12–14 mm; forearm, 31–35 mm; weight, 4–8 g. See figure 26.

Habits and Habitat. The eastern pipistrelle is a common bat in the eastern United States, albeit locally restricted. The biology of this species in hibernation is well known, but relatively little is known of its natural history in summer. Individuals are thought to forage primarily in open wooded areas and along woodland borders, frequently near or over water. Daytime retreats may be primarily in the foliage of trees, but small maternity colonies have been found in buildings. In the Southeast, these bats have been found roosting in Spanish moss by day. This species usually begins foraging early in the evening and can be recognized by its small size and weak, erratic flight.

Caves, mines, and rock crevices are used as hibernacula in winter, as well as night roosts in summer. Seasonal movements are poorly known, but *P. subflavus* migrates only locally to and from places of hibernation. During torpor, individuals are usually single, although small groups have been reported. They seek relatively warm and humid areas in the hibernaculum, and beads of water frequently collect on hibernating individuals. In Kansas, the eastern pipistrelle enters winter quarters in September and quits them in May and early June. In one study, females were found to live about 10 years and a few males as long as 15.

Reproduction. Birth of young, one to three (usually two), takes place in June and early July. Copulation occurs in autumn as the bats prepare for hibernation, and possibly at times during the winter. Offspring are volant within three to four weeks after birth.

Suggested References. Barbour and Davis (1969); Fujita and Kunz (1984); Jones and Pagels (1968); Lowery (1974).

Eptesicus fuscus / Big Brown Bat

Distribution. This common bat is distributed across the United States and southern Canada southward to northern South America. It occurs throughout the five-state region. See map 19.

Description. A large bat, dark to pale brownish dorsally, slightly paler ventrally. Ears dark colored and hairless; membranes dark brown. Total length, 112–130 mm; tail, 39–50 mm; hind foot, 9–13 mm; ear, 16–20 mm; forearm, 42–50 mm; weight, 16–30 g or more. Females average about 5 percent larger than males. See figure 27.

Habits and Habitat. This is perhaps the most common bat in the plains states; look for it anywhere suitable roosting sites and sources of food and water are available. This is a hardy animal; it is active later in the autumn than other hibernating species, and even on warm winter days. There is some movement within and between hibernacula in winter.

E. fuscus roosts in a variety of man-made structures as well as in caves, rock fissures, tree hollows, and behind loose bark. Hibernacula generally are in buildings, caves, or mines. In hibernation, individuals hang singly or in small groups or wedge themselves into cracks and crevices within the retreat. Maternity colonies are formed in spring. Males and barren females evidently are solitary in the warm months.

This bat is an early flier and can be recognized by its relatively slow, strong, steady flight. Some chatter audibly when flying. After leaving the daytime roost, these bats seek water and then forage at heights rarely exceeding 30 feet over water or clearings, along riparian vegetation, or around lights in urban areas. Most activity is early in the evening but may continue intermittently throughout the night. Known longevity in *E. fuscus* is 19 years.

Reproduction. Mating takes place in autumn or over the winter, and sperm is stored in the female. Nearly hairless young, weighing between 3 and 4 grams, are born in June or early July. The number varies geographically in this species—two in the eastern part of the range and one in the west. Young bats become volant at three to four weeks after birth and reach adult size in about 70 days.

Suggested References. Barbour and Davis (1969); Jones et al. (1983); Kunz (1974a); Phillips (1966).

Lasiurus borealis / Red Bat

Distribution. The red bat has the broadest distribution of any New World chiropteran, ranging from Canada southward to southern South America. It occurs throughout the plains states except in treeless areas in the West. See map 20.

Description. A medium-sized bat with long, pointed wings and short, rounded ears; uropatagium heavily furred dorsally. Upper parts bright reddish orange to chestnut (males usually more reddish than females); venter paler than dorsum; yellowish white patch on each shoulder. Total length, 103–124 mm; tail, 43–60 mm; hind foot, 8–10 mm; ear, 10–14 mm; forearm, 37–42 mm; weight, 6–14 g. See figure 28.

Habits and Habitat. This is a migratory species. It occurs in the plains states from March or April to as late as October but abandons all but possibly the extreme southern part of the region in the cold months. There is increasing evidence, however, that some individuals hibernate at middle latitudes. Those that do so may be seen abroad, feeding and taking water, on warm days.

Red bats roost in trees, either singly or in family groups of a female with young. Elms seem to be preferred, but box elder, fruit trees, and a variety of other woody vegetation are also used. Roost sites are in shaded places from four to more than 40 feet above the ground. These bats begin to forage early, before the sun goes down, when they can be observed flying near woodlots and trees bordering streams, city streets, and the like. Most activity is concluded within two hours after sunset.

Females and young occur throughout much of the five states in summer, although distribution in the West is restricted to woody riparian habitats and urban areas. Adult males are usually absent, their whereabouts unknown, until late summer. These bats are generally free of ectoparasites. Blue jays are important predators, especially of young.

Reproduction. Copulation occurs during autumn migration or on wintering grounds and has been observed between bats in flight. One to five young have been reported, more than in any other bat; the average is between three and four, usually born in June. There are two pair of mammae as in other *Lasiurus.*

Suggested References. Mumford and Whitaker (1982); Shump and Shump (1982*a*).

Lasiurus cinereus / Hoary Bat

Distribution. The hoary bat has a broad yet disjunct range. One population occurs in much of North America, from central Canada south to Guatemala, another in western and central South America, and a third in Hawaii. Because it is a strong flier and long-distance migrant, records of wayward individuals well outside the normal distribution are common. *L. cinereus* ranges throughout the five-state region as either a resident or migrant. See map 21.

Description. A large bat with long, narrow wings and short, rounded ears that are edged with black. Dorsum yellowish brown to mahogany, frosted with silver (thus hoary); venter whitish to yellowish; yellowish white patch on shoulder; membranes dark brownish. Uropatagium heavily furred dorsally. Total length, 133–150 mm; tail, 46–65 mm; hind foot, 11–14 mm; ear, 17–20 mm; forearm, 52–57 mm; weight averaging about 25 g. See figure 29.

Habits and Habitat. Like other *Lasiurus,* this species seeks daytime retreats in woody vegetation. It roosts in solitude except for females with young. Roosting sites are well covered above, open below, and generally 10 to 15 feet above the ground.

This species emerges later to forage than most bats and is swift of flight. In a study in Iowa, the period of greatest activity was three to seven hours after sunset, with a second surge before individuals returned to roost. The frequent chatter of these bats in flight is audible to humans. Moths have been reported to be the principal food, but beetles, bugs, neuropterans (lacewings), and flies were also found in stomachs of specimens from southeastern Montana.

This bat is strongly migratory, sometimes apparently flying in groups, especially in autumn. Males and females are segregated in summer for the most part; males migrate later and are generally found at higher altitudes or latitudes than females. Adults of both sexes have been reported from northwestern Nebraska to northwestern South Dakota in this area. It is suspected that *L. cinereus* winters mostly in Mexico, but this has not been certainly established, nor is much known of migratory routes.

Reproduction. Females usually bear twins, which are born from late May to early July. Breeding probably takes place during autumn migration but may also occur on wintering grounds.

Suggested References. Jones et al. (1983); Shump and Shump (1982*b*).

Lasiurus seminolus / Seminole Bat

Distribution. This monotypic species occurs in the southeastern United States, northward along the East Coast to Pennsylvania and New York and westward to eastern Texas and extreme southeastern Oklahoma. See map 21.

Description. Much the same as for *L. borealis* except dorsum rich mahogany brown in color, hairs sometimes tipped with grayish white; posterior parts of venter somewhat paler, throat and chest whitish; males and females similar in coloration. Total length, 89–114 mm; tail, 35–50 mm; hind foot, 7–10 mm; ear, 9–13 mm; forearm, 36–45 mm; weight, 8–12 g. See figure 30.

Habits and Habitat. This bat is abundant in the Deep South where the interior of clumps of Spanish moss provides favored roosting sites. Individuals also roost in other woody vegetation, generally at heights of four to 15 feet above the ground. Like other tree bats, *L. seminolus* is solitary except for females with young. The same or different bats may occupy the same roost on successive days, and at different times roosts may be occupied by other species of *Lasiurus*.

There is some evidence that Seminole bats in the northern part of the range of the species move southward in winter, but little is known of these movements. They do not hibernate and thus are active the year around, but individuals will become torpid during especially cold weather.

This species emerges early in the evening and usually seeks its insect prey at the treetop level, 25 to 40 feet above the ground. The flight is direct and usually rather swift. Several authors have noted that this lasiurine is less easily captured in mist nets than the red bat because of the height of the flight pattern.

Also like other tree bats, *L. seminolus* has a set of predators different from that of colonial species. Blue jays are thought to take some Seminole bats, and other avian predators may also be important. Adverse weather and the commercial collection of Spanish moss, however, are probably the most important factors contributing to mortality.

Reproduction. Females give birth to young in late May or June. Litter size averages a little more than three (range one to four). Young are fully furred at two weeks of age and are almost identical to adults in color.

Suggested References. Barbour and Davis (1969); Lowery (1974).

Nycticeius humeralis / Evening Bat

Distribution. The evening bat ranges throughout much of the eastern United States, from Michigan and Pennsylvania southward to Florida, Texas, and into northeastern Mexico. In the plains states, it occurs in southeastern Nebraska and through much of eastern and central Kansas and Oklahoma. See map 22.

Description. Dorsum dark brownish, venter slightly paler. Somewhat resembles big brown bat, but smaller and has only one (instead of two) pair of upper incisors that are separated from the canines. Also resembles several species of *Myotis,* but has only 30 instead of 38 teeth. Total length, 83–96 mm; tail, 35–40 mm; hind foot, 7–9 mm; ear, 12–14 mm; forearm, 34–37 mm; weight, 7–14 g. See figure 31.

Habits and Habitat. Evening bats roost during the day in hollows in trees, behind loose bark, and in man-made structures. Maternity colonies, frequently numbering hundreds of bats, are established in old buildings and in hollow trees.

In flight, *N. humeralis* normally courses over clearings, farm ponds, and openings in trees bordering watercourses. It is an inhabitant of the eastern deciduous forest, and in the western part of its range in Kansas, Nebraska, and Oklahoma, this bat is more or less restricted to riparian situations. It is a rather slow and deliberate flier and begins to forage at late twilight.

The evening bat is migratory, and individuals leave northern parts of the range for unknown destinations to the south in late September and October. Some may winter as far north as Oklahoma. Adult males are not known from the northern part of the warm-weather distribution; they may remain in the South while females travel northward to bear young. Evening bats are active in all months of the year in the southeastern United States, but torpid individuals are known from southern Arkansas. The extent to which hibernation is a widespread phenomenon is, however, unknown.

Reproduction. Females give birth to one to three (usually two) young from early June to early July. Breeding takes place in autumn or winter but, as in many other temperate-zone bats, fertilization is delayed until spring. Young are pink and hairless at birth, with eyes closed, and weigh about 2 grams. They are capable of flight in three weeks.

Suggested References. Mumford and Whitaker (1982); Watkins (1972).

Plecotus rafinesquii / Rafinesque's Big-eared Bat

Distribution. This is a species of the southeastern United States, occurring northward to Indiana and westward to the eastern parts of Oklahoma and Texas. See map 23.

Description. A medium-sized bat with tremendously enlarged ears as in *P. townsendii.* Two large lumps on snout. First upper incisors bicuspid (unicuspid in *P. townsendii*). Upper parts grayish, basal portion of hairs blackish and strongly contrasting with tips; venter white. Long hairs project beyond toes on hind feet. Total length, 80–110 mm; tail, 42–54 mm; hind foot, 8–13 mm; ear, 27–37 mm; forearm, 38–43 mm; weight, 8–13 g. See figure 32.

Habits and Habitat. This species appears to prefer roosts in the twilight zone, even in winter. Unoccupied buildings, culverts, and other man-made structures are used, but these bats also roost in caves, tree hollows, and other natural shelters. They seem to prefer caves in the northern part of the range. Colonies range in size from a few individuals up to 100 or more.

These bats emerge after dark to forage and return to roosts before dawn. The flight pattern of adults varies from swift and agile to nearly hovering. When a nursery colony is disturbed, females may take flight with young attached, but, as in other bats, they are not known to carry young while foraging. Little is known of the food habits of this species. Molt takes place from July to September.

P. rafinesquii is a hardy bat. In the northern part of the range, individuals are usually found in hibernation within 100 feet of the entrance of caves and mines. In the Deep South, some bats of this species are active at all times of the year, whereas others are torpid even in summer.

Snakes evidently occasionally feed on *P. rafinesquii* as do raccoons, opossums, and cats. Because of its roosting habits, this species is especially susceptible to disturbance by humans. Known longevity is a little more than 10 years.

Reproduction. Copulation takes place in both autumn and winter. The length of gestation is unknown. A single young, weighing about 2.5 grams, is born in late May or early June. The young have permanent teeth and first become volant at three weeks of age.

Suggested References. Barbour and Davis (1969); Jones (1977).

Plecotus townsendii / Townsend's Big-eared Bat

Distribution. This big-eared bat has a broad distribution in western North America from British Columbia southward to south-central Mexico and from the Pacific coast eastward to the plains states; isolated populations also occur on the Ozark Plateau and in the central Appalachians. In the five states, the species is known from western South Dakota, northwestern Nebraska, southern Kansas, western Oklahoma, and east-central Oklahoma. See map 24.

Description. A medium-sized bat with tremendously enlarged ears, resembling only its relative *P. rafinesquii.* Two large lumps on snout. Dorsum usually pale brownish, only slightly darker than venter; ears and membranes brownish. Total length, 95–105 mm; tail, 40–50 mm; hind foot, 9–12 mm; ear, 30–38 mm; forearm, 40–45 mm; weight, 8–12 g. See figure 33.

Habits and Habitat. This is a cavernicolous species throughout most of its known range, and its distribution probably is limited by the availability of caves and analogous man-made structures such as mines. In the five-state region, this bat occurs principally on the Black Hills, in the gypsum cave area of southern Kansas and western Oklahoma, and on the Ozark Plateau.

   P. townsendii hibernates in winter in caves or mines, singly or in small groups. There is some movement in winter, even between hibernacula. In spring, groups of females select sites for maternity colonies; males and barren females generally are solitary in the warm months. Caves and mines are the usual summer roosting haunts, but buildings are used occasionally.

   In flight the large ears are held erect and pointed forward parallel to the body; in hibernation they are typically curled along the neck like the horns of a ram. This species does not leave daytime roosts until well after dark and thus rarely is observed in flight.

Reproduction. The breeding season extends from October to February, just before or during hibernation. The period of gestation is uncertain (up to 100 days reported) because of less than precise knowledge of time of fertilization. A single young is born in late June or July. Neonates are grotesque in appearance because of their large, floppy ears and disproportionately large feet and thumbs.

Suggested References. Humphrey and Kunz (1976); Jones et al. (1983); Kunz and Martin (1982).

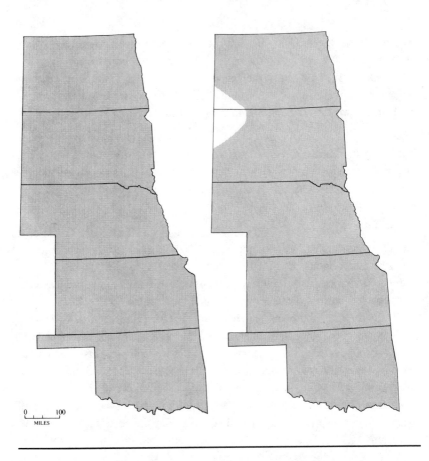

Map 19. *(Left).* Distribution of the big brown bat, *Eptesicus fuscus.*

Map 20. *(Right).* Distribution of the red bat, *Lasiurus borealis.*

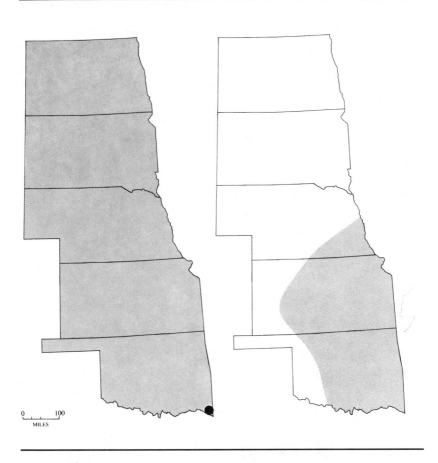

Map 21. *(Left).* Distribution of the hoary bat, *Lasiurus cinereus,* and the Seminole bat, *Lasiurus seminolus* (dot).

Map 22. *(Right).* Distribution of the evening bat, *Nycticeius humeralis.*

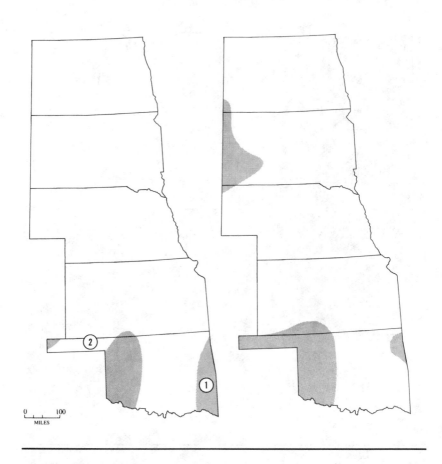

Map 23. *(Left).* Distribution of Rafinesque's big-eared bat, *Plecotus rafinesquii* (1), and the pallid bat, *Antrozous pallidus* (2).

Map 24. *(Right).* Distribution of Townsend's big-eared bat, *Plecotus townsendii*.

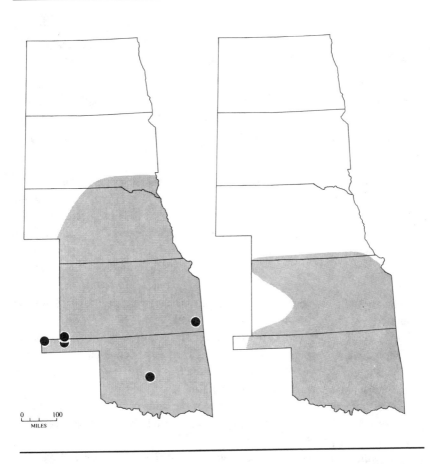

0   100
MILES

Map 25. *(Left).* Distribution of the Brazilian free-tailed bat, *Tadarida brasiliensis,* and the big free-tailed bat, *Tadarida macrotis* (dots).

Map 26. *(Right).* Distribution of the nine-banded armadillo, *Dasypus novemcinctus.*

Antrozous pallidus / Pallid Bat

Distribution. This bat occurs in western North America, from southernmost British Columbia southward to central Mexico. In the plains region, it is known only from western Oklahoma and adjacent Barber County, Kansas. See map 23.

Description. A large, pallid-colored bat with prominent ears. Color yellowish to pale dusky brown above, pale to buffy white ventrally. Total length, 106–129 mm; tail, 40–56 mm; hind foot, 11–16 mm; ear, 26–31 mm; forearm, 49–58 mm; weight, 16–22 g. See figure 34.

Habits and Habitat. *Antrozous pallidus* is common at lower elevations in the Southwest and adjacent Mexico. It favors areas of rocky outcrops, ranging from desert to oak and pine forest. In the five states, this species is known only from the gypsum cave region of northwestern Oklahoma and adjacent Kansas and from the Wichita Mountains.

Crevices in rocks are favored daytime roosts, but buildings, caves, mines, and hollow trees are also used. Maternity colonies, frequently in buildings, begin to form in April. Hibernacula, in the same general area as summer quarters, are known to be in caves, mines, and man-made structures.

A. pallidus emerges late in the evening, flying three or four feet above the ground toward water or a feeding area. Shortly after emergence, some individuals begin to appear at night roosts, which may be almost any open shelter. Favored night roosts include open buildings, covered porches, mines, rock shelters, bridges, and the like. Sometimes the same roost used during the day is also occupied at night. Nursing females evidently return to their young during nightly periods of inactivity.

A. pallidus is recognizable at night in the beam of a spotlight by its pale color, large size, and slow flight. It is one of the few bats that readily alight on the ground to feed; thus, terrestrial insects are a significant part of the diet.

Reproduction. Copulation takes place in autumn prior to entry into hibernation. Females normally bear two young (about 20 percent of all births are single) from late May to early July. The young bats mature more slowly than those of other plains species but can fly well at six weeks of age.

Suggested References. Barbour and Davis (1969); Hermanson and O'Shea (1983); Martin and Schmidly (1982).

Tadarida brasiliensis / Brazilian Free-tailed Bat

Distribution. This free-tailed species has one of the broadest distributions of any New World bat, occurring from Argentina and Chile northward through Middle America and the Antilles to the southern and western United States. In the five-state region, it is known as far north as northern Nebraska and southeastern South Dakota. See map 25.

Description. Upper parts usually dark grayish brown; venter slightly paler; membranes dark brown. Ears not joined at base. Total length, 90–108 mm; tail, 30–40 mm; hind foot, 8–11 mm; ear, 13–18 mm; forearm, 40–45 mm; weight, 8–14 g. See figure 35.

Habits and Habitats. Populations of this bat known from the plains states are migratory, individuals arriving in spring and departing in late summer or early autumn. The colder months evidently are spent at mostly unknown locations in Mexico. The northernmost known summer colonies are in Oklahoma and adjacent southern Kansas; other records from the latter state, the four known localities of record in Nebraska, and the one reported from South Dakota are evidently of spring migrants that "overshot" their intended destination, or of young-of-the-year dispersing in late summer.

Females form large maternity colonies, some containing hundreds of thousands—even millions—of bats, such as those at Carlsbad Caverns, New Mexico, and Bracken Cave, Texas. Males seem to be widely dispersed in summer, congregating in relatively small groups. Caves seem to be the preferred sites for colonies, but large cracks and crevices in rocks and several kinds of man-made structures are also used.

Food consists of a variety of small flying insects, such as ants, beetles, bugs, and moths. The fecal matter (guano) is rich in nitrogen, and where large congregations of this species occur, it can be harvested as a commercial fertilizer. Thus, the vernacular name "guano bat" is sometimes used. Like other plains chiropterans, this bat molts once annually, usually in July (males) and in August (females).

Reproduction. Breeding occurs on wintering grounds in February and March, and the single offspring is born in June after a gestation period of up to 100 days. Young become volant about a month after birth.

Suggested References. Barbour and Davis (1969); Bee et al. (1981); Jones et al. (1983).

Tadarida macrotis / Big Free-tailed Bat

Distribution. This bat has a known range extending from northern South America northward to the western and central United States. In the plains states, it is known only from two localities in Kansas (one recent report from there was in error) and three in Oklahoma (one from the Panhandle was previously unreported), but it has been recorded also from Colorado and Iowa and is to be looked for anywhere in the southern half of the region. See map 25.

Description. Upper parts reddish brown to dark brown (usually), even blackish; venter slightly paler; membranes dark brown. Two pair of lower incisors in contrast to three in the smaller *T. brasiliensis.* Ears joined basally at midline. Total length, 125–138 mm; tail, 46–54 mm; hind foot, 12–16 mm; ear, 28–30 mm; forearm, 58–64 mm; weight to 20 g or more. See figure 36.

Habits and Habitat. This free-tailed bat inhabits rough, rocky country. Preferred roost sites evidently are in crevices in rock cliffs. *T. macrotis* migrates, but little is known of its migratory routes or wintering grounds. Most records from the northern part of the known range in the United States probably relate to errant migrants. The earliest and latest months of reported occurrence in New Mexico are May and October, respectively, and from southwestern Texas they are June and September.

When foraging, this bat usually emits loud, piercing chatter, which is said to be distinctive. Moths probably make up much of the diet, but a variety of insects are consumed, including some ground-dwelling kinds that may be captured by the bats on the sides of cliffs. Like other species of molossids, individuals are readily taken in mist nets, especially those that are placed over water.

Maternity colonies, sometimes numbering more than 100 females, are formed in spring. These frequently are revealed by the loud chattering of the occupants and by accumulations of guano in and below the crevice in which the colony is located. Some sites are apparently used year after year.

Reproduction. Females bear a single young in June or July. Lactating individuals have been reported from July to September. Volant young have not been reported as taken until August.

Suggested References. Barbour and Davis (1969); Easterla (1973).

Figure 24. Silver-haired bat, *Lasionycteris noctivagans* (T. H. Kunz).

Figure 25. Western pipistrelle, *Pipistrellus hesperus* (B. J. Hayward).

Figure 26. Eastern pipistrelle, *Pipistrellus subflavus* (R. J. Baker).

Figure 27. Big brown bat, *Eptesicus fuscus* (T. H. Kunz).

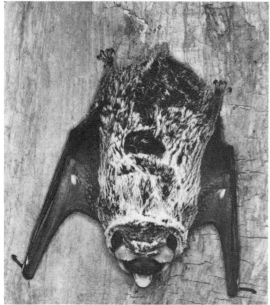

Figure 28. Red bat, *Lasiurus borealis,* family group (T. H. Kunz).

Figure 29. Hoary bat, *Lasiurus cinereus* (J. L. Tveten).

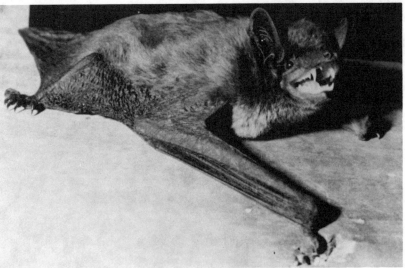

Figure 30. Seminole bat, *Lasiurus seminolus* (R. W. Barbour).

Figure 31. Evening bat, *Nycticeius humeralis* (T. H. Kunz).

Figure 32. Rafinesque's big-eared bat, *Plecotus rafinesquii* (R. W. Barbour).

Figure 33. Townsend's big-eared bat, *Plecotus townsendii* (J. P. Farney).

Figure 34. Pallid bat, *Antrozous pallidus* (R. W. Barbour).

Figure 35. Brazilian free-tailed bat, *Tadarida brasiliensis* (J. L. Tveten).

Figure 36. Big free-tailed bat, *Tadarida macrotis* (R. W. Barbour).

Figure 37. Nine-banded armadillo, *Dasypus novemcinctus* (J. L. Tveten).

Order Edentata

The order Edentata comprises three or four modern families, depending on the authority consulted, and is confined to the New World. Representatives of only one family occur outside tropical regions. Living edentates are represented by 13 genera and about 30 species. The order has a long fossil history.

The one family occurring in temperate North America, Dasypodidae, includes the familiar nine-banded armadillo, the only edentate found north of the tropics. Some members of the order are toothless (anteaters), as the ordinal name implies, but all others (sloths and armadillos) possess teeth (premolars and molars) in the posterior parts of the jaw. These teeth are, however, peglike, single rooted, and lack enamel. Deciduous (milk) teeth are present only in armadillos, the permanent cheekteeth of which total 28 to 36. The ordinal name Xenarthra is sometimes used for this group in a more restrictive sense than Edentata.

Dasypus novemcinctus / Nine-banded Armadillo

Distribution. The nine-banded armadillo ranges from South America northward to the southeastern and south-central United States. It has expanded its distribution northward in the plains region in this century and has recently been recorded as far north as southern Nebraska. See map 26.

Description. A distinctive mammal that cannot be confused with any other species in the plains states. Most of animal covered by bony carapace (or shell) consisting of anterior scapular shield, nine flexible bands, and pelvic shield; tail encased in series of bony rings; bony plate on head; rest of body covered by tough skin, with hard scutes on lower parts of legs and on feet; all toes heavily clawed. General dorsal color grayish brown, paler ventrally. Total length, 615–800 mm; tail, 245–370 mm; hind foot, 75–100 mm; ear, 30–40 mm; weight to 17 lb, but usually 7 to 10. See figure 37.

Habits and Habitat. This species occurs principally in woodlands, open savannas, and scrub areas. It is predominantly but not exclusively nocturnal. Food consists mostly of insects and other invertebrates, but fruit, berries, mushrooms, eggs of ground-nesting birds, and perhaps a few vertebrates also are eaten. Armadillos do not hibernate.

   D. novemcinctus digs its own burrows and also roots and digs in the ground in search of food. Active burrow systems have two or more openings, only one of which is regularly used. A nest of leaves and grasses is constructed in the burrow. Natural shelters among rocks and the like also are used as denning and retreat sites.

   Armadillos have few natural enemies. They can run with surprising speed when pursued, generally seeking safety in burrows or dense underbrush. When caught in the open, individuals can curl up in such a way that the carapace provides substantial protection from potential predators. Where common, armadillos frequently are killed on highways by motor vehicles.

Reproduction. Breeding occurs in middle to late summer, but implantation of the fertilized ovum is delayed about 14 weeks. Normally four young, identical quadruplets from one fertilized egg, are born in late winter after 120 days of gestation. The young are precocial at birth and reach sexual maturity in one year.

Suggested References. McBee and Baker (1982).

Figure 38. Swamp rabbit, *Sylvilagus aquaticus* (K. H. Maslowski).

Figure 39. Desert cottontail, *Sylvilagus audubonii* (T. W. Clark).

Figure 40. Eastern cottontail, *Sylvilagus floridanus* (J. K. Jones, Jr.). Note molt lines.

Figure 41. Nuttall's cottontail, *Sylvilagus nuttallii* (Valan Photos, photograph by E. Schmidt).

Figure 42. Snowshoe hare, *Lepus americanus* (J. Prescott).

Figure 43. Black-tailed jackrabbit, *Lepus californicus* (Kansas Fish and Game Commission, photograph by K. Steibben).

Figure 44. White-tailed jackrabbit, *Lepus townsendii*, winter pelage (U.S. Fish and Wildlife Service).

Order Lagomorpha

Lagomorphs occur naturally on all continents except Australia (where they have been introduced) and Antarctica. The order, once thought to be closely related to rodents, has a fossil history dating back to the Paleocene. Like rodents, lagomorphs have large, ever-growing incisors, high-crowned cheekteeth, and a long diastema between the incisors and the cheekteeth. Rodents have but one pair of upper incisors, however, and lagomorphs have two, the second pair peglike and located directly behind the first.

There are two modern families—Ochotonidae (pikas) and Leporidae (hares and rabbits). Only leporids are found in the plains states. In all, the order is comprised of 12 Recent genera and about 62 Recent species.

Two genera, *Lepus* (hares) and *Sylvilagus* (rabbits), with a total of seven species are native to the plains region. Hares are generally larger than rabbits and have precocial young, whereas the offspring of rabbits are altricial.

Key to Lagomorphs / Rabbits and Hares

1. Hind foot less than 115 mm (less than 105 in all but some *Sylvilagus aquaticus*); interparietal bone distinct 2
1'. Hind foot 105 mm or more (more than 115 in all but smallest *Lepus americanus*); interparietal bone indistinct, fused to parietal 5
2. Anterior projection on supraorbital process minute or lacking; posterior projection on supraorbital process completely fused to braincase; size large, hind foot averaging more than 100 mm . . . . *Sylvilagus aquaticus*
2'. Anterior projection on supraorbital process present; posterior projection of supraorbital process mostly free of (or incompletely fused to) braincase; size medium, hind foot averaging less than 100 mm 3
3. Auditory bullae relatively large and inflated; ear longer than 61 mm . . . . *Sylvilagus audubonii*

3'. Auditory bullae relatively small and not inflated; ear usually shorter than 61 mm 4

4. Total length usually more than 400 mm; ear relatively sparsely furred within; diameter of external auditory meatus less than crown length of upper molars . . . . *Sylvilagus floridanus*

4'. Total length usually less than 400 mm; ear densely furred within; diameter of external auditory meatus greater than crown length of upper molars . . . . *Sylvilagus nuttallii*

5. Ear less than 90 mm; hind foot usually less than 125 mm; no anterior projection on supraorbital process . . . . *Lepus americanus*

5'. Ear more than 90 mm; hind foot usually more than 125 mm; pronounced anterior projection on supraorbital process 6

6. Dorsum of tail white (or, if darker, with mid-dorsal line that does not extend onto back); simple fold on occlusal surface of first upper incisor; mesopterygoid fossa relatively broad, usually 11.5 mm or more . . . . *Lepus townsendii*

6'. Dorsum of tail black, with black patch extending onto back; bifurcate or trifurcate fold on occlusal surface of first upper incisor; mesopterygoid fossa relatively narrow; usually 11.0 mm or less . . . . *Lepus californicus*

NOTE: The European rabbit, *Oryctolagus cuniculus*, is not included in the foregoing key because wild populations probably do not occur in the plains states (see account of introduced species).

Sylvilagus aquaticus / Swamp Rabbit

Distribution. The swamp rabbit is a species of the south-central United States, ranging from East Texas to Georgia, and northward to extreme southern Indiana. In the plains states, it occurs only in eastern Oklahoma and extreme southeastern Kansas. See map 27.

Description. Upper parts blackish to reddish brown, paler ventrally. Size large for genus. Total length, 450–540 mm; tail, 50–75 mm; hind foot, 90–115 mm; ear, 60–80 mm; weight, 1,700–2,700 g. See figure 38.

Habits and Habitat. The swamp rabbit is aptly named; it occurs most often in floodplain forests, densely forested bottomlands, briar and honeysuckle patches, and canebrakes. The animals rest by day in "forms" beneath bushes, in hollow logs or trees, or even atop stumps.

These rabbits are not discriminating herbivores. They feed on both herbaceous and woody vegetation roughly in proportion to their abundance in the habitat. The diet includes grasses, sedges, shrubs, and twigs and bark of trees.

Floods, hunters, and a variety of predators all take their toll on populations of swamp rabbits. In addition, the animals harbor a variety of arthropod and helminth parasites. Longevity in the wild is not known, but the average life span must be fairly short; fecundity is high, yet only half of the animals in one population studied were juveniles. Adults molt in both spring and autumn.

Home ranges of two to 20 acres have been reported and the animals are territorial. Males form a linear social hierarchy, the dominant male in a given area doing most of the mating.

Reproduction. Swamp rabbits breed throughout the warmer months. Females are polyestrous and ovulation is induced. Gestation lasts 35 to 40 days. Mean litter size is about three. Females show postpartum estrus and may produce four or even five litters annually.

Neonates are altricial—blind, helpless, and thinly furred. Young are reared in a nest under a log or the roots of a tree. Eyes open after about a week and the young leave the nest at two weeks, before they are even weaned. There are distinct nestling, juvenile, and subadult pelages. The young can breed as early as six months of age.

Suggested References. Chapman and Feldhamer (1981); Mumford and Whitaker (1982); Toll, Baskett, and Conaway (1960).

Sylvilagus audubonii / Desert Cottontail

Distribution. This species occurs over arid parts of western North America, from Montana southward to central Mexico, and from the High Plains of Oklahoma, Kansas, and Nebraska to the Pacific Coast. See map 27.

Description. A medium-sized cottontail; palest in color of local species; upper parts pale grayish washed with yellow, with sparse wash of black hairs; venter whitish; throat orangish brown. Total length, 390–435 mm; tail, 40–60 mm; hind foot, 90–100 mm; ear, 60–70 mm; weight, 950–1,375 g. See figure 39.

Habits and Habitat. Typical habitats in the plains region are weedy margins of upland fields and pastures, brushy country, and thickets in dry ravines. The desert cottontail occupies situations much more arid than the habitats of either Nuttall's or the eastern cottontail, species with which its range abuts in the plains states. The diet varies with habitat and is not selective, emphasizing grasses in open country and a variety of herbaceous and woody vegetation elsewhere. Succulent new growth is preferred. Moisture from food supplies needed water. Foraging is usually crepuscular to nocturnal.

Most medium-sized to large predators take desert cottontails. At times they are a staple for coyotes, hawks, and large owls. Badgers, weasels, and snakes take nestling young. Rapid flight is the main defense. The animals rest in burrows (usually remodeled from those of badgers, coyotes, or prairie dogs), as well as in simple "forms" beneath shrubs. Diseases exact a toll and desert cottontails are widely pursued as small game. Average longevity is less than one year.

Home range varies from one to 15 acres; densities to seven per acre have been reported. These animals are not strongly territorial. Females are tolerant of one another, but males are pugnacious.

Reproduction. Ovulation is induced and females are polyestrous, showing postpartum estrus. Breeding continues throughout the warmer months. Females bear two or three litters of one to five (mean about three) young per year. The altricial young are reared in a nest lined with grasses and fur. The eyes open at 10 days, and the young leave the nest at two weeks. Sexual maturity is attained at about six months of age.

Suggested References. Chapman, Hockman, and Edwards (1982); Chapman and Willner (1978); Jones et al. (1983).

Sylvilagus floridanus / Eastern Cottontail

Distribution. This cottontail has a broad distribution, from the eastern seaboard west to the Rockies and from southern Canada southward to Costa Rica. It occurs virtually throughout the plains region. *S. floridanus* is broadly sympatric with the swamp rabbit, less so with the desert cottontail, and is mostly parapatric with Nuttall's cottontail. See map 28.

Description. Upper parts grayish to brownish, with liberal sprinkling of blackish hairs; dark rusty nape; venter white. Size medium; total length, 400–450 mm; tail, 40–70 mm; hind foot, 85–105 mm; ear, 50–60 mm; weight, 900–1,500 g. See figure 40.

Habits and Habitat. This is a cottontail of the eastern deciduous forest. Suitable habitat in the plains states is increasingly restricted westward to riparian ecosystems.

Foraging is crepuscular for the most part. The diet includes a variety of plants. Succulent forbs and grasses are taken during the growing season; in colder months the animals browse on shrubs and trees, eating twigs, buds, and bark. Most water is obtained incidental to the diet. Like other rabbits, this species reingests specialized, vitamin-rich fecal pellets.

Eastern cottontails are primarily solitary. Home ranges of females are five to 15 acres; those of males range to 100 acres (but usually are much smaller). Breeding females may be territorial, and males defend their personal space actively, although home ranges overlap broadly. Densities of about five per acre have been reported.

S. floridanus is an important food for foxes, eagles, coyotes, hawks, and owls. Weasels and snakes take the young. This is the most widely hunted game mammal in the United States, and many individuals are killed on highways. Mean natural longevity surely is less than one year. Three-fourths of the young die at less than five months of age.

Reproduction. Females can bear seven or more litters of one to nine (commonly four or five) young each year, throughout the warmer months. Gestation takes 28 to 39 days. The altricial young are reared in a fur-lined nest. They are blind, helpless, and weigh about 40 grams. They grow quickly, however, eat vegetation at two weeks, and are independent of the mother by four or five weeks of age.

Suggested References. Chapman, Hockman, and Edwards (1982); Chapman, Hockman, and Ojeda C. (1980).

Sylvilagus nuttallii / Nuttall's Cottontail

Distribution. Nuttall's cottontail (sometimes referred to as mountain cottontail) is a mammal of mountains and basins of western North America, ranging from Alberta to Arizona and New Mexico, and from the Sierra-Cascades to the Black Hills and the High Plains of the Upper Missouri Valley in North Dakota. Apparently the species is nowhere sympatric with the closely related eastern cottontail. See map 29.

Description. Grayish brown above, white below; generally paler (fewer blackish hairs and chest less reddish) than the eastern cottontail; darker in color than the desert cottontail. Hind feet densely haired. Size medium for genus. Total length, 350–400 mm; tail, 35–65 mm; hind foot, 80–100 mm; ear, 60–70 mm; weight, 650–1,000 g. See figure 41.

Habits and Habitat. This is a species of sagebrush lands on the northern Great Plains and the adjacent mountain forests and woodlands. Because cottontails are difficult to identify, habitat relationships are poorly studied; in the plains states, however, Nuttall's cottontail generally occupies continuous brushlands, woodlands, and woodland edges. Detailed studies of species of the genus *Sylvilagus* are warranted where they occur in near proximity, as they do on the Black Hills and in adjacent areas.

These animals are mostly crepuscular. Sagebrush is a dietary staple, but forbs, grasses, other shrubs, and a variety of other woody vegetation also are eaten. Reingestion of fecal matter occurs.

Individuals rest in "forms" beneath shrubs, among rocks, or in burrows. When flushed, they flee in a circuitous path, the white tail and concealing coloration of the dorsum confusing would-be predators. Still, many are killed by coyotes, bobcats, foxes, hawks, and owls, as well as by human hunters and vehicles on roadways.

Reproduction. The breeding season spans the warmer months. Mean litter size is four to five (known range one to eight). The polyestrous females may bear four or five litters annually. Ovulation is induced, as in other rabbits. A fur-lined nest in a hollow, usually beneath a shrub, protects the altricial young. Development has not been detailed but presumably is similar to that of other cottontails. Occasionally, females breed in their first summer.

Suggested References. Chapman (1975); Chapman, Hockman, and Edwards (1982); Jones et al. (1983).

Lepus americanus / Snowshoe Hare

Distribution. The snowshoe hare has a boreal and montane distribution, ranging across subarctic North America from Alaska to Newfoundland and then southward along major mountain ranges to California, New Mexico, and North Carolina. In the plains states, it occurs primarily in northern North Dakota. See map 30.

Description. Dorsum rusty brown with blackish brown wash in summer, venter grayish white. Winter pelage pure white except for black tips of ears. Overall size smaller than that of other hares; ears shorter and feet relatively longer. Total length, 370–465 mm; tail, 25–40 mm; hind foot, 100–125 mm; ear, 75–90 mm; weight, 1.5–4.5 lb. See figure 42.

Habits and Habitat. This is a species of dense coniferous forests or deciduous thickets of alder or willow. These hares spend the day in a simple "form" beneath shrubbery, in a hollow log, or in a burrow abandoned by another mammal. They forage at night, eating herbaceous vegetation during the growing season and browsing twigs, buds, and bark in winter. Foraging routes are marked by numerous runways. Predators include lynx, martens, red foxes, and coyotes. These hares host numerous parasites, including arthropods externally and flatworms and roundworms internally.

Snowshoe hares are solitary except during the breeding season. They are not strongly territorial, but they do show mutual avoidance. Densities vary by a factor of 25 from high to low points in the population cycle, over roughly a 10-year period. Peak populations frequently result in densities of five or six hares per acre. Disease and winter food shortages lower survivorship, leading to a decline of dense populations; at such times, the lynx is the major predator.

Molt from brown pelage to the snow white coat of winter takes place in autumn, apparently cued by the length of the day. The reverse occurs in spring. A similar pattern occurs in some other species of the genus *Lepus*, including the white-tailed jackrabbit.

Reproduction. The breeding season is early March to late August. Females are polyestrous, bearing one to three litters of one to seven young annually. Ovulation is induced. The gestation period is 36 days. The precocial young are weaned at one month of age, weighing nine times more than at birth.

Suggested References. Aldous (1937); Baker (1983); Keith and Windberg (1978).

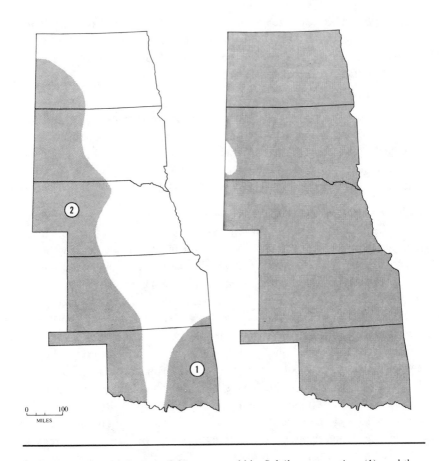

Map 27. *(Left).* Distribution of the swamp rabbit, *Sylvilagus aquaticus* (1), and the desert cottontail, *Sylvilagus audubonii* (2).

Map 28. *(Right).* Distribution of the eastern cottontail, *Sylvilagus floridanus.*

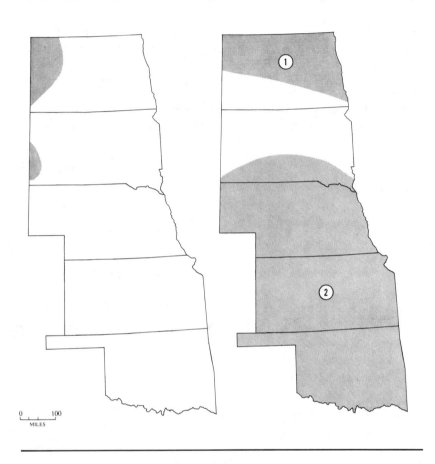

Map 29. *(Left).* Distribution of Nuttall's cottontail, *Sylvilagus nuttallii.*

Map 30. *(Right).* Distribution of the snowshoe hare, *Lepus americanus* (1), and the black-tailed jackrabbit, *Lepus californicus* (2).

Lepus californicus / Black-tailed Jackrabbit

Distribution. This jackrabbit occupies semiarid western North America, ranging from central Mexico northward to Washington and Montana west of the Rockies and to South Dakota in the east. See map 30.

Description. Dorsum gray to blackish tinged with buff; sides grayish; venter white; tail with black dorsal stripe extending onto back. Slightly smaller than *L. townsendii.* Total length, 535–585 mm; tail, 70–90 mm; hind foot, 125–135 mm; ear, 110–125 mm; weight, 4–7 lb. See figure 43.

Habits and Habitat. These are animals of open country, frequently occurring on short-grass prairie with scattered shrubs, yucca, or cacti. Their presence is encouraged by heavy grazing. They tend to avoid areas of heavy brush or woods, where their principal defenses, keen eyesight and speed of escape, are ineffective. The animals rest by day in a simple "form" at the base of a shrub or rock.

By night they emerge to feed on grasses, forbs, and crops, especially alfalfa. In winter they eat dried herbage, woody twigs, buds, and cacti. Like other lagomorphs, these jackrabbits produce two kinds of feces. Hard, dry waste pellets are voided at night; soft feces are produced by day, taken directly from the anus, and reingested. The soft feces seem to contain vitamins synthesized by an intestinal microflora.

Able to run 35 to 40 miles per hour, jackrabbits can often escape predators, but they are nonetheless captured regularly by coyotes, foxes, hawks, and eagles. Weasels and owls take young. Parasites include fleas, lice, ticks and mites, warbles, and worms. Some diseases (tick fever, tularemia) are transmissible to humans.

Jackrabbits are valuable to humans for sport and sometimes for food, but they can also be a nuisance, damaging crops and nursery stock. They do degrade overgrazed pastures by spreading prickly pear, but they also void viable grass seeds in their feces.

Reproduction. Black-tailed jackrabbits bear one to four litters of one to eight young annually. Gestation takes 41 to 47 days. Ovulation is induced. Like those of hares generally, the young are precocial—they are born well haired and mobile, with eyes open. They eat solid food at 10 days of age.

Suggested References. Hansen and Flinders (1969); Jones et al. (1983); Tiemeier et al. (1965); Vorhies and Taylor (1933).

Lepus townsendii / White-tailed Jackrabbit

Distribution. This is a species of the Northern Great Plains and the Great Basin, distributed from California to the Mississippi River and from Saskatchewan to the Upper Rio Grande Valley of New Mexico. White-tailed jackrabbits formerly ranged southward across the plains states to southern Kansas but now occur predominantly north of the Platte River. See map 31.

Description. In summer, pale buffy gray above, white below; tail with at most a mid-dorsal line of blackish gray. In winter, pure white over most of range, except for black tips of ears. Size large, largest of local hares; total length, 540–640 mm; tail, 70–110 mm; hind foot, 125–165 mm; ear, 95–110 mm; weight to 10 lb. Seasonal molts result in color change. See figure 44.

Habits and Habitat. These jackrabbits occur in open grasslands and sagebrush, but they avoid forests and woodland. They seem to be less well adapted to cultivated areas than *L. californicus,* and their range has diminished over the past century as that of the black-tailed jackrabbit has increased. Part of this change may be due to general climatic warming on the Great Plains within historic time.

   White-tailed jackrabbits are basically crepuscular, feeding in early morning and again in the evening. The diet consists chiefly of grasses and shrubs, and some alfalfa where available. In winter, twigs and bark are eaten. Overall, they do not cause much damage to agriculture.

   L. townsendii avoids predators with escape speeds up to 40 miles per hour. Still, white-tailed jackrabbits are preyed upon by coyotes, eagles, and hawks, and the young are taken by a wide variety of carnivores. Parasites and diseases, including tularemia, also take a toll. They are hunted by humans for sport and food, and the fur has been used commercially to make felt.

Reproduction. The breeding season is from late February to mid-June; the breeding structure is promiscuous. Ovulation is induced by copulation. Females usually bear two to four young (range one to nine) per litter. The young are fairly precocial and are born well haired with the eyes open, and weigh about 100 grams. Growth is rapid and full size is reached by three to four months of age.

Suggested References. Bear and Hansen (1966); James and Seabloom (1969*a,* 1969*b*); Jones et al. (1983).

Figure 45. Least chipmunk, *Tamias minimus* (E. P. Haddon).

Figure 46. Colorado chipmunk, *Tamias quadrivittatus* (Valan Photos, photograph by R. C. Schmidt).

Figure 47. Eastern chipmunk, *Tamias striatus* (E. C. Birney).

Figure 48. Yellow-bellied marmot, *Marmota flaviventris* (R. G. Van Gelder).

Figure 49. Woodchuck, *Marmota monax* (K. H. Maslowski and W. W. Goodpaster).

Figure 50. Wyoming ground squirrel, *Spermophilus elegans* (J. L. Tveten).

Figure 51. Franklin's ground squirrel, *Spermophilus franklinii* (R. W. Barbour).

Figure 52. Richardson's ground squirrel, *Spermophilus richardsonii* (K. A. Fagerstone).

Figure 53. Spotted ground squirrel, *Spermophilus spilosoma* (D. P. Streubel).

Figure 54. Thirteen-lined ground squirrel, *Spermophilus tridecemlineatus* (U.S. Fish and Wildlife Service).

Figure 55. Rock squirrel, *Spermophilus variegatus* (W. W. Goodpaster).

Figure 56. Black-tailed prairie dog, *Cynomys ludovicianus* (U.S. Fish and Wildlife Service, photograph by D. E. Beggins).

Figure 57. Gray squirrel, *Sciurus carolinensis* (W. E. Clark).

Figure 58. Fox squirrel, *Sciurus niger* (L. Miller).

Figure 59. Red squirrel, *Tamiasciurus hudsonicus* (R. B. Fischer).

Figure 60. Northern flying squirrel, *Glaucomys sabrinus* (R. Altig).

Order Rodentia

Rodents represent the largest (in numbers of taxa included) and most diverse of living orders of mammals. There are more than 30 Recent families (the exact number depends on where familial boundaries are drawn), about 490 genera, and some 1,620 species. The known fossil record, which is moderately good, extends back to the late Paleocene.

Broadly distributed, the order is native to all of the world's major land masses except Antarctica, New Zealand, and some arctic and oceanic islands, and rodents have been introduced by humans in most places where they were not found originally. They range in habits from taxa that are fossorial and semiaquatic to those that are scansorial or that glide, but most rodents are adapted to a terrestrial mode of existence. Many are obligate herbivores, but some also eat insects and other small animals. Members of the order are characterized by a single pair of ever-growing incisors, both above and below, a distinct diastema between the incisors and the cheekteeth, and a dental formula that never exceeds 1/1, 0/0, 2/1, 3/3, total 22.

Seven families of rodents are native to the plains states and representatives of two others have been introduced there (and are briefly treated in a special section at the end of this guidebook). The large number of included species (59) that are native to the plains region makes construction of keys cumbersome unless they are first broken down to the family level. There is considerable controversy in the literature about whether the family Cricetidae, recognized here, should be regarded as distinct from the Muridae.

Key to Families of Rodents

1. Modified for semiaquatic life; hind feet webbed; lower incisor more than 6.0 mm in width at alveolus 2

1'. Not especially modified for semiaquatic life (except *Ondatra*); hind feet not webbed; lower incisor less than 5.5 mm (less than 4.0 mm in all except Erethizontidae) in width at alveolus 3

2. Tail flattened dorsoventrally, its breadth approximately 25 percent of its length; infraorbital canal smaller than foramen magnum . . . . Castoridae

2'. Tail not flattened dorsoventrally, its breadth less than 10 percent of its length; infraorbital canal larger than foramen magnum . . . . Myocastoridae*

3. Sharp quills on dorsum and tail; infraorbital canal larger than foramen magnum . . . . Erethizontidae

3'. No quills on any part of body; infraorbital canal never larger than foramen magnum 4

4. Hairs on tail usually distichous; skull with distinct postorbital processes . . . . Sciuridae

4'. Hairs on tail not distichous (except in *Neotoma cinerea*); skull lacking distinct postorbital processes 5

5. External fur-lined cheek pouches present; cheekteeth 4/4 6

5'. No external fur-lined cheek pouches; cheekteeth 4/3 or 3/3 7

6. Tail more than three-fourths length of head and body; hind feet larger than forefeet; tympanic bullae exposed on posterodorsal part of skull . . . . Heteromyidae

6'. Tail much less than three-fourths length of head and body; hind feet smaller than forefeet; tympanic bullae not exposed on posterodorsal part of skull . . . . Geomyidae

7. Tail much longer than head and body; hind feet noticeably elongate; cheekteeth 4/3 . . . . Zapodidae

7'. Tail about equal to, or shorter than, head and body; hind feet not noticeably elongate; cheekteeth 3/3 8

8. Annulations of scales on tail nearly or completely concealed by pelage (except in *Ondatra,* in which the tail is laterally flattened); cheekteeth with two longitudinal rows of cusps or prismatic . . . . Cricetidae

8'. Annulations of scales easily visible on sparsely haired tail; cheekteeth with three longitudinal rows of cusps . . . . Muridae*

Key to Sciurids / Squirrels

1. Skin between forelimbs and hind limbs noticeably loose, forming gliding membrane; narrow interorbital region V-shaped 2

1'. Skin between forelimbs and hind limbs not noticeably loose;
     interorbital region not V-shaped 3
2.   Hair of venter white to base; total length less than 260 mm; greatest
     length of skull less than 36 mm .... *Glaucomys volans*
2'. Hair of venter gray, white only at tips; total length more than 260 mm;
     greatest length of skull more than 36 mm .... *Glaucomys sabrinus*
3.   Skull large and relatively massive, greatest length more than 70 mm;
     hind foot usually more than 75 mm; weight more than 2.5 pounds .. 4
3'. Skull smaller, greatest length less than 70 mm; hind foot less than 75
     mm; weight less than 2.5 pounds 5
4.   General color yellowish, face black with white markings on muzzle;
     two pair of abdominal mammae; maxillary toothrows divergent
     anteriorly .... *Marmota flaviventris*
4'. General color brownish, face brown to black; no white markings on
     muzzle; one pair of abdominal mammae; maxillary toothrows
     parallel .... *Marmota monax*
5.   Tail short, about 25 percent length of body, tip black; maxillary
     toothrows strongly convergent posteriorly, more than 15 mm in length,
     cheekteeth laterally expanded .... *Cynomys ludovicianus*
5'. Tail moderate to long, more than 25 percent length of body, not
     distinctly tipped with black; maxillary toothrows more or less parallel
     (at least not strongly convergent posteriorly), less than 12 mm in
     length, cheekteeth not laterally expanded 6
6.   Dorsal pelage always striped; stripe(s) continuing onto face;
     infraorbital foramen (no extensive canal) piercing zygomatic plate .. 7
6'. Dorsal pelage striped, mottled, spotted, or more or less uniform; if
     striped, the stripes not continuing onto face; distinct infraorbital canal
     passing between zygomatic plate and rostrum 9
7.   Dorsal stripes not continuous to base of tail; tail less than 40 percent of
     total length; premolars 1/1 .... *Tamias striatus*
7'. Dorsal stripes continuous to base of tail; tail more than 40 percent of
     total length; premolars 2/1 8
8.   Hind foot 32 mm or less; greatest length of skull
     less than 33 mm .... *Tamias minimus*
8'. Hind foot 33 mm or more; greatest length of skull
     more than 35 mm .... *Tamias quadrivittatus*
9.   Total length more than 340 mm; greatest length of skull more than 50
     mm (except in some *Tamiasciurus*) 10

9'. Total length less than 340 mm; greatest length of skull less than 50 mm 14

10. Dorsal color dappled or mottled; zygomatic arches not parallel, converging anteriorly; crown of second upper molar noticeably wider than long 11

10'. Dorsal color more or less uniform or grizzled; zygomatic arches parallel, not convergent anteriorly; crown of second upper molar as long as wide 12

11. Color grayish dappled with black and white; habitat in tallgrass prairie; anterior premolar with two cusps .... *Spermophilus franklinii*

11'. Color reddish buff mottled with black and white; habitat rimrock country of Oklahoma Panhandle; anterior premolar with one cusp .... *Spermophilus variegatus*

12. Total length less than 400 mm, greatest length of skull less than 55 mm; anterior border of orbit opposite P4 .... *Tamiasciurus hudsonicus*

12'. Total length more than 430 mm, greatest length of skull more than 55 mm; anterior border of orbit opposite M1 13

13. Pelage predominantly gray above, white below; tips of hairs of tail white; two upper premolars usually present (the first, P3, much reduced and sometimes absent) .... *Sciurus carolinensis*

13'. Pelage orange-brown above, yellowish or buffy below; tips of hairs of tail orange; only one upper premolar (P4) present ...... *Sciurus niger*

14. Dorsal pelage marked with large stripes or spots; length of maxillary toothrow less than 8.5 mm 15

14'. Dorsal pelage uniform or grizzled color; length of maxillary toothrow more than 8.5 mm 16

15. Dorsal pelage marked with series of alternating dark brown, pale brown, and broken pale and dark brown longitudinal stripes; postorbital constriction less than 12 mm ....
Spermophilus tridecemlineatus

15'. Upper parts beige to cinnamon, with scattered white spots of moderate size; postorbital constriction more than 12 mm ....
Spermophilus spilosoma

16. Color grayish brown; call a weak, short chirp; occurring in western Nebraska .... *Spermophilus elegans*

16'. Color yellowish brown; call a loud, longer chirp; occurring in North and South Dakota .... *Spermophilus richardsonii*

Key to Geomyids / Pocket Gophers

1. Faces of upper incisors smooth (or sometimes with faint groove along medial margin); hind foot usually less than 30 mm . . *Thomomys talpoides*
1'. Faces of upper incisors with distinct longitudinal groove(s); hind foot usually greater than 30 mm 2
2. Dorsum yellowish with middorsal blackish wash; upper incisors with one longitudinal groove . . . . *Cratogeomys castanops*
2'. Dorsum tan to reddish or chocolate brown, without mid-dorsal blackish wash; upper incisors with two longitudinal grooves 3
3. Dorsal exposure of jugal bone shorter than width of rostrum below infraorbital foramen; occurring in eastern Oklahoma; diploid chromosome number 74 . . . . *Geomys breviceps*
3'. Dorsal exposure of jugal bone longer than width of rostrum below infraorbital foramen; not occurring in eastern Oklahoma; diploid chromosome number 70 or 72 . . . . *Geomys bursarius*

Key to Heteromyids / Pocket Mice and Kangaroo Rats

1. Tail bushy at tip; total length more than 240 mm; hind foot more than 35 mm 2
1'. Tail not bushy at tip; total length less than 240 mm; hind foot less than 30 mm 3
2. Four toes on each hind foot; tail more than 160 mm . . *Dipodomys elator*
2'. Five toes on each hind foot (fifth is midway up foot, and little more than claw is exposed); tail less than 160 mm . . . . *Dipodomys ordii*
3. Total length more than 180 mm; pelage bristly, harsh to the touch . . . . *Perognathus hispidus*
3'. Total length less than 150 mm; pelage silky, not harsh to the touch . . . 4
4. Buffy patch behind ear conspicuous, often larger than ear; interparietal bone narrower than interorbital breadth . . . . *Perognathus flavus*
4'. Buffy patch behind ear usually inconspicuous, smaller than ear; interparietal breadth about same as interorbital breadth 5
5. Dorsal pelage olive-colored; auditory bullae generally not meeting anteriorly at midline . . . . *Perognathus fasciatus*
5'. Dorsal pelage buff to brownish; auditory bullae generally meeting anteriorly at midline . . . . *Perognathus flavescens*

Key to Cricetids / Native Mice, Rats, and Voles

1. Cheekteeth cuspidate (except *Neotoma,* in which they are semiprismatic); tail usually more than 40 percent of total length (except *Onychomys*) 2

1'. Cheekteeth prismatic; tail usually less than 35 percent of total length (except *Ondatra,* in which it is laterally flattened) 21

2. Cheekteeth cuspidate; total length less than 300 mm 3

2'. Cheekteeth semiprismatic; total length more than 300 mm 17

3. Pelage somewhat harsh to touch; claws brown; molars nearly equal in size, square, relatively large and low crowned . . . . *Sigmodon hispidus*

3'. Pelage soft to touch; claws pale, translucent; first molar nearly twice as long as third, molars not square, relatively small and high crowned 4

4. Tail less than one-third total length; coronoid process of mandible conspicuously high . . . . *Onychomys leucogaster*

4'. Tail more than one-third total length; coronoid process of mandible not conspicuously high 5

5. Faces of upper incisors conspicuously grooved 6

5'. Faces of upper incisors not grooved 9

6. Size smaller, total length usually less than 120 mm; tail relatively short, less than half total length 7

6'. Size larger, usually more than 120 mm; tail relatively long, half total length or more 8

7. Ridge on outer margin of first two lower molars; occurring in southeastern Oklahoma . . . . *Reithrodontomys humulis*

7'. No ridge on outer margin of first two lower molars; occurring mostly other than in southeastern Oklahoma . . . . . *Reithrodontomys montanus*

8. First and second folds of third upper molar equal in size, extending halfway across crown; dorsal color golden to reddish brown; tail moderately bicolored . . . . *Reithrodontomys fulvescens*

8'. First fold of third upper molar shorter than second, extending less than halfway across crown; dorsal color grayish brown; tail distinctly bicolored . . . . *Reithrodontomys megalotis*

9. Size large, total length 225 mm or more; cusps of upper molars opposite . . . . *Oryzomys palustris*

9'. Size moderate to small, total length less than 225 mm; cusps of upper molars alternate 10

10. Ears same color as head, reddish to golden buff; posterior palatine foramina nearer posterior edge of palate than anterior palatine foramina . . . . *Ochrotomys nuttalli*

10'. Ears colored somewhat distinctly from head, more grayish and usually rimmed with white; posterior palatine foramina about equidistant between posterior edge of palate and anterior palatine foramina 11

11. Tail longer, distinctly more than half total length 12

11'. Tail shorter, usually less than or equal to half total length 13

12. Ankles white; upper molar toothrow less than 4.0 mm . . . . *Peromyscus pectoralis*

12'. Ankles grayish; upper molar toothrow more than 4.0 mm . . . . *Peromyscus attwateri*

13. Ear markedly long, as long as or longer than hind foot 14

13'. Ear moderate, shorter than hind foot 15

14. Ear 25 mm or more; dorsal color buff . . . . *Peromyscus truei*

14'. Ear usually 23 mm or less, dorsal color grayish . . *Peromyscus difficilis*

15. Size larger, hind foot 22 mm or longer; greatest length of skull more than 28 mm . . . . *Peromyscus gossypinus*

15'. Size smaller; hind foot less than 22 mm; greatest length of skull less than 28 mm 16

16. Average size larger; tail indistinctly bicolored . . . *Peromyscus leucopus*

16'. Average size smaller; tail distinctly bicolored . . *Peromyscus maniculatus*

17. Tail bushy; soles of feet furred from heel to proximal tubercle; diastema markedly longer than row of cheekteeth . . . *Neotoma cinerea*

17'. Tail not bushy; soles of feet furred only to heel; diastema same length as row of cheekteeth 18

18. Nasal septum intact 19

18'. Nasal septum with maxillovomerine notch 20

19. Dorsal color of adults gray; anterior palatine spine not forked . . . . *Neotoma micropus*

19'. Dorsal color of adults buffy to brown; anterior palatine spine forked . . . . *Neotoma floridana*

20. Hairs of chest and throat white based; no dark line around mouth; anterointernal fold of first upper molar shallow . . . . *Neotoma albigula*

20'. Hairs of chest and throat gray based; dark line around mouth; anterointernal fold of first upper molar deep . . . . . . *Neotoma mexicana*

21. Tail naked, laterally flattened, more than 150 mm . . . . *Ondatra zibethicus*

21'. Tail well furred, not laterally flattened, less than 100 mm 22
22. Tail approximately same length as hind foot; upper incisor with distinct groove on anterior surface . . . . *Synaptomys cooperi*
22'. Tail at least slightly longer than hind foot; anterior surface of upper incisors smooth or only faintly grooved 23
23. Tail short, less than 10 mm longer than hind foot; dorsal pelage pale gray; sole of hind foot densely haired . . . . *Lemmiscus curtatus*
23'. Tail usually more than 10 mm longer than hind foot (except in *Microtus pinetorum*); dorsal pelage reddish, brownish, or grayish; sole of hind foot not densely haired 24
24. Dorsal stripe reddish to reddish brown, contrasting with gray sides; cheekteeth rooted in adults . . . . *Clethrionomys gapperi*
24'. Dorsum lacking distinct reddish stripe contrasting with gray sides; cheekteeth unrooted, ever growing 25
25. Tail less than 29 mm (usually less than 25); pelage soft, smooth, reddish brown dorsally . . . . *Microtus pinetorum*
25'. Tail more than 26 mm (usually more than 29); pelage coarse, grizzled, brownish, grayish, or blackish dorsally 26
26. Tail 25 to 35 percent of body length; underparts usually buff to ochraceous . . . . *Microtus ochrogaster*
26'. Tail more than 35 percent of body length; underparts grayish to whitish 27
27. Tail usually more than 50 percent of body length; second upper molar with four closed triangles and lacking posterior loop . . . . *Microtus longicaudus*
27'. Tail less than 50 percent of body length; second upper molar with distinct posterior loop that often appears as a fifth triangle . . . . *Microtus pennsylvanicus*

Key to Zapodids / Jumping Mice

1. Dorsal pelage slightly grizzled, resulting from grayish hairs located in the dorsal stripe; lateral lines faintly orange; ears with border of white hairs . . . . *Zapus princeps*
1'. Dorsal pelage not grizzled; lateral lines distinctly orange; ears not bordered with white hairs . . . . *Zapus hudsonius*

Tamias minimus / Least Chipmunk

Distribution. The least chipmunk has a broad boreal and montane distribution, ranging from the Yukon to Ontario and southward to Wisconsin, the Dakotas, Nebraska, Arizona, and New Mexico. It is the most widespread of American chipmunks. See map 32.

Description. Color highly variable geographically, from ashy gray to quite dark; all races marked with white, black, grayish, and buff stripes; grayish white beneath. Smallest of local chipmunks; total length, 190–210 mm; tail, 80–100 mm; hind foot, 30–32 mm; ear, 14–18 mm; weight, 30–55 g. See figure 45.

Habits and Habitat. This chipmunk has a broader ecological amplitude than most other squirrels. It occurs in forest-edge communities, rocky ravines, barren badlands, and brushlands. In fact, within its broad geographic range, it is found in most ecosystems except unbroken forest and open grassland.

The diet emphasizes seeds and fruit. Frequently the heads are stripped from composites such as dandelions. Food is carried to favored feeding stations (a stump, rock, or log) in capacious cheekpouches. Some green vegetation is eaten, and also insects. Food is stored in the burrow.

Chipmunks are diurnal. Nights are spent in a burrow beneath a rock or stump. In cold, snowy weather, activity ceases, but individuals arouse periodically to feed on stored food. In spring, they may emerge through the snowpack to forage. They molt in spring and autumn.

Least chipmunks are not colonial, but they do have dense populations and exhibit social behavior. Home ranges (one to several acres) overlap broadly. Interactions are often vocal but seldom involve actual combat. Densities are five to 15 per acre. These chipmunks are nearly as likely to climb trees for protection as to use rock shelters or burrows. Predators include hawks, weasels, martens, snakes, and foxes. There are a variety of internal and external parasites and microbial diseases. Longevity is unknown.

Reproduction. Like most squirrels, least chipmunks are monoestrous, breeding in April or May, soon after emergence from the winter den. Gestation lasts about one month. The three to nine (usually four to six) young are altricial, weighing about 2 grams each. Weaning begins at about one month and at two months juveniles are independent.

Suggested References. Carleton (1966); Nadler et al. (1977); Sheppard (1972); Skryja (1974).

Tamias quadrivittatus / Colorado Chipmunk

Distribution. This species occurs in the foothills of the Southern Rocky Mountains and adjacent highlands. In addition, the range extends eastward along the mesas of southern Colorado and northern New Mexico, reaching its easternmost limit in the vicinity of Kenton, Oklahoma. See map 32.

Description. Upper parts reddish buff; distinct stripes of white, black, and reddish buff; venter whitish; head grayish. Size medium for genus; total length 210–245 mm; tail, 90–110 mm; hind foot, 33–36 mm; ear, 20–23 mm; weight about 70 g. See figure 46.

Habits and Habitat. Surprisingly little detailed information is available for this species. Over much of its range, the Colorado chipmunk occurs with other, similar chipmunks. Problems of identification have hindered careful field study. The best place to study the natural history of this chipmunk might well be on the Black Mesa of Oklahoma and in adjacent Colorado.

This is a species of rocky pine or juniper woodlands. The animals burrow beneath rocks, roots, or shrubs, and there they store food, rear young, and spend nights and colder winter weather asleep. There are two seasonal molts annually, in spring or early summer and in autumn.

The diet is opportunistic: a variety of seeds, berries, and nuts, including juniper "berries" (actually cones); some herbage (a major source of moisture); and insects. Predation has not been detailed, but presumably hawks, weasels, coyotes, foxes, badgers, and snakes take a toll. The animals are a bit less arboreal than least chipmunks and usually take refuge beneath rocks.

Social organization, home range, and other aspects of population biology have not been investigated. Populations seem to be less dense than those of the least chipmunk, probably no more than two or three per acre.

Reproduction. Reproduction has been studied only in the Southwest. There breeding begins in February or March and in April the young are born after a gestation period of 30 to 33 days. One would expect the breeding season in Oklahoma to be about a month later. Weight at birth is about 3 grams, and neonates are blind and helpless. Young are weaned when approximately two months old.

Suggested References. Armstrong (1975, 1982).

Tamias striatus / Eastern Chipmunk

Distribution. The eastern chipmunk ranges in suitable habitat from Quebec to Louisiana and from the East Coast to the extreme eastern parts of the plains states, including the Neosho Valley of Oklahoma and Kansas, the Missouri Valley of Kansas and Nebraska, and the Red River Valley of the Dakotas. In the five-state region, the eastern chipmunk is sympatric with the least chipmunk only in northeastern North Dakota. See map 33.

Description. Upper parts reddish brown; black and tan stripes becoming indistinct on head. Largest of chipmunks of plains states; total length, 250–300 mm; tail, 95–110 mm; hind foot, 35–40 mm; ear, 12–15 mm; weight, 90–110 g. See figure 47.

Habits and Habitat. This is a species of brushy ravines, hilly woodlands, and rocky outcrops. It does not occur in open country. Hence its range in the plains states is restricted.

These animals are less agile than their western cousins and less arboreal. They burrow beneath tree roots, rocks, and buildings. There they rest and store food—nuts, fruits, and grains (including corn and wheat). Winter food stores up to a bushel in volume have been reported. Some individuals actually hibernate in northern parts of the range, but farther south they are merely inactive. In summer, insects, mushrooms, and carrion are eaten. The annual molt is in spring.

Home ranges are 0.5 to 1.5 acres and overlap broadly. The burrow is defended strongly and vocally, and a dominance hierarchy develops. Densities in the plains states are only two to five per acre. Hawks feed on eastern chipmunks as do weasels, foxes, and raccoons. The animals host numerous ectoparasites and helminths. Warbles (botfly larvae) are common beneath the skin. Despite high mortality, maximum longevity is in excess of 10 years.

Reproduction. Females have two litters per year in the southern part of their range, but only one in the north. Mating begins in late March or early April. Two to seven (the mean is four to five) altricial young are born after a gestation period of one month. Neonates weigh only 3 grams, but the young weigh 10 times that within a month, when weaning begins and the young come above ground; at two months of age they disperse.

Suggested References. Forbes (1966); Synder (1982).

Marmota flaviventris / Yellow-bellied Marmot

Distribution. This montane mammal ranges from southern British Columbia and Alberta southward to California and New Mexico. In the plains states, it is isolated on the Black Hills. The yellow-bellied marmot and the closely related woodchuck are not sympatric on the Great Plains, although they are narrowly so in western Canada. See map 34.

Description. Paler than woodchuck; reddish to yellowish grizzled brown above; nearly clear yellowish on throat; paling beneath to buff; feet brown. Total length, 470–680 mm; tail, 140–225 mm; hind foot, 70–85 mm; ear, 25–35 mm; weight 8–12 lb (females average about one-third lighter than males). See figure 48.

Habits and Habitat. The yellow-bellied marmot is a species of montane meadows on the Black Hills, but occurs in subalpine and alpine situations in the Rockies. Typical habitat includes boulders for cover and lush vegetation for food. Burrow systems are extensive, to three feet deep and 15 feet long, ending in a nest chamber, often beneath a boulder.

The diet includes both grasses and forbs. Picky eaters, marmots avoid toxic plants and select species that are succulent and actively growing. They double their weight in summer, storing fat for hibernation, which lasts from September to May.

These are social mammals. Males are strongly territorial, and quite aggressive toward other males. Territories are about 1.5 acres. The typical territory is occupied by a male, a harem of several females, and their offspring. Some animals, however, are solitary, and others live as mated pairs. Reproductive success is greater for colonial than for solitary marmots.

Predators include coyotes, badgers, hawks, eagles, and bobcats. Weasels and martens prey on the young. Colonial animals protect each other by sounding an alarm. Dispersing individuals are at greater risk. A diversity of arthropod and helminth parasites infest the animals. The greatest source of mortality may be hibernation stress. Longevity is eight to 10 years.

Reproduction. Females are monoestrous. Mating occurs just after emergence from hibernation. Gestation lasts one month, and the altricial young are blind, naked, and weigh about 35 grams. They are nearly weaned by the time they emerge in early July, aged 30 days, weighing 15 times their birth weight.

Suggested References. Frase and Hoffmann (1980); Jones et al. (1983).

Marmota monax / Woodchuck

Distribution. The woodchuck is a boreal and eastern species, occurring from Alaska to extreme northern Idaho, eastward across Canada to Labrador, and southward to Mississippi and Alabama. The species occurs only along the eastern margin of the five-state region. See map 34.

Description. Dorsum and throat grizzled yellowish to reddish or blackish brown; venter paler brown; feet black. Size generally larger than yellow-bellied marmot, but tail relatively shorter. Total length, 575–650 mm; tail, 125–155 mm; hind foot, 85–95 mm; ear, 28–34 mm; weight 4–12 lb (wide variability due to seasonal fat accumulation). See figure 49.

Habits and Habitat. Woodchucks occupy a wide range of habitats although they do avoid open plains. Forest edges, often along rocky bluffs or ravines, are prime habitat. There woodchucks burrow beneath rocks, stumps, or buildings. They also burrow in lush meadows, well away from cover. Burrows (which may be 30 feet long) are marked by large piles of soil at the main entrance. This mound serves as a vantage point. Secondary escape exits are unmarked.

Woodchucks are primarily diurnal, feeding on grasses and forbs, especially legumes. They may damage fields and gardens by foraging and trampling. These animals are neither as social nor as vocal as yellow-bellied marmots. Adults den alone. A hierarchy of dominance makes relations among neighbors predictable. Home ranges overlap broadly.

Predators include foxes, coyotes, large hawks, bobcats, and humans, who kill woodchucks for sport and food, and accidentally in traffic. Parasite loads tend to be heavy, typical for burrowing mammals with permanent dens.

Woodchucks hibernate for four to six months a year, having doubled their body weight with fat accumulated over the summer. The winter den is a sealed chamber in the burrow system. The single annual molt is in spring.

Reproduction. Mating occurs in March or early April, after arousal from hibernation. Gestation lasts one month. The two to nine (average four to five) young are altricial but grow rapidly and are weaned at six weeks. At two months, dispersal occurs. Animals that survive hibernation stress, predators, and human harassment may live six years or more.

Suggested References. de Vos and Gillespie (1960); Grizzell (1955); Hamilton and Whitaker (1980); Mumford and Whitaker (1982).

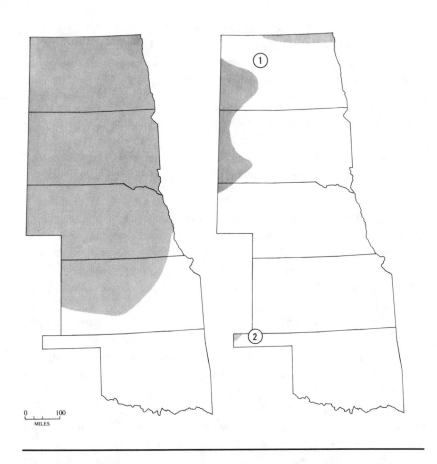

Map 31. *(Left).* Distribution of the white-tailed jackrabbit, *Lepus townsendii.*

Map 32. *(Right).* Distribution of the least chipmunk, *Tamias minimus* (1), and the Colorado chipmunk, *Tamias quadrivittatus* (2).

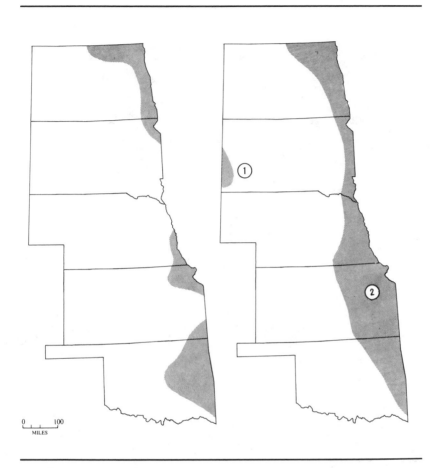

Map 33. *(Left).* Distribution of the eastern chipmunk, *Tamias striatus.*

Map 34. *(Right).* Distribution of the yellow-bellied marmot, *Marmota flaviventris* (1), and the woodchuck, *Marmota monax* (2).

0 ___ 100
MILES

Map 35. *(Left).* Distribution of the Wyoming ground squirrel, *Spermophilus elegans* (1); Richardson's ground squirrel, *Spermophilus richardsonii* (2); and the rock squirrel, *Spermophilus variegatus* (3).

Map 36. *(Right).* Distribution of Franklin's ground squirrel, *Spermophilus franklinii.*

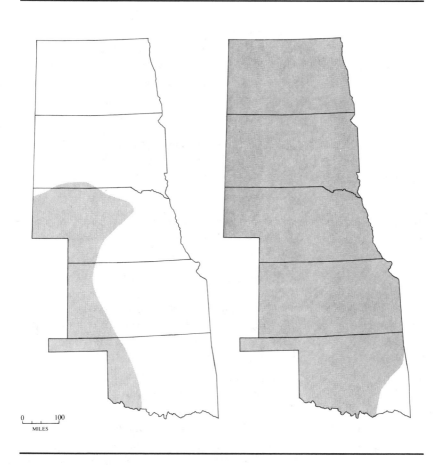

Map 37. *(Left).* Distribution of the spotted ground squirrel, *Spermophilus spilosoma.*

Map 38. *(Right).* Distribution of the thirteen-lined ground squirrel, *Spermophilus tridecemlineatus.*

Spermophilus elegans / Wyoming Ground Squirrel

Distribution. The Wyoming ground squirrel has been reported from the plains states only from Nebraska, where its present status is questionable. It also occurs in the Central and Southern Rockies, the Wyoming Basin, and the northern Great Basin. Populations of this species were once considered to represent *S. richardsonii*, which overlaps geographically with *S. elegans* only in southwestern Montana. See map 35.

Description. Nondescript ground squirrel without stripes, spots, or prominent tail. Upper parts brownish gray, paling to yellowish gray below. Size moderate for genus. Total length, 275–295 mm; tail, 60–85 mm; hind foot, 40–45 mm; ear, 10–18 mm; weight, 230–270 g. See figure 50.

Habits and Habitat. These squirrels are typical of sagebrush country and bunchgrass rangeland, especially on well-drained soils. There they form dense colonies, each burrow marked by a mound of bare soil and containing a central nest chamber. Males live alone, whereas females and young or several subadult siblings may live together.

The animals are hibernators, entering the winter burrow as early as July (if critical weight is reached) and remaining there until March. Young animals and females that have lactated enter hibernation later than do males; poor forage postpones hibernation. The diet includes a variety of vegetable matter, including seeds, stems, leaves, flowers, the roots of both forbs and grasses, and the bark of a variety of shrubs. Individuals also eat insects and readily take carrion.

Highly vocal animals, they call to one another continually during aboveground activity, sounding alarm against predators. Tail flicks carry meaning in aggressive encounters. Predators include hawks, coyotes, badgers, weasels, and snakes. Fleas are abundant, as in most social species. Plague carried by some fleas decimates colonies and is transmissible to humans.

Reproduction. Breeding occurs as females emerge from hibernation. A single litter of one to 11 young is born after a gestation period of three to four weeks. The young are tiny (6 grams), naked, blind, and have the ears closed. A thin pelage develops within two weeks and by one month the young emerge from the natal burrow weighing 80 to 100 grams. Males are polygynous, although peripheral males breed with only one or two females.

Suggested References. Koeppl and Hoffmann (1981); Zegers (1984).

Spermophilus franklinii / Franklin's Ground Squirrel

Distribution. This species occurs from Alberta, Saskatchewan, and Manitoba southward to Kansas, Missouri, and Illinois. It generally occupies the eastern parts of the plains states, but occurs westward in Nebraska to the Panhandle. See map 36.

Description. Large, bushy-tailed ground squirrel. Upper parts grayish dappled with white and blackish specks; venter buff. Total length, 365–415 mm; tail, 125–145 mm; hind foot, 45–60 mm; ear, 13–18 mm; weight, 150–540 g. See figure 51.

Habits and Habitat. A species of the tall-grass prairie, Franklin's ground squirrel must be much less abundant than it was prior to breaking the prairie for agriculture. Habitat now is abandoned fields, railroad rights-of-way, and prairie cemeteries. Furthermore, this is a solitary mammal of wary and retiring habits, and its dappled coloration makes it hard to observe in dense vegetation. In view of all this, it is not surprising that little is known about the biology of this ground squirrel.

The animals are diurnal and terrestrial. They burrow extensively in well-drained soils, often near thickets or woodland edges. Burrows have several entrances marked with mounds of soil. Populations of six animals per acre have been reported. The diet includes leafy vegetation, fruits, seeds, and roots. In summer, considerable animal matter is taken, including insects, eggs and nestlings of birds, small mammals, and carrion. Probably they are the most carnivorous of the ground squirrels.

Adults enter hibernation as early as July (males first), and do not emerge until April. Thus, they pass fully two-thirds of the year inactively. Predators include badgers, coyotes, foxes, weasels, hawks, and large snakes. *S. franklinii* carries the usual range of parasites—fleas, mites, lice, cestodes, nematodes, and protozoans.

Reproduction. Breeding occurs within a few weeks of emergence from hibernation, in April or May. Females are monoestrous and produce a litter of two to 13 (typically six to nine) altricial young after a gestation period of four weeks. Born blind and naked, the young are thinly furred and two to three weeks later emerge from the natal burrow to forage on their own, storing fat against the needs of hibernation.

Suggested References. Haberman and Fleharty (1972); Iverson and Turner (1972); Murie (1973); Turner, Iverson, and Severson (1976).

Spermophilus richardsonii / Richardson's Ground Squirrel

Distribution. This ground squirrel occurs on the northern Great Plains, ranging from Alberta, Saskatchewan, and Manitoba southward to Montana in the west and Minnesota in the east. In the five-state region, it is found in the Dakotas, primarily north and east of the Missouri River. See map 35.

Description. A nondescript ground squirrel, confused only with *S. elegans,* from which it differs in vocalization (a loud, longer descending chirp rather than a weaker, shorter chirp), slightly larger size, slightly darker (more brownish, less grayish) color, and in chromosomal and biochemical details. Total length, 290–325 mm; tail, 75–85 mm; hind foot, 45–48 mm; ear, 10–15 mm; weight 260–635 g. See figure 52.

Habits and Habitat. This is a species of open country—grasslands, pastures, grainfields, and disturbed sites. Suitable habitat provides vegetation for food and well-drained soils for burrows. The general ecology is similar to that of the closely related Wyoming ground squirrel. It forms dense colonies of 10 to 20 animals per acre and burrows extensively. Burrow entrances may be only a few feet apart, and when the residents stand erect on entrance mounds the ground seems to be covered with squirrels. The diet includes all parts of both grasses and forbs. Seeds are important as the animals fatten for hibernation. Insects are consumed in quantity and also carrion. This squirrel can do considerable damage in grainfields.

These animals are territorial, defending an area about the burrow. During the mating season, males patrol an area including the home ranges of several females. Defense includes vocalization, postural threats, tail-flicks, chasing, and combat.

Most diurnal predators, including coyotes, hawks, badgers, weasels, and snakes, prey on these squirrels. Both helminth and arthropod parasites infest them and they are susceptible to various microbial diseases, including plague.

Reproduction. This species breeds upon emergence from hibernation. A single litter is produced each year; most females in the colony produce litters. After a gestation period of three to four weeks, a litter of six to eight (range three to 11) altricial young is born. They grow rapidly and begin to forage on their own within a month, weighing about 80 grams.

Suggested References. Michener (1979, 1980); Michener and Michener (1977).

Spermophilus spilosoma / Spotted Ground Squirrel

Distribution. This species ranges from extreme southern South Dakota to San Luis Potosí in Mexico and from Arizona to the Texas Gulf Coast. The animals occur primarily in the western parts of the plains states, reaching their easternmost limit in Antelope County, Nebraska. See map 37.

Description. Distinguished from other ground squirrels in the region by white dorsal spots scattered on grayish tan background. Pelage pale on sides; venter white. Smallest ground squirrel of plains states. Total length, 200–225 mm; tail, 60–70 mm; hind foot, 30–33 mm; ear, 8–12 mm; weight, 150–200 g. See figure 53.

Habits and Habitat. Spotted ground squirrels typically inhabit sandy soils in semiarid grasslands or grassland-shrub ecotones, often where there are sagebrush, prickly pear, and yucca. Overgrazing favors them. They excavate extensive burrow systems with the main entrance usually beneath a shrub or rock. Burrows up to 12 feet long and about two feet deep may have several entrances.

Food consists mostly of seeds and green vegetation, but some insects also are eaten. Some food is stored in the grass-lined nest chamber. The animals are diurnal, active in the morning and late afternoon, retiring to the burrow at night and during midday heat. Hibernation seems to be less profound than in some other ground squirrels; most individuals seem to arouse periodically after activity slows in September. Final arousal occurs in April. The animals exhibit vernal and autumnal molts.

Predators include hawks, snakes, badgers, coyotes, and perhaps swift foxes. Several kinds of helminth and arthropod parasites have been reported. *S. spilosoma* seems to be less abundant than other small ground squirrels, but that may be because it is cryptically colored and individuals seldom venture far from their burrows. Home ranges are three to four acres. The animals defend their burrows, but they are not strongly territorial.

Reproduction. Unlike most other squirrels, females may have two litters, especially in the southern part of the range. Breeding commences in April. Gestation takes four weeks, after which a litter of four to 12 (mean about seven) young is born; neonates weigh about 4 grams. They emerge from the natal burrow at six weeks, weighing 40 to 50 grams.

Suggested References. Jones et al. (1983); Streubel and Fitzgerald (1978a).

Spermophilus tridecemlineatus / Thirteen-lined Ground Squirrel

Distribution. This is a species of the interior grasslands, ranging from the southern Prairie Provinces southward to the Texas Gulf Coast and from the Wyoming Basin eastward to Ohio. It occurs throughout the five-state region except in southeastern Oklahoma. See map 38.

Description. Small, slender ground squirrel marked with alternating dark and pale stripes; lines of white spots along each of the dark stripes. General color yellowish brown above; venter pale orange to nearly white. Total length, 225–290 mm; tail, 80–100 mm; hind foot, 32–37 mm; ear, 8–12 mm; weight doubles from spring to autumn and ranges from 80 to 200 g. See figure 54.

Habits and Habitat. This is a grassland species abundant along disturbed rights-of-way and other such areas. Once this was probably one of several small mammals (including prairie dogs and grasshopper mice) that benefited from the presence of migratory herds of bison.

Runways lead from burrows to foraging areas. Burrows are up to 30 feet long and three feet deep, often in a hillside with a southern or eastern exposure. The animals generally are solitary and actively defend the burrow, although home ranges (three to 10 acres) overlap broadly and densities range from 10 per acre upward.

By day these squirrels forage for seeds, leaves, and roots of grasses and forbs. In summer and autumn, the diet may be dominated by insects. They also eat carrion and prey upon mice and nestling birds. A number of predators capture these ground squirrels, among them badgers, coyotes, weasels, hawks, swift foxes, and snakes. The animals host an abundance of ecto- and endoparasites. Floods, traffic, and hibernation stress take a toll. Still, over most of the Great Plains this is the most common ground squirrel, sometimes sufficiently abundant to be a pest.

Reproduction. These squirrels breed upon emergence from hibernation in March or April. Ovulation is induced by copulation. Gestation lasts about four weeks, and litter size averages eight to nine (range five to 13). One litter per year is the rule. The altricial young weigh only about 4 grams, but development is rapid and the young are weaned in about one month.

Suggested References. Scheck and Fleharty (1979); Streubel and Fitzgerald (1978b).

Spermophilus variegatus / Rock Squirrel

Distribution. This is a squirrel of the Mexican roughlands, but it occurs northward to the western United States, reaching northern distributional limits in Idaho and northern Colorado. In the plains states, it is known only from the mesa country of the Oklahoma Panhandle, ranging eastward to Beaver County. See map 35.

Description. A large, bushy-tailed ground squirrel, similar to no sympatric species. Upper parts grayish brown, washed with reddish and dabbled with white and black specks and lines; venter buff. Total length, 440–500 mm; tail, 175–240 mm; hind foot, 55–61 mm; ear, 29–31 mm; weight to about 900 g in autumn, about half that in spring. See figure 55.

Habits and Habitat. Rock squirrels inhabit broken canyon country, often in areas with rocky slopes and vegetation of junipers and oakbrush. They burrow beneath boulders or roots and emerge by day to forage or bask in the sun. The nest is lined with grasses, shredded bark, or leaves.

These are unusual ground squirrels because their appearance is rather like that of tree squirrels. They forage in trees and bushes (and thus may be important pests in orchards). They are not social; they are not territorial (although they do defend a personal space); and they form no dominance hierarchy. They are also not strong hibernators; rather they arouse about every week through the period of torpidity, which lasts from one to six months.

Densities are highly variable, ranging to two or three animals per acre in suitable habitat, and twice that before the young disperse. Home ranges are one to two acres in area and overlap broadly.

The diet changes through the season, reflecting availability rather than strong preferences. Seeds, nuts, berries, carrion, and insects are eaten. Rock squirrels are preyed upon by bobcats, badgers, coyotes, and hawks, but predation on adults probably is not an important check on populations. The amount of suitable rimrock or rocky habitat may be limiting, however.

Reproduction. Two litters per year have been reported, but whether that is the rule is not known. Litters of four or five young are typical. The gestation period probably lasts about 30 days. Young are weaned at approximately eight weeks.

Suggested References. Johnson (1981); Steiner (1975).

Cynomys ludovicianus / Black-tailed Prairie Dog

Distribution. This is the most widespread of prairie dogs, ranging from southern Saskatchewan southward across the plains to northern Mexico. See map 39.

Description. A stocky, short-tailed, short-eared squirrel. Dorsum grizzled yellowish to brownish buff, belly whitish. Relatively short, black-tipped tail. Only the much smaller Wyoming and Richardson's ground squirrels look at all similar. Total length, 310–410 mm; tail, 60–100 mm; hind foot, 50–65 mm; ear, 8–14 mm; weight, 600–1,200 g. See figure 56.

Habits and Habitat. This prairie dog is an animal of the semiarid prairie. It thrives on overgrazed rangeland and once must have prospered in the wake of disturbance by migratory bison. These rodents avoid stands of tall grass.

Prairie dogs are highly social, typically living in "towns" that once covered thousands of acres. Large towns are subdivided into "wards" five to 10 acres in size, usually delimited by topographic features. Wards, in turn, are subdivided into "coteries," with a half dozen (to about three dozen) members. Animals in a coterie defend a group territory. These noisy rodents make a variety of barking and chirping sounds. Within the coterie, there is much play, nuzzling, grooming, and mutual tooth-scratching.

Burrows, marked by large mounds that serve as sentinel posts, are three to six feet deep and as long as 15 feet, oriented for ventilation. Nest chambers are lined with grasses. There the animals spend the night, rest at midday, and sleep extensively in winter weather. They may not actually hibernate (although fat is stored), but they may remain dormant for several weeks at a time.

Food consists of a variety of plants, predominantly succulent species. Forbs are preferred over grasses, and shrubs, although not eaten, are clipped to maintain visibility. Hence, prairie dogs in moderate numbers actually improve well-managed rangeland. Badgers, coyotes, hawks, and humans are the chief predators. Once black-footed ferrets probably were an important check on populations.

Reproduction. Mating takes place in March or early April. Females are monoestrous, bearing four to six (range two to 10) offspring annually. Young emerge in five or six weeks to forage for themselves and are weaned about a week later. Females may breed as yearlings.

Suggested References. King (1955); Koford (1958); Smith (1967).

Sciurus carolinensis / Gray Squirrel

Distribution. This species occurs throughout the eastern United States and southern Canada. It is found in the eastern part of the five-state region, following the Missouri River to central North Dakota and the Solomon River to central Kansas. See map 40.

Description. Slightly smaller size and gray dorsal pelage distinguish it from the fox squirrel; venter white. Total length, 445–500 mm; tail, 190–230 mm; hind foot, 60–70 mm; ear, 30–35 mm; weight, 380–720 g. See figure 57.

Habits and Habitat. The gray squirrel and the fox squirrel are sympatric throughout most of their ranges. *S. carolinensis* ranges farther north than the fox squirrel, but not as far west. Gray squirrels seem to be less tolerant of open woodland and are less able to colonize riparian corridors on the plains. Beyond that, the two species have similar habitat requirements and often occur together in the same woodlot. Gray squirrels spend less time on the ground than do fox squirrels.

Dens are leaf-nests or fiber-lined tree holes, which may be the enlarged nest cavities of woodpeckers or other birds. Individuals den alone and generally are not social. They are not territorial but defend a personal space.

The food consists mostly of nuts, some other fruits, fungi, and occasional insects and carrion. Nuts are cached for winter. A keen sense of smell aids in the retrieval of buried nuts; those not recovered may germinate.

A number of predators take gray squirrels—hawks, owls, foxes, coyotes, bobcats, feral house cats, and weasels—but the mortality of adults is low because they spend so little time on the ground. Numerous parasites have been reported. Prolonged rainy periods may take a toll of nestlings, but adults have a long life expectancy, usually five or six years, and some individuals may survive twice that long.

Reproduction. Females often produce two litters in a breeding season that extends from late December to early autumn. Gestation lasts 45 to 50 days. Like those of other squirrels, the young are altricial. Two to four young (range one to eight) make up a typical litter. The young are weaned at two months of age and disperse when a new litter is born.

Suggested References. Jones et al. (1983); Packard (1956); Uhlig (1955).

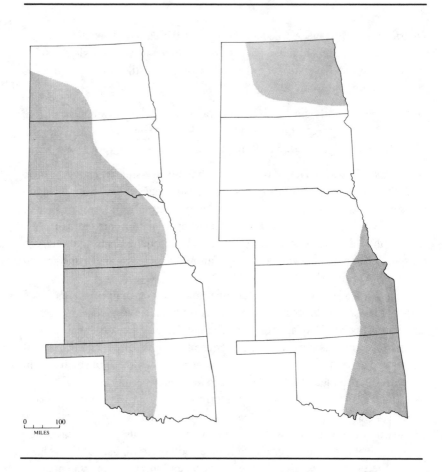

0 ⌞__⌟ 100
MILES

Map 39. *(Left).* Distribution of the black-tailed prairie dog, *Cynomys ludovicianus.*

Map 40. *(Right).* Distribution of the gray squirrel, *Sciurus carolinensis.*

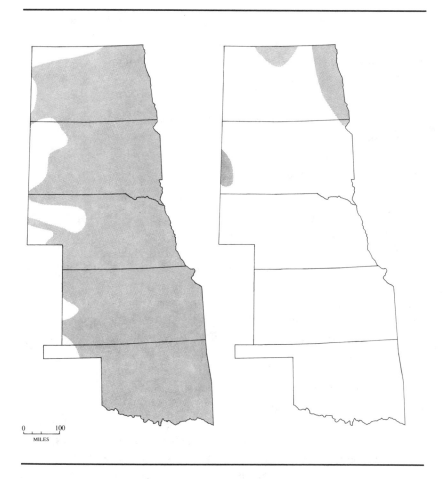

0 ⟞⟝ 100
MILES

Map 41. *(Left).* Distribution of the fox squirrel, *Sciurus niger.*

Map 42. *(Right).* Distribution of the red squirrel, *Tamiasciurus hudsonicus.*

Sciurus niger / Fox Squirrel

Distribution. This squirrel ranges over much of the eastern and midwestern United States, from the eastern seaboard to the foot of the Rockies and from southern Manitoba to northern Durango, Mexico. The animals occur in suitable habitat throughout much of the plains region. See map 41.

Description. Larger size and grizzled, reddish orange to reddish brown color distinguish it from the gray squirrel. Venter orange to nearly white. Total length, 490–530 mm; tail, 220–245 mm; hind foot, 67–75 mm; ear, 27–32 mm; weight, 500–1,000 g. See figure 58.

Habits and Habitat. Fox squirrels are restricted to deciduous forest and riparian and urban woodland. By far the most abundant and widespread squirrel of the plains states, they spend most of their time in trees (although they come to the ground to forage, cache nuts, or move to other trees). The diet includes nuts, fruits, seeds, berries, buds, fungi, flowers, carrion, birds' eggs, and insects.

The animals rest by night in tree hollows or leaf nests indistinguishable from those of gray squirrels. *S. niger* is active throughout the year and strictly diurnal. Stormy weather may force squirrels to remain in the nest for several days at a time, but on cold, clear days they move about, burrowing beneath the snow to reach stored food. Annual molt occurs in spring.

These squirrels are primarily solitary but not strongly territorial. They do, however, defend the nest and a personal space. Home ranges are 10 to 20 acres; prime habitat may support two or three squirrels per acre. Predators include foxes, bobcats, coyotes, weasels, raccoons, opossums, hawks, owls, and occasionally snakes. Humans influence populations through hunting, mortality on roadways, and land development (especially the construction of reservoirs).

Reproduction. Females produce two litters per year, mating in December or January and again in April or May. Gestation is 45 days, and litters average three (range one to six) young. Neonates are altricial, weighing only about 15 grams. They are reared in the nest until three months of age. Weaning begins at 10 weeks. The survival rate of juveniles is not high, but the longevity of adults in the wild is four to seven years.

Suggested References. Allen (1943); Longley (1963); Moore (1957); Packard (1956).

Tamiasciurus hudsonicus / Red Squirrel

Distribution. This is a boreal and montane species, occurring from Alaska and Labrador southward to South Carolina, New Mexico, and Arizona. In the plains states, there are two widely disjunct populations, one in North Dakota and the other on the Black Hills. See map 42.

Description. A small, dark-colored tree squirrel. Dorsal color reddish; venter and edge of tail white; lateral line black. Total length, 300–400 mm; tail, 128–180 mm; hind foot, 45–60 mm; ear, 25–30 mm; weight, 160–340 g. See figure 59.

Habits and Habitat. Typical habitat is coniferous forest, so red squirrels are mostly segregated from the larger gray and fox squirrels. Occasionally, in areas of complex habitat, two or three species of tree squirrels are found together.

Nests are usually built of twigs and conifer needles and lined with plant fibers. The diet is primarily conifer seeds but includes seeds of deciduous trees, fungi (which may be hung on branches to dry), insects, birds' eggs, nestlings, tender young bark, and buds. Several bushels of cones may be cached in a "midden" between down logs or next to a stump, covered with cone scales and needles. Middens are usually adjacent to feeding stations.

Red squirrels are highly territorial—defending nest, midden, and a tract of trees one to three acres in area. Intruders are loudly scolded and actively chased away. Territorial defense breaks down only in the breeding season. The animals are diurnal and active year around.

Raptors and carnivores prey on red squirrels, and several kinds of parasites infest them. Forest fires and inclement spring weather are the principal controls on populations.

Reproduction. The breeding season is extended, individual females coming into estrus from midwinter to early autumn. Males are attracted to estrous females and admitted to their territories just long enough to mate. Some females may have two litters per year, but that probably is not typical. One to 10 (usually four or five) altricial young are born after a gestation period of about five weeks. Young are dependent on the mother until approximately three months of age, when she helps them to set up territories of their own.

Suggested References. Finley (1969); Layne (1954); Rusch and Reeder (1978); Smith (1968, 1970).

Glaucomys sabrinus / Northern Flying Squirrel

Distribution. This flying squirrel has a distribution from Alaska across Canada to Labrador, and southward to North Carolina, California, and Utah. A relict population occurs on the Black Hills, and *G. sabrinus* is also found in northeastern North Dakota. See map 43.

Description. Dorsum pinkish to brownish gray; venter creamy to grayish white, hairs gray at their bases. Total length, 290–315 mm; tail, 130–142 mm; hind foot, 36–46 mm; ear, 16–29 mm; weight, 100–165 g. See figure 60.

Habits and Habitat. The northern flying squirrel occurs in coniferous forests (as on the Black Hills) and in mixed deciduous-coniferous forests (as on the Turtle Mountains). It is not sympatric in the plains states with the southern flying squirrel.

These animals are highly arboreal, strictly nocturnal, and active throughout the year. Nests are in tree holes or built of twigs and bark, located six to 30 feet above ground, and lined with grasses, moss, and lichens. They sometimes use nests abandoned by red squirrels.

The diet is composed mainly of lichens and fungi; hence, there is considerable terrestrial activity. A variety of seeds, fruits, and cones are eaten, as are flowers, buds, insects, young birds, and eggs. Food storage is not well developed. The home range is five to 10 acres and the animals probably are not strongly territorial. Behavioral ecology generally has not been studied, although the animals are known to overwinter with their mothers, and winter aggregations may form, as in *G. volans.*

Owls, foxes, martens, and weasels all have been reported as predators. These squirrels are not large enough to be sought by human hunters. Both arthropod and helminth parasites have been reported.

Reproduction. Apparently females may have two litters per year. The breeding season is March to May and young are born from May to July, after a gestation period of five to six weeks. Litter size averages about four (range three to six). Neonates are altricial and weigh 5 to 6 grams. At six weeks of age they leave the nest and begin to forage on their own. At 10 to 12 weeks they begin to practice gliding maneuvers. They first breed as yearlings. Longevity may be six years.

Suggested References. Baker (1983); Weigl (1978).

Glaucomys volans / Southern Flying Squirrel

Distribution. This is a species of the eastern United States and central Mexico; there is a hiatus in the range from central Tamaulipas (Mexico) to east-central Texas. In the plains states, southern flying squirrels occur in southern Nebraska, eastern Kansas, and central and eastern Oklahoma. See map 43.

Description. Upper parts brownish gray; hairs of venter white to bases. Slightly smaller than *G. sabrinus;* total length, 215–235 mm; tail, 80–100 mm; hind foot, 28–34 mm; ear, 15–20 mm; weight, 50–85 g. See figure 61.

Habits and Habitat. Southern flying squirrels occur in heavy deciduous forest, especially oak-hickory forest. They are strongly arboreal. On the ground their movements are rather clumsy, but they move from tree to tree with graceful glides as long as 40 or 50 yards, alighting on a tree trunk, and then scrambling up to glide again.

Flying squirrels are strictly nocturnal. In the beam of a flashlight, the eyes glow reddish orange. A variety of chirps, raspy squeals, and low "chuck" sounds reveal their presence. *G. volans* is a cavity nester. These squirrels use nests abandoned by woodpeckers or owls (and also birdhouses), which they line with fine fibers of bark, or with grasses or moss. In winter, they aggregate to nest, apparently to conserve body heat. They do not hibernate but do become inactive in blustery winter weather. The single annual molt occurs in autumn, from September to November.

The diet consists mostly of acorns, hickory nuts, and beechnuts, which are stored on the ground or in tree holes, but during the growing season the squirrels also eat buds, flowers, berries, fungi, birds' eggs and nestlings, and insects. Carrion is taken year around. Owls are important predators and raccoons and opossums take them in their nests. Predation generally is not heavy, however, and the animals are fairly long-lived—five years or more in the wild. They are not strongly territorial.

Reproduction. There are two breeding periods during the year, but individual females breed only once a year, in late winter or midsummer. Gestation takes about 40 days. A typical litter is three or four (range two to seven) young. The altricial neonates grow rapidly and are weaned at six to eight weeks. Young breed first as yearlings.

Suggested References. Dolan and Carter (1977); Weigl (1978).

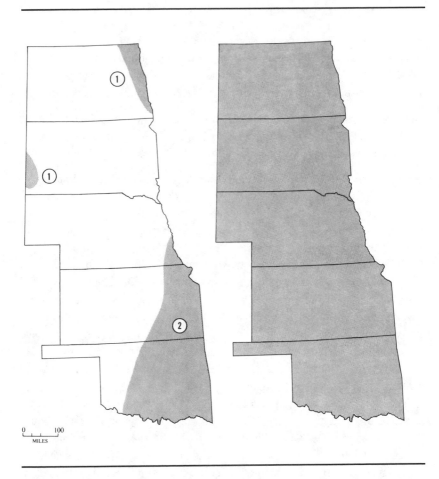

Map 43. *(Left).* Distribution of the northern flying squirrel, *Glaucomys sabrinus* (1), and the southern flying squirrel, *Glaucomys volans* (2).

Map 44. *(Right).* Distribution of the beaver, *Castor canadensis.*

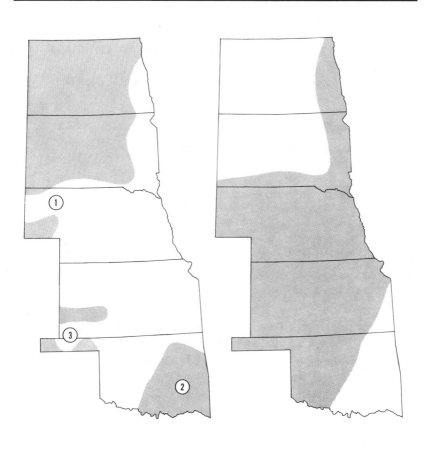

Map 45. *(Left).* Distribution of the northern pocket gopher, *Thomomys talpoides* (1); Baird's pocket gopher, *Geomys breviceps* (2); and the yellow-faced pocket gopher, *Cratogeomys castanops* (3).

Map 46. *(Right).* Distribution of the plains pocket gopher, *Geomys bursarius.*

Thomomys talpoides / Northern Pocket Gopher

Distribution. The northern pocket gopher is a species of the intermontane West and adjacent northern plains, ranging from the Prairie Provinces of Canada southward (at increasingly higher elevations) to New Mexico, and from the Sierra and Cascade mountains eastward to Minnesota. See map 45.

Description. Highly variable in color and size. Color dark brown on Black Hills to pale grayish in Nebraska Panhandle. Size varies from large (total length, 210–240 mm; tail, 40–75 mm; hind foot, 27–32 mm) in western North Dakota to small (total length, 175–205 mm; tail, 50–65 mm; hind foot, 25–28 mm) in northwestern Nebraska. Ears measure 5–8 mm; weight is 60–175 g. Males average much larger than females. See figure 62.

Habits and Habitat. Soil type is more important than vegetation for the distribution of pocket gophers. *T. talpoides* is a species of mountain soils on the Black Hills. It occurs on rocky soils and heavy clay in western Nebraska, where it is mostly surrounded by the range of *Geomys bursarius*. In the Dakotas, *Thomomys* occurs in all kinds of soils.

These are highly fossorial rodents, with eyes and ears reduced and the forefeet modified for digging. Burrow systems may be 300 feet long and up to six feet deep. Separate chambers contain food stores, feces, and the nest. Openings are numerous but most are plugged with soil. Loose soil is stored in tunnels in snowpack. With snowmelt, this soil sinks to ground level where it appears as characteristic "eskers," common evidence of the presence of *Thomomys*. Pocket gophers are primarily solitary and exhibit mutual avoidance. Densities may reach 50 per acre.

These gophers are nonselective vegetarians, feeding on a variety of roots, bulbs, tubers, and leaves. Food is carried in the capacious cheek pouches. Badgers, coyotes, and weasels prey on pocket gophers. Young animals dispersing above ground are taken by owls. Flooding kills adults and especially nestlings. Parasites include lice, ticks, mites, fleas, and helminths.

Reproduction. Females are monoestrous, producing a litter of four to seven young after a gestation period of three weeks. Young are weaned at six weeks and at two months are forced from the maternal burrow. They first reproduce as yearlings.

Suggested References. Andersen (1978); Gettinger (1975); Hansen and Ward (1966); Vaughan (1967).

Geomys breviceps / Baird's Pocket Gopher

Distribution. Baird's pocket gopher occurs from the vicinity of Norman, Oklahoma, eastward across the Cherokee Plains into Arkansas and southward to the Gulf Coast of Louisiana and Texas. This species and the plains pocket gopher are allopatric; the two are in contact in central Oklahoma with minimal hybridization. See map 45.

Description. Similar to the closely related plains pocket gopher; species differ in chromosome number (diploid number 74 in *G. breviceps,* 70 or 72 in *G. bursarius*), cranial details, and size (*G. breviceps* is smaller). Total length, 190–250 mm; tail, 60–75 mm; hind foot, 25–30 mm; weight, 200–400 g. Males 10 to 12 percent larger than females. Mostly dark brown in color. Not figured.

Habits and Habitat. Studies to determine ecological differences (if any) between Baird's and plains pocket gophers have not yet been done. Baird's pocket gopher lives in deep sandy to loamy soils, avoiding gravels and clays.

These are strongly fossorial rodents that spend nearly all of their lives in tunnels two to four inches in diameter and up to a yard deep. A single gopher can move two to three tons of soil per year. The deeper main tunnel leads to a nest chamber, storage chambers, and a latrine. Shallower lateral foraging tunnels course among the underground plant parts (roots, tubers, rhizomes) that are the principal food. A small amount of herbage also is taken above ground. Food is transported in the cheek pouches. Soil and rocks, on the contrary, are carried in the teeth. That is possible because the incisors pierce the lips and hence the lips can be closed behind them.

A subterranean existence protects them from most predators, and badgers are absent from much of the range of this particular species of pocket gopher. Flooding must be an important check on populations. A wide variety of parasites is known, but diseases have not been studied.

Reproduction. Females average about one and a half litters of 2.7 (range one to five) young per year. The gestation period has not been documented, but probably is about 30 days. The breeding season is from February to July.

Suggested References. Bohlin and Zimmerman (1982); Davis (1940); Hart (1978); Honeycutt and Schmidly (1979); Wood (1949).

Geomys bursarius / Plains Pocket Gopher

Distribution. The plains pocket gopher is mostly allopatric with other kinds of pocket gophers. It ranges from southern Manitoba to southern Texas and from Indiana westward to the foot of the Rockies. Some recent evidence suggests subdivision of the plains pocket gopher into two species, *G. bursarius* in the east and *G. lutescens* in the west. See map 46.

Description. Dorsal color dark brown to reddish brown to buff; belly paler. On average, largest gopher of the plains states; total length, 235–300 mm; tail, 62–102 mm; hind foot, 35–43 mm; weight, 170–420 g. Males 5 to 10 percent larger than females. Eastern *G. bursarius* average larger and darker than those to the west. See figure 63.

Habits and Habitat. This is the common pocket gopher of deep soils in the plains states. It is not abundant in cultivated fields, but it does occupy hayfields, roadside ditches, pastures, and bottomlands. Vegetation is less important than soil texture for suitability of habitat.

Tunnels are at two depths, the main one a yard or more beneath the surface. From this branch lateral foraging tunnels through the root zone about 10 inches below ground. The nest is a grass-lined chamber separate from the food storage and latrine areas. Excavation is with forefeet and teeth. A burrow system houses a single pocket gopher (except mothers with nursing young). Population densities range up to 15 per acre.

Food is mostly roots, bulbs, and tubers of forbs and grasses. There is some surface foraging but the animals seldom move far from the burrow, maintaining contact with the entrance with the sensitive tail.

For badgers, pocket gophers are a dietary staple. Coyotes, weasels, owls, and snakes also eat them. Parasites include fleas, ticks, mites, lice, and endoparasitic worms.

Reproduction. Breeding occurs from midwinter to spring. Females give birth annually to a single litter of three or four (range one to six) altricial young— hairless, with eyes, ears, and cheek pouches closed. They are weaned about two months of age and then disperse, breeding first as yearlings. Maximum longevity is in excess of two years.

Suggested References. Downhower and Hall (1966); Heaney and Timm (1983); Hendrickson (1972); Kennerly (1964); Wilks (1963). Also see suggested references for *G. breviceps*.

Figure 61. Southern flying squirrel, *Glaucomys volans* (New York Zoological Society).

Figure 62. Northern pocket gopher, *Thomomys talpoides* (U.S. Fish and Wildlife Service).

Figure 63. Plains pocket gopher, *Geomys bursarius* (D. C. Lovell and R. S. Mellott).

Figure 64. Yellow-faced pocket gopher, *Cratogeomys castanops* (R. L. Robbins).

Figure 65. Olive-backed pocket mouse, *Perognathus fasciatus* (R. E. Wrigley).

Figure 66. Plains pocket mouse, *Perognathus flavescens* (B. L. Clauson).

Figure 67. Silky pocket mouse, *Perognathus flavus* (T. H. Kunz).

Figure 68. Hispid pocket mouse, *Perognathus hispidus* (R. J. Baker).

Figure 69. Texas kangaroo rat, *Dipodomys elator* (Texas Parks and Wildlife Department).

Figure 70. Ord's kangaroo rat, *Dipodomys ordii* (T. H. Kunz).

Figure 71. Beaver, *Castor canadensis* (J. L. Tveten).

Figure 72. Marsh rice rat, *Oryzomys palustris* (R. J. Esher).

Figure 73. Fulvous harvest mouse, *Reithrodontomys fulvescens* (R. Altig).

Figure 74. Eastern harvest mouse, *Reithrodontomys humulis* (J. L. Tveten).

Figure 75. Western harvest mouse, *Reithrodontomys megalotis* (T. H. Kunz).

Cratogeomys castanops / Yellow-faced Pocket Gopher

Distribution. This is a species of the southern High Plains, ranging from southwestern Kansas and the Oklahoma Panhandle southward to central Mexico. See map 45.

Description. Upper parts yellowish, with black-tipped hairs common toward midline; belly whitish to buff. Total length, 245–290 mm; tail, 65–85 mm; hind foot, 35–40 mm; weight, 200–325 g. Males average 10 to 15 percent larger than females. Incisors with single groove on face. *Cratogeomys* sometimes treated as subgenus of *Pappogeomys*. See figure 64.

Habits and Habitat. This is a pocket gopher of variable habitat. In parts of the Southwest it uses deep sandy loams. Where its range approaches that of the plains pocket gopher, however, it lives in heavier upland soils. The animals generally avoid rocky soils and irrigated and forested areas. Vegetation may be less important to distribution than soil type.

The bulk of forage is found underground—roots, tubers, and rhizomes of numerous plant species. Food is carried in cheek pouches. Burrows are 12 to 24 inches deep, up to four inches in diameter, and marked by mounds at intervals of 10 to 20 feet. The forefeet are used in digging, soil is pushed with the chest, and rocks are carried in the teeth.

Like other gophers, these are solitary animals. Territorial defense is strong. Yellow-faced pocket gophers are somewhat colonial, however, living in concentrations of five or six per acre. Adult females live in the center of the colony, males and subadults on the periphery.

Except for occasional badgers, enemies are few. Dispersing young move above ground and hence are taken by coyotes, owls, and other predators. Parasites include lice, ticks, fleas, and helminths. Flooding sometimes is a major factor in mortality. Mean longevity of females is more than a year, that of males about eight months. Gophers molt seasonally in spring and autumn.

Reproduction. Breeding occurs from midwinter to midautumn, with a peak in March and April. Females are seasonally polyestrous, bearing up to three litters per year. The young disperse as juveniles. Females of early litters may breed late in their natal season.

Suggested References. Birney, Jones, and Mortimer (1971); Honeycutt and Williams (1982); Moulton, Choate, and Bissell (1983); Russell (1968); Smolen, Genoways, and Baker (1980).

Perognathus fasciatus / Olive-backed Pocket Mouse

Distribution. This species occurs from south-central Canada southward to northeastern Utah and the Colorado–New Mexico border. In the plains states, it is known only from the Dakotas (west of the tallgrass prairie) and northwestern Nebraska. See map 47.

Description. A small, silky-haired pocket mouse with a middorsal band of blackish and olive-colored hairs and a pronounced, yellowish lateral stripe; underparts white. Auditory bullae not meeting anteriorly. Auditory bullae smaller and interparietal bone broader than in *P. flavus;* size smaller than in *P. hispidus.* Total length, 125–142 mm; tail, 57–68 mm; hind foot, 16–18 mm; ear, 7–8 mm; weight, 10–14 g. See figure 65.

Habits and Habitat. This pocket mouse is most common on short-grass rangeland. Specimens have also been trapped in thickets of wild rose and sagebrush, in cropland, and among yucca and cactus at the edge of ponderosa pine forest. Entrances to burrows usually are not marked by mounds of excavated soil and are found in groups of two or three on slightly elevated ground. Entrances are plugged during the day. A burrow system may cover an area 20 feet across and tunnels may extend six feet below the surface.

This and other pocket mice use their fur-lined cheek pouches to carry food into the burrow. Food items transported consist of mainly seeds of grasses and forbs, including needlegrass, croton, butterfly weed, knotweed, lamb's-quarters, pigweed, Russian thistle, and junegrass. Excess food is cached in a separate chamber off the main tunnel of the burrow system.

Individuals of this species are solitary. Population densities reportedly range from 0.5 to two animals per acre. Molt and predation have not been described in detail. Owls may be the most important predator, although snakes and other carnivorous vertebrates doubtless prey on this mouse as well. Ectoparasites include mites, ticks, and fleas.

Reproduction. No comprehensive study of reproduction has been undertaken. Pregnant females have been trapped from mid-May through July and have carried from two to nine fetuses (average five). One female had 12 placental scars of two ages, suggesting that there may be two or more litters per year.

Suggested References. Maxwell and Brown (1968); Pefaur and Hoffmann (1974, 1975); Turner and Bowles (1967); Williams and Genoways (1979).

Perognathus flavescens / Plains Pocket Mouse

Distribution. The plains pocket mouse occurs from the Mississippi River in Minnesota and Iowa southwestward to the Front Range in Colorado and the Staked Plains of Texas, westward through New Mexico into the Four Corners area of Arizona, New Mexico, Utah, and Colorado. In the plains region, the species inhabits all but the western and northern Dakotas and the eastern parts of Nebraska, Kansas, and Oklahoma. See map 48.

Description. Resembles *P. fasciatus* except lacks olive-colored or blackish hairs on dorsum, has less pronounced buff-colored lateral line, and has auditory bullae that meet anteriorly. Bullae and buffy spot behind ear smaller and interparietal bone broader than in *P. flavus*. Total length, 114–130 mm; tail, 52–65 mm; hind foot, 16–18 mm; ear, 6–8 mm; weight, 7–12 g. See figure 66.

Habits and Habitat. This pocket mouse inhabits communities characterized by sandy soil with a vegetative cover of grasses and especially sagebrush or yucca. It is most common on the Nebraska Sandhills and other areas of sand-sage prairie. The abundance of this and other small pocket mice often is underestimated because they are only infrequently taken in conventional traps. Pocket mice, however, readily enter pitfalls buried in sand, especially if drift fences are set to direct them toward the pitfalls.

Little is known about the natural history of this species. Its burrows have several entrances that are kept plugged during the day. Separate chambers are excavated for the nest and for caches of food. The diet apparently consists mostly of seeds, but a few insects also are eaten in summer.

Most activity is at night, when these mice are exposed to predation by owls and other nocturnal predators. One study revealed that plains pocket mice made up 2.7 percent of the diet of the great horned owl in central Nebraska. There is no evidence for hibernation; however, animals maintained in a laboratory at 5° to 15°C became lethargic, suggesting a capacity for winter torpor.

Reproduction. Little is known about reproduction in this species. Adult females apparently bear one or two litters in spring and summer. The number of young per litter is thought to range from two to five.

Suggested References. Beer (1961); Czaplewski (1976); Jones et al. (1983); Williams (1978).

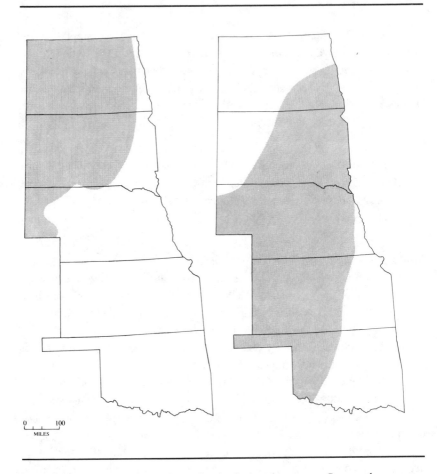

0 |___|___| 100
MILES

Map 47. *(Left).* Distribution of the olive-backed pocket mouse, *Perognathus fasciatus.*

Map 48. *(Right).* Distribution of the plains pocket mouse, *Perognathus flavescens.*

Map 49. *(Left).* Distribution of the silky pocket mouse, *Perognathus flavus.*

Map 50. *(Right).* Distribution of the hispid pocket mouse, *Perognathus hispidus.*

Perognathus flavus / Silky Pocket Mouse

Distribution. This inhabitant of semidesert grasslands ranges northward from central Mexico through the southwestern United States and across the southern and central Great Plains. Its distribution in the five-state region extends eastward into the central parts of Oklahoma, Kansas, and Nebraska. See map 49.

Description. Smallest of the pocket mice on the Great Plains. Pelage soft and silky, usually yellowish in color dorsally; underparts white; lateral line less well defined than in other species; dorsum often washed with black hairs in northern populations. Distinctive buffy spot usually present behind ear. Auditory bullae larger than in other small *Perognathus* and meeting anteriorly; interparietal bone narrow. Total length, 105–130 mm; tail, 46–60 mm; hind foot, 14–16 mm; ear, 6–7 mm; weight, 6–10 g. See figure 67.

Habits and Habitat. This is the least abundant and least well known of the pocket mice on the Great Plains. Unlike other species, it seems to tolerate diverse soil types and plant communities. In one study in Wyoming, it was most abundant in loamy short-grass rangeland with little bare soil; nearby areas with sandy soil or brushy vegetation were inhabited by *P. flavescens* or *P. fasciatus.* In southwestern Texas, it is most common in rocky soils unsuited for habitation by other plains species of *Perognathus.* Possibly this mouse does not require sand or bare soil for dusting and cleansing its pelage as do other pocket mice on the plains.

Silky pocket mice can be caught most easily by hand; their small size limits the effectiveness of conventional traps, and the habitats in which they occur often are not suitable for the use of pitfalls. Contents of cheek pouches of trapped mice invariably consist of seeds, which are carefully shelled so the endosperm can be eaten.

Reproduction. Pocket mice generally do not breed in captivity. Therefore, details of reproduction in this and other species are based on meager field records and are incomplete. Females apparently bear only one litter per year (usually in spring) in New Mexico, but they are thought to bear two litters per year (spring and summer) in Texas. Fetus counts of two to six have been recorded. Gestation probably lasts about four weeks.

Suggested References. Forbes (1964); Maxell and Brown (1968); Schmidly (1977).

Perognathus hispidus / Hispid Pocket Mouse

Distribution. This species ranges from North Dakota to central Mexico and from Missouri to the Rocky Mountains. In the plains states, it occurs west of the Missouri River from southwestern North Dakota southward, except in eastern Kansas and Oklahoma. See map 50.

Description. Largest of the pocket mice in the plains region. Pelage bristly, yellowish interspersed with black hairs above, and with distinct buffy lateral line; underparts white. Total length, 190–237 mm; tail, 90–115 mm; hind foot, 23–30 mm; ear, 12–14 mm; weight, 35–60 g. See figure 68.

Habits and Habitat. This pocket mouse has been reported to occur in rocky and loamy soils, but it is most abundant where soil is sandy and scattered open areas permit dusting. It inhabits various upland habitats, including those characterized by tall or short grasses, forbs, shrubs, cacti, or yucca, but seemingly avoids dune sands and riparian habitats.

The diet consists mostly of seeds, which are selected rather than gathered at random. A thorough study in Texas revealed that winter foods comprise seeds of mesquite, sunflower, sagebrush, sorghum, and millet, whereas in spring the diet included seeds of blanketflower and bluestem plus nearly 14 percent insects. Seeds of other plants are eaten in other areas.

Stored seeds are eaten in winter, when hispid pocket mice seldom venture above ground. In one study conducted in Kansas from 1965 through 1969, none was trapped between 9 December and 3 April. Burrows have two or three entrances that are kept plugged, and are often marked by conspicuous mounds. Carnivorous mammals and owls prey on these solitary mice, and ticks and other arthropods parasitize them.

Reproduction. Information on reproduction in this species is primarily anecdotal. Litter size has been reported to vary from two to nine. The reproductive season on the northern Great Plains extends from spring through late summer; in Kansas, adult males have enlarged testes from March through October, pregnant females have been taken from April through August, and lactating females have been trapped in July and August. Length of the breeding season suggests that females bear two or more litters per year.

Suggested References. Alcoze and Zimmerman (1973); Blair (1937); Glass (1947); Kaufman and Fleharty (1974); Maxell and Brown (1968).

Dipodomys elator / Texas Kangaroo Rat

Distribution. This rat is known only from north-central Texas and one locality in adjacent Oklahoma. The Oklahoma record is from Comanche County and is based on a specimen taken near the turn of the century. Recent attempts to locate this species in that state have failed, although it is common in several Texas counties just across the Red River. See map 51.

Description. Upper parts buff, washed with blackish; venter white. Tail long, about 160 percent of head and body length, with conspicuous white "banner" on tip. Four toes on each hind foot. Total length, 260–345 mm; tail, 161–205 mm; hind foot, 42–49 mm; ear, 10–15 mm; weight usually 65–90 g but may exceed 100. See figure 69.

Habits and Habitat. This kangaroo rat occurs primarily in and adjacent to pastureland supporting mesquite. Animals have been taken in dense brush and grasses along roadsides—always within a short distance of more open areas—and along the weedy borders of cultivated fields.

Clay-based soils seem to be preferred for burrowing but some sandy areas also are occupied. The burrow, constructed at the base of a mesquite bush, is rarely plugged in the daytime and may be complex, containing many interconnecting tunnels, storage areas for food caches, and a nest located near the bottom of the system of tunnels. Burrow systems averaged 18 inches deep in firm soil in one Texas study. Based on trapping records, the average home range of adults is about 0.20 acre. Scratching and dust-bathing areas frequently are found near burrow entrances.

This rat is nocturnal and active the year around, even in snow; the greatest period of activity evidently is two to three hours after dark. Food consists principally of the seeds of grasses (including cultivated grains), forbs, and perennials, but fruits and leaves apparently are eaten as well as an occasional insect.

Reproduction. Virtually nothing is known about reproduction in this species. We have records of pregnant females, which carried two to four fetuses, from February, June, July, and September. Juveniles have been collected in the months of May through November.

Suggested References. Chapman (1972); Dalquest and Collier (1964); Martin and Matocha (1972); Packard and Roberts (1973); Roberts and Packard (1973).

Dipodomys ordii / Ord's Kangaroo Rat

Distribution. This species occurs from southern Saskatchewan and Alberta to central Mexico and from the plains states to the Sierra Nevada. In the five-state region, this distribution includes southwesternmost North Dakota, the western half of South Dakota, the western two-thirds of Nebraska, and the western half of Kansas and Oklahoma. See map 52.

Description. Five toes on each hind foot (fifth midway up foot and little more than claw exposed). Dorsum yellowish buff, often with blackish wash; tail with dark dorsal and ventral stripes; sides of tail, venter and flank stripes white. Total length, 240–280 mm; tail, 130–156 mm; hind foot, 40–45 mm; ear, 12–16 mm; weight, 50–80 g. See figure 70.

Habits and Habitat. Ord's kangaroo rat is closely associated with sandy soil. It is abundant on the Nebraska Sandhills and in other areas where bare sand permits dusting. Its burrows open at the base of sagebrush, yucca, or bunchgrass, or in banks or cuts. Entrances are plugged whenever burrows are occupied. Winter foods consist mostly of seeds, which are gathered roughly in proportion to their abundance in the environment. In spring, the diet is more selective and includes more than 18 percent insects.

Kangaroo rats are highly adapted to arid conditions and can live indefinitely without free water. They obtain metabolic water from the oxidation of food, and they conserve it by means of efficient kidneys and by remaining within cool, damp burrows during the day. The open habitats where these rats live provide sparse cover from predators. Saltatorial bipedal locomotion is used to evade pursuers, but owls, snakes, coyotes, badgers, and others nevertheless exact a toll.

Reproduction. Time of reproduction varies geographically. Pregnant females have been trapped in June and July in South Dakota, in May through September in Nebraska, and in March through May and July through October in Kansas. In the Oklahoma and Texas panhandles, most pregnancies evidently occur from August through March. Apparently there are two or more litters per year, at least in the southern part of the region. Litter size ranges from one to five.

Suggested References. Alcoze and Zimmerman (1973); Hoditschek and Best (1983); Kennedy and Schnell (1978); Schmidt-Nielsen and Schmidt-Nielson (1952); Setzer (1949).

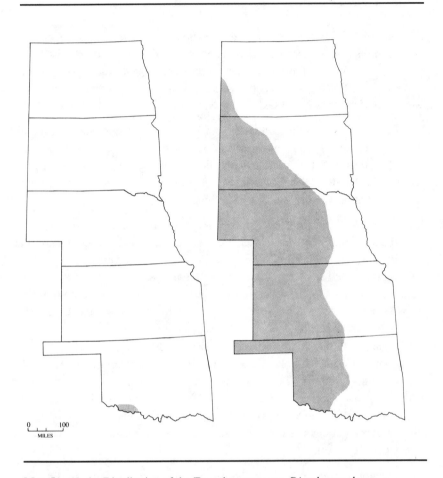

0   100
MILES

Map 51. *(Left).* Distribution of the Texas kangaroo rat, *Dipodomys elator.*

Map 52. *(Right).* Distribution of Ord's kangaroo rat, *Dipodomys ordii.*

Map 53. *(Left)*. Distribution of the marsh rice rat, *Oryzomys palustris* (1), and the plains harvest mouse, *Reithrodontomys montanus* (2).

Map 54. *(Right)*. Distribution of the eastern harvest mouse, *Reithrodontomys humulis* (1), and the western harvest mouse, *Reithrodontomys megalotis* (2).

Castor canadensis / Beaver

Distribution. The beaver occurs in suitable habitats throughout much of North America, southward to northern Mexico. It inhabits permanent bodies of water on the Great Plains. See map 44.

Description. Largest rodent in North America; aquatic specializations include webbed feet, eyes protected by nictitating membranes, nostrils and ears capable of being closed underwater, and broad, scaly, flat tail. Paired anal scent glands (castors) present. Dorsum dark or rusty brown; underparts grayish brown. Total length, 940–1,210 mm; tail, 290–400 mm; hind foot, 170–192 mm; ear, 33–37 mm; weight averages about 40 lb but may exceed 90. Seasonal molts are in spring and autumn. See figure 71.

Habits and Habitat. Beavers generally are more abundant along watercourses on the plains than in areas farther east because the preferred foods of this rodent (for example, cottonwoods and willows) are more plentiful on the plains than in eastern deciduous forests. Aspens are favored where available in the plains states, such as on the Black Hills. Bark is eaten, and other parts are used in construction of dams and lodges.

Beavers construct dams to retard the flow of water, producing ponds. Ponds protect lodges or bank dens from predators, facilitate transport of building materials and foods, and enable swimming both in summer and beneath the ice in winter. Ponds also elevate the water table and thereby enhance the growth of nearby vegetation, which includes the species favored as food. Lodges provide a protected, above-water resting area with two or more underwater entrances. Bank dens are cavities excavated or enlarged beneath the bank of a stream, often with only one underwater entrance.

Exploitation of beavers for their commercially valuable fur was responsible for the early exploration of much of North America. Aside from humans, the principal predators are coyotes, domestic dogs, bobcats, lynx, and mountain lions. Mink sometimes prey on young.

Reproduction. Breeding begins in January, and litters containing one to six (usually three or four) young are born after a gestation period of approximately 120 days. Only one litter is produced annually. Females do not breed until the second season after their birth, or even later in large populations.

Suggested References. Henderson (1960); Jenkins and Busher (1979).

Oryzomys palustris / Marsh Rice Rat

Distribution. This is a species of the southeastern United States. It reaches its northern limits in Pennsylvania; in the plains states, it occurs only in eastern Oklahoma. See map 53.

Description. Upper parts grayish brown to buff, mixed with black; paling on sides; white to buff ventrally. Tail sparsely haired, usually brownish above, white below. Total length, 225–260 mm; tail, 110–145 mm; hind foot, 25–37 mm; ear, 10–16 mm; weight, 40–75 g. See figure 72.

Habits and Habitat. Typical habitat of these rice rats is wetlands, including marshes, swamps, wet margins of gravel pits, and roadside ditches. Common mammalian associates are hispid cotton rats and fulvous harvest mice. Rice rats swim well, entering the water not just to escape but also to forage. Sometimes these rats burrow, but they also build softball-sized nests of grass beneath shrubs or debris.

These are omnivorous rodents that eat seeds (mostly grasses, but some forbs), green vegetation, and fungi. Some authors have reported a diet of well over half insects. Fish, crayfish, nestling birds, eggs, young turtles, and carrion are also taken in quantity.

Home ranges are from half an acre to an acre. Densities range around one to seven per acre. Behavioral ecology is not well documented, but rice rats seem to be mutually intolerant. They are primarily nocturnal. The chief predator may be the barn owl. At one locality, rice rats provided 97.5 percent of the diet of these owls. Marsh hawks, water moccasins, red foxes, raccoons, striped skunks, and mink also prey on them. A wide variety of arthropod and helminth parasites have been reported. Some of the parasitic worms are contracted from eating fish and crayfish.

Reproduction. Rice rats are highly fecund. They can breed throughout the year, although reproduction peaks in late winter and early spring. Population densities seem to influence reproductive effort. Females undergo postpartum estrus. Gestation takes three to four weeks, depending upon whether or not the female is lactating. Litter size averages about five. Neonates are altricial and weigh about 3.5 grams. At a week and a half the eyes open and weaning begins. Sexual maturity is reached at 50 to 60 days of age. Longevity is not known.

Suggested References. Wolfe (1982).

Reithrodontomys fulvescens / Fulvous Harvest Mouse

Distribution. This species ranges from Missouri and Arizona southward to Nicaragua. In the plains states, it occurs in southeastern Kansas and in eastern and central Oklahoma. See map 55.

Description. Largest harvest mouse of the plains states and the species with the relatively longest tail. Upper parts golden brown with black-tipped hairs on middorsal area; face and sides reddish orange; venter grayish white; tail moderately bicolored. Total length, 135–200 mm; tail, 70–120 mm; hind foot, 16–20 mm; ear, 11–17 mm; weight to about 25 g. See figure 73.

Habits and Habitat. Fulvous harvest mice occur in grasslands interspersed with brush, including weedy gullies, abandoned fields, and grassland-woodland ecotones. Where they occur with plains harvest mice, they occupy moister sites with more rank vegetation. Common associates are the cotton rat and the rice rat.

The species is almost exclusively nocturnal. Nests are baseball-sized globes of grasses and sedges. Entrances are plugged when the mouse is within. These mice climb stems to feed on grass seeds. Some seeds of forbs and other green vegetation also are eaten, as are insects in warmer months.

Densities to 60 per acre have been reported, but densities of about 12 per acre are more common through most of the year. Home range averages about half an acre. Social behavior is poorly known, but there seems to be a great deal of mutual tolerance, and there is some indication of pair-bonding. Predation and parasitism are poorly studied, but owls are known to feed on them and they do carry fleas.

Reproduction. Two litters per year may be the rule for most females. Breeding peaks in spring and autumn. Litter size is two to four. Gestation probably lasts about three weeks, based on the known period in closely related species. Neonates weigh about 2 grams and are naked and blind. Growth is rapid, however; the eyes open at 12 days and by two weeks the young can climb well and soon are weaned. There are two maturational molts, and adults undergo seasonal molts in spring and autumn. Life expectancy is brief; most individuals live no more than two or three months, and one year would represent old age.

Suggested References. Spencer and Cameron (1982).

Reithrodontomys humulis / Eastern Harvest Mouse

Distribution. This harvest mouse occurs in the Southeast, ranging from Maryland and Ohio southward to Florida and westward to southeastern Oklahoma and eastern Texas. See map 54.

Description. Dorsum brown, heavily washed with blackish; white to grayish below. Tail not distinctly bicolored. A small harvest mouse, as small as or smaller than the plains harvest mouse. Total length, 105–130 mm; tail, 45–60 mm (less than half the total length); hind foot, 15–17 mm; ear, 8–9 mm; weight, 6–10 g. See figure 74.

Habits and Habitat. Like many other harvest mice, this is a species of abandoned fields, weedy roadsides, and brushy clearings. Nests are built of woven grasses suspended from plants or placed on the ground. Like the plains harvest mouse, this species seldom seems to be abundant, with densities of two or three per acre.

These mice are not strongly territorial. Indeed, they are highly tolerant of one another. Groups of two to six individuals huddle to sleep in cold weather, thereby conserving energy. The animals are nocturnal except in coldest weather, when individuals forage by day. The diet consists of seeds, along with a few insects and a little green vegetation. Like other mice, disturbed females may cannibalize young.

A variety of animals, including owls, snakes, weasels, and foxes, prey on eastern harvest mice, and both arthropods and helminths parasitize them. Longevity is not known but probably averages no more than a month or two; mortality is highest among nestlings. More than a quarter of the animals that actually leave the nest survive to six months, and maximum recorded longevity is more than 15 months.

Reproduction. Reproduction may occur throughout the year, but it is concentrated in late spring and early autumn and depressed in midsummer. Litter size averages about three (range one to eight) young, which are born after a gestation period of about three weeks. The young weigh only a little more than a gram at birth. A litter at term, however, may weigh half as much as the mother, about the highest reproductive efficiency known in mammals. Growth is rapid and the young are weaned at two to four weeks of age.

Suggested References. Dunaway (1968); Kaye (1961); Layne (1959).

Reithrodontomys megalotis / Western Harvest Mouse

Distribution. This harvest mouse ranges across the northern and central plains and through the intermontane West, southward to central Mexico. It is mostly allopatric with eastern and fulvous harvest mice but broadly overlaps the plains harvest mouse in distribution. See map 54.

Description. A fairly large harvest mouse, second in size only to *R. fulvescens* in the plains states. Dorsum grayish to reddish, with only obscure darker middorsal area. Underparts white and tail bicolored (the dorsal stripe nearly covers top of tail). Total length, 120–170 mm; tail, 55–95 mm; hind foot, 14–20 mm; ear, 11–14 mm; weight, 11–15 g. See figure 75.

Habits and Habitat. Western harvest mice occur in a wide variety of situations, from abandoned fields to well-developed mid- and tall-grass prairie, weedy field margins, and highway rights-of-way. Habitat may include some shrubs, but fewer than the habitats of eastern and fulvous harvest mice. Western harvest mice occupy situations more xeric than either *R. fulvescens* or *R. humulis,* but more mesic than *R. montanus.* Common mammalian associates are *Microtus ochrogaster* (prairie vole) and *Cryptotis parva* (least shrew).

Strictly nocturnal, this harvest mouse rests by day in a baseball-sized nest woven of grasses and other plant fibers and lined with thistledown. The nest is usually suspended a few inches above the ground. The diet consists primarily of seeds (including native grasses, forbs, and small grains such as oats, wheat, and barley), insects, and occasional herbage. The animals forage throughout the year. Western harvest mice are not territorial and are remarkably tolerant of one another. They are known to huddle together for warmth.

Predators include owls, hawks, shrikes, jays, weasels, skunks, badgers, foxes, coyotes, and snakes. Probably occasional communal nesting adds to the generally high parasite loads.

Reproduction. Breeding takes place throughout the warmer months. Mean litter size is about five (usual range three to seven). Females show postpartum estrus. Gestation takes 24 to 25 days. In the laboratory, one female produced 59 young in 14 litters in one year, but such fecundity would not be expected in the wild. Young are altricial, weighing only 1.5 grams. They are weaned at three weeks; females may breed at one month of age.

Suggested References. Webster and Jones (1982).

Reithrodontomys montanus / Plains Harvest Mouse

Distribution. This is a species of the central and southern Great Plains. It ranges from northwestern South Dakota south to northern Mexico, and from Missouri to Arizona. Thus it occurs throughout much of the five-state region. See map 53.

Description. A tiny mouse, smaller than either western or fulvous harvest mice. Upper parts grayish brown, becoming darker toward dorsal midline; venter white to grayish. Tail distinctly bicolored, with narrow, dark dorsal stripe less than one-fourth diameter of tail. Total length, 110–140 mm; tail, 48–63 mm; hind foot, 14–17 mm; ear, 12–15 mm; weight, 10–12 g. See figure 76.

Habits and Habitat. This is a species of well-developed upland grasslands. It responds well to grazed rangelands, with exposed rocks and prickly pear, but the cover of grasses must be greater than about 50 percent. Eastern, western, and fulvous harvest mice all usually occupy more mesic sites than those of the plains harvest mouse. Typical mammalian associates are the deer mouse, hispid pocket mouse, northern grasshopper mouse, thirteen-lined ground squirrel, and black-tailed prairie dog.

The diet probably consists mostly of seeds, although there have been no detailed studies. Like other harvest mice, it probably takes some insects as well. These animals are strictly nocturnal.

Either this mouse is generally rare, or it is decidedly trap-shy, for it never appears to occur in dense populations. The home range averages about half an acre. Like other harvest mice, *R. montanus* shows little agonistic behavior. A male may be caged with a female even when she has nestling young, which is rare among cricetine rodents. Enemies include owls, weasels, snakes, grasshopper mice, and most other predatory vertebrates.

Reproduction. The breeding season spans the warmer months, from February to November. Females are polyestrous. Gestation lasts three weeks. Young are altricial, weighing only about a gram (one-third the weight of a penny) at birth. They are born pink and hairless, with eyes, ears, and anus unopened, but by two weeks they are sufficiently developed to be weaned. Females are known to produce litters when they are as young as 12 weeks of age.

Suggested References. Goertz (1963); Hibbard (1938); Hill and Hibbard (1943); Leraas (1938); Moulton et al. (1981).

Peromyscus attwateri / Texas Mouse

Distribution. This is a species of the Ozarks and uplands of southeastern Kansas, central and eastern Oklahoma, and central Texas. The distribution probably is discontinuous across that range, due to the predilection of the Texas mouse for rocky habitats. See map 56.

Description. Similar to *P. truei* and *P. difficilis* but larger; tail relatively longer (longer than head and body), ears relatively short (considerably shorter than hind foot); most closely resembles *P. pectoralis* (which has shorter hind feet, usually less than 23 mm, paler color, white ankles, and more sharply bicolored tail) and *P. boylii* (brush mouse, which has shorter hind feet, white belly, smaller average skull, and distinctive karyotype). Dorsum buff; venter pale grayish to white. Total length, 187–218 mm; tail, 96–112 mm; hind foot, 23–27 mm; ear, 15–17 mm; weight 20–30 g. See figure 77.

Habits and Habitat. Apparently closely related to the brush mouse, *P. attwateri* shares its affinity for brushy hillsides and ravines. The two mice were thought to represent a single species until chromosomal differences were noted. The brush mouse is yet undocumented in the plains states but should be expected because it is known from southeastern Colorado.

These animals are highly tolerant of one another and seem not to be particularly territorial. Densities of one to three per acre have been reported, and home ranges are about half an acre, arranged linearly along cliffs and ledges. The diet includes seeds, berries, and a little green vegetation. Insects make up one-third of the food during the warmer months. When abundant, acorns predominate in the winter diet.

Records of predation are few and involve the broad-winged hawk and the coachwhip snake. The Texas mouse, however, doubtless falls prey to a wide variety of predatory mammals, reptiles, and birds, although it must derive some protection from its rocky habitat.

Reproduction. Probably females are polyestrous. There are peaks of breeding in spring and early autumn, but the species may breed nearly year around. Gestation probably takes about four weeks. Litter size is three to six. The young are altricial, but development is rapid. Age at sexual maturity is unknown. Mean lifespan has been estimated to be 6.8 months, and estimated maximum longevity is 18 months.

Suggested References. Schmidly (1974a).

Peromyscus difficilis / Rock Mouse

Distribution. The rock mouse ranges from Oaxaca northward in the Sierra Madre of eastern and western Mexico to the Front Range of Colorado. In the plains states, it is known only from the Black Mesa, at the western end of the Oklahoma Panhandle. See map 55.

Description. Similar to *P. truei;* adults grayish to brownish gray above, never clear buff (at most buff on sides); venter whitish. Ear about same length as hind foot; tail bicolored, brownish above, roughly same length as head and body. Total length, 170–200 mm; tail, 80–100 mm; hind foot, 20–23 mm; ear, 22–24 mm; weight, 25–30 g. See figure 78.

Habits and Habitat. These are mice of brushy, rocky country, living over a wide range of moisture conditions in situations where boulders are present. Typical vegetation of such habitats includes Gambel's oak, skunkbush, and snowberry. Rock mice feed on seeds and also eat insects, fungi, and green vegetation. Some food is stored in a den in a hollow beneath a boulder or in an abandoned woodrat den (or even in the wall of an occupied den). The animals are nocturnal and are active throughout the year.

Despite its extensive geographic range, this species has been the subject of little research. Few studies have been done of its relationships with sympatric species of *Peromyscus*. Where it occurs, the rock mouse may be abundant, but it does not seem to be continuously distributed in apparently suitable habitat.

Doubtless a wide variety of vertebrate predators feed on rock mice, but like other species of rocky habitats, predation pressure may be low. Parasitism has not been studied.

Reproduction. The breeding season continues through the warmer months. Males come into breeding condition in March or April. Females begin to breed in April and are polyestrous, continuing to breed throughout the season until August. Probably there is postpartum estrus. Litters of two to six altricial young are born after a gestation period of three to four weeks. Females born early in the season probably breed later that same summer. Most mice surely do not survive two full summers. A mouse 12 to 15 months old would be aged indeed.

Suggested References. Armstrong (1975); Cinq-Mars and Brown (1969).

Peromyscus gossypinus / Cotton Mouse

Distribution. This is a species of the southeastern United States, ranging from southeastern Oklahoma and East Texas to the East Coast, and from Virginia to Florida. See map 57.

Description. Largest of short-tailed *Peromyscus* of plains states. Color, dark brown above, white below; tail brown above, whitish below. Greatest similarity with *P. leucopus,* which differs in shorter hind foot (usually less than 22 mm) and smaller average size. Total length, 160–205 mm; tail, 68–97 mm; hind foot, 22–26 mm; ear, 16–18 mm; weight, 20–40 g. See figure 79.

Habits and Habitat. The cotton mouse occupies a variety of habitats, generally with heavy cover—deciduous bottomland forests, swamps, thickets, and weedy field margins as well as rocky ravines. Climbing and swimming are well developed, suiting the animals to quite moist habitats. Like other species of *Peromyscus,* this is an opportunistic omnivore, eating fruits, seeds, fungi, insects, and carrion roughly as available in the habitat.

Predation is poorly documented, but doubtless a variety of forest- and woodland-dwelling mammalian, avian, and reptilian predators exact a toll. Mites, chiggers, ticks, fleas, and a variety of worms are known to parasitize cotton mice. Populations as high as about 40 per acre have been reported, but usual densities are about one-tenth that high. Home ranges of about one acre seem to be typical. Territoriality has not been reported, but in competition with *P. leucopus* the cotton mouse is behaviorally dominant, excluding white-footed mice from lowland forests. These nocturnal animals spend the day and rear their young in nests built of plant fibers beneath stumps, logs, brush, or debris.

Reproduction. Cotton mice breed throughout the warmer months. There is postpartum estrus. Gestation takes about 30 days in lactating mothers, 23 days in nonlactating females. Mean litter size is about four (range one to seven). Neonates are altricial—blind, hairless, and weighing about 2 grams. Weaning occurs at four weeks of age. Females as young as 10 weeks have been known to breed. Long-term studies of populations have not been made, but longevity probably is similar to that of other species of *Peromyscus*—a few months on the average, with the maximum a little more than a year.

Suggested References. Wolfe and Linzey (1977).

Peromyscus leucopus / White-footed Mouse

Distribution. This mouse ranges widely in eastern and central North America, except for the Gulf Coast and Florida. Its northern limits are in Nova Scotia and Saskatchewan, and it ranges southward to the Yucatan Peninsula. *P. leucopus* occurs throughout most of the plains region, but westwardly it is increasingly restricted to riparian woodlands along major rivers. See map 58.

Description. Color variable, becoming paler brownish westward across plains; sides paler than back; venter white; tail indistinctly bicolored. Total length, 160–185 mm; tail, 65–80 mm; hind foot, 17–21 mm; ear, 15–17 mm; weight, 27–36 g. Easily confused with the generally smaller deer mouse and the usually larger cotton mouse; for comparisons, see accounts of those species. See figure 80.

Habits and Habitat. The white-footed mouse occupies a wide variety of ecological conditions but mostly occurs in habitats with a three-dimensional structure such as forest, woodland, brushy country, and shelterbelts. The slightly smaller deer mouse, by contrast, inhabits more open country.

These rodents are mostly nocturnal, spending the day in canteloupe-sized nests of plant fibers beneath rocks or stumps or in hollow logs. They are active throughout the year. White-footed mice forage for seeds, berries, fruits, nuts, insects, and occasionally carrion. Green vegetation and dew provide the bulk of their water needs. Much foraging is done in brushy vegetation, where the long tail is used for balance. The home range is from 0.2 to 2 acres, and territoriality is weakly developed at best.

Nearly all woodland predators take white-footed mice. They are staple fare for owls and snakes and are eaten also by foxes, skunks, weasels, and opossums. Fleas, mites, ticks, and warbles infest them externally and a variety of endoparasites live within.

Reproduction. These animals breed throughout the warmer months, with peaks in March–April and September–October. Females are polyestrous and show postpartum estrus. Gestation is about four weeks for nursing mothers, but only 22 or 23 days for nonlactating females. Mean litter size is about four (range one to seven). Weaning takes place at four weeks, and newly weaned females sometimes breed almost immediately.

Suggested References. Baar and Fleharty (1976); Baker (1983); King (1968); Miller and Getz (1969).

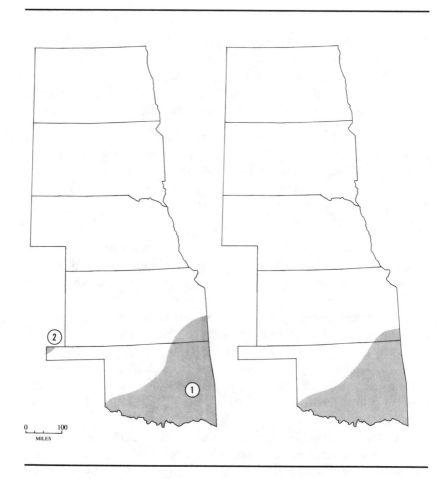

Map 55. *(Left).* Distribution of the fulvous harvest mouse, *Reithrodontomys fulvescens* (1), and the rock mouse, *Peromyscus difficilis* (2).

Map 56. *(Right).* Distribution of the Texas mouse, *Peromyscus attwateri.*

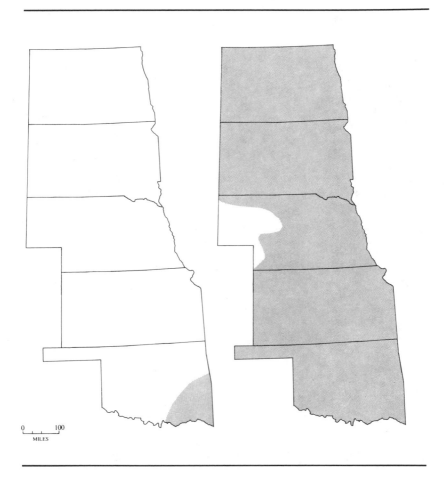

Map 57. *(Left).* Distribution of the cotton mouse, *Peromyscus gossypinus*.

Map 58. *(Right).* Distribution of the white-footed mouse, *Peromyscus leucopus*.

Map 59. *(Left).* Distribution of the deer mouse, *Peromyscus maniculatus*.

Map 60. *(Right).* Distribution of the white-ankled mouse, *Peromyscus pectoralis* (1), and the piñon mouse, *Peromyscus truei* (2).

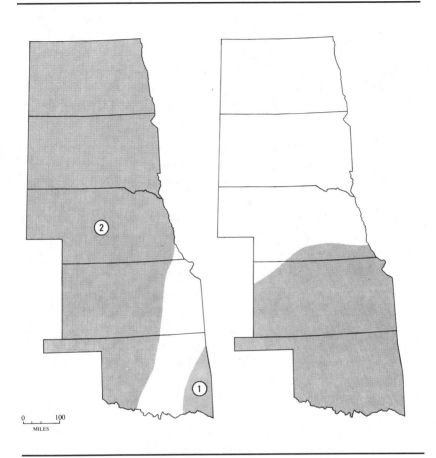

Map 61. *(Left).* Distribution of the golden mouse, *Ochrotomys nuttalli* (1), and the northern grasshopper mouse, *Onychomys leucogaster* (2).

Map 62. *(Right).* Distribution of the hispid cotton rat, *Sigmodon hispidus*.

Peromyscus maniculatus / Deer Mouse

Distribution. This is the most wide-ranging of *Peromyscus* species and one of the most widespread of North American mammals. It occurs from the Yukon and Mackenzie rivers southward to Oaxaca, Mexico, and east-west from coast to coast. It is absent from the Deep South, a region occupied by the oldfield mouse, but it occurs throughout the plains states except in the southeastern part of Oklahoma. See map 59.

Description. Highly variable in size and color in the plains states. Dorsum nearly black in eastern Kansas to yellowish on the High Plains and brownish gray in the western Dakotas; venter white; tail sharply bicolored. Size variable; largest animals in western part of region. Total length, 125–175 mm; tail, 50–75 mm; hind foot, 16–20 mm; ear, 13–19 mm; weight, 15–25 g. Easily confused with the white-footed mouse, which is usually larger with a relatively longer and less sharply bicolored tail, and duller, more grayish dorsum. See figure 81.

Habits and Habitat. Doubtless the most abundant terrestrial vertebrate in the plains states, deer mice occur from arid grasslands to floodplains, cultivated fields, and farmhouse pantries. Generally, the species is absent only from wetlands and from places where a larger, specialized relative is present.

Deer mice retreat to rest by day and during inclement weather into nests situated under rocks, stumps, or debris, but they are active year around. They are omnivorous, emphasizing insects in summer and seeds in winter. Seeds are stored for winter and so is body fat.

These mice are the most common prey for upland predators, and they harbor a broad spectrum of arthropod and helminth parasites. Population densities average roughly three per acre. Home ranges of 0.1 to 10 acres have been reported.

Reproduction. Breeding takes place throughout the warmer months, with peaks in spring and early autumn. Females bear several litters of one to nine (average about four) altricial young annually after gestation periods of about 23 days. The young are weaned at four weeks and females as young as five weeks are known to have bred. Average longevity may be less than two months, and one year marks advanced old age.

Suggested References. Hansen and Fleharty (1974); Jones et al. (1983); King (1968); Myers and Master (1983).

Peromyscus pectoralis / White-ankled Mouse

Distribution. The white-ankled mouse ranges from extreme southern Oklahoma (Love County) southward through central Texas to central Mexico. See map 60.

Description. A large, long-tailed mouse, pale buff above, white below; tail sharply bicolored; similar in appearance to *P. attwateri* but has smaller hind feet (23 mm or shorter) and grayish ankles. Ear relatively shorter than that of *P. truei* or *P. difficilis.* Total length, 185–219 mm; tail longer than head and body, 92–117 mm; hind foot, 19–23 mm; ear, 14–18 mm; weight 20–30 g. See figure 82.

Habits and Habitat. This is a rock-dwelling species, as are the other long-tailed *Peromyscus* of the plains states. Its typical habitat is semiarid brush and cedar-oak thickets in rimrock country and along ledges in ravines. The locality from which the species has been taken in Oklahoma had vegetation of post oak and greenbriar.

The biology of this mouse is as poorly known as that of any species of *Peromyscus* in the United States. In Texas it is known to eat juniper berries, acorns, and hackberries and in Mexico it has been reported to eat cactus fruits. Probably individuals are rather opportunistic feeders, eating a variety of fruits, seeds, and herbage, and taking insects as available.

Behavioral ecology has not been studied. Nothing is known of home range, territoriality, or agonistic interactions. Nor have predators been studied, although one would suppose that a variety of vertebrate predators (owls, weasels, snakes, coyotes, foxes) would feed on these mice as opportunity allowed. Ectoparasitism by fleas and chiggers is known. As in other species of *Peromyscus,* there are two maturational molts, a post-juvenile molt and a post-subadult molt. Adults undergo seasonal molts in spring or early summer and in autumn.

Reproduction. Breeding probably takes place throughout the warmer months of the year and in Mexico the species may breed year around. Reported embryo counts range from three to seven (average five), and young per litter averages 2.9 (range two to five). Gestation is probably about 23 days, as in other *Peromyscus* of similar body size. Developmental patterns have not been observed, and neither have longevity nor population dynamics.

Suggested References. Kilpatrick and Caire (1973); Schmidly (1974*b*).

Peromyscus truei / Piñon Mouse

Distribution. The piñon mouse is a species of the southwestern United States and Mexico, ranging from Oregon to Oaxaca and from California eastward to the canyons of the Texas Panhandle. In the plains states, it occurs only in the western part of the Oklahoma Panhandle. See map 60.

Description. Upper parts rich tan; tail sharply bicolored, black above, whitish below, about the same length as head and body; venter whitish; ear long, decidedly longer than hind foot, longest of any Peromyscus in plains region. Total length, 185–200 mm; tail, 90–100 mm; hind foot, 23–25 mm; ear, 25–30 mm; weight, 18–30 g. See figure 83.

Habits and Habitat. This mouse occurs mostly in rough canyon and rimrock country with pygmy conifers. The animals nest in hollow juniper logs and among roots, build nests of shredded bark, and feed on the pungent berries of juniper, as well as other seeds and insects. They frequently live around wood-rat dens.

Mean home range of males is 2.5 acres, and the range of females is about half as large. The animals probably are not territorial; like other species of *Peromyscus,* they are quite tolerant of one another in captivity.

Predation has not been studied in detail. Doubtless owls, weasels, coyotes, and bobcats are common predators, but their rocky habitat may protect piñon mice from high predation pressure. Ectoparasitism by a variety of fleas and mites has been reported.

Reproduction. P. truei breeds throughout the warmer months. Females are polyestrous and some individuals exhibit postpartum estrus. Litter size ranges from one to six (average about four) altricial young, born after a gestation period of 25 to 27 days in females that are not lactating (and a few days longer in those that are). Neonates are pink, blind, and helpless. Mothers may carry individual young in their teeth or may drag the whole litter about, each tiny young grasping a teat. Eyes open about three weeks of age and the young are weaned in about five weeks (when they are about 85 percent of adult size). Females in juvenal pelage have been known to breed. Longevity averages less than a year and only rare individuals survive to breed in two successive summers.

Suggested References. Armstrong (1982); Hoffmeister (1981).

Figure 76. Plains harvest mouse, *Reithrodontomys montanus* (J. L. Tveten).

Figure 77. Texas mouse, *Peromyscus attwateri* (R. J. Baker).

Figure 78. Rock mouse, *Peromyscus difficilis* (K. H. Maslowski and W. W. Goodpaster).

Figure 79. Cotton mouse, *Peromyscus gossypinus* (J. L. Tveten).

Figure 80. White-footed mouse, *Peromyscus leucopus* (T. H. Kunz).

Figure 81. Deer mouse, *Peromyscus maniculatus* (D. C. Lovell and R. S. Mellott).

Figure 82. White-ankled mouse, *Peromyscus pectoralis* (J. L. Tveten).

Figure 83. Piñon mouse, *Peromyscus truei* (W. W. Goodpaster).

Figure 84. Golden mouse, *Ochrotomys nuttalli* (R. Altig).

Figure 85. Northern grasshopper mouse, *Onychomys leucogaster* (T. H. Kunz).

Figure 86. Hispid cotton rat, *Sigmodon hispidus* (J. K. Jones, Jr.).

Figure 87. White-throated woodrat, *Neotoma albigula* (Texas Parks and Wildlife Department, photograph by R. D. Porter).

Figure 88. Bushy-tailed woodrat, *Neotoma cinerea* (R. W. Barbour).

Figure 89. Eastern woodrat, *Neotoma floridana* (R. W. Wiley).

Figure 90. Mexican woodrat, *Neotoma mexicana* (R. J. Baker).

Figure 91. Southern Plains woodrat, *Neotoma micropus* (J. L. Tveten).

Ochrotomys nuttalli / Golden Mouse

Distribution. This is a species of the southeastern United States, ranging from Virginia and Illinois southward to the Gulf Coast and westward to extreme eastern Oklahoma. See map 61.

Description. Beautiful little mice closely related to *Peromyscus;* sometimes considered subgenus of *Peromyscus.* Dorsal pelage golden to reddish, thick; venter white, sometimes washed with buff; tail indistinctly bicolored. Total length, 145–180 mm; tail, 60–80 mm; hind foot, 14–20 mm; ear, 16–18 mm; weight, 17–25 g. See figure 84.

Habits and Habitat. Golden mice occupy a wide spectrum of habitats, most with heavy undergrowth—woodland, mesic ravines, field margins, mixed forest, thickets of woody second growth. Commonly, cotton mice live in such situations as well. Where sympatric locally, cotton mice may exclude golden mice.

These mice are rather strongly arboreal. Globular nests of shredded plant matter often are built in trees. There these nocturnal animals spend the day and pass periods of inclement weather. In addition to the nest, there often is an arboreal feeding platform, to which the mice retire to eat after bouts of food gathering. The diet consists mostly of seeds; insects are taken in season. Food storage has been reported.

Predation has not been studied in detail, but golden mice certainly are taken by a variety of forest-dwelling carnivorous vertebrates. In addition, they harbor external and internal parasites, including arthropods, helminths, and protists. Despite arboreal habits, severe flooding is known to decimate populations. Reported densities usually range from one to 10 per acre, with highest numbers in dense underbrush. Home ranges are around one acre.

Reproduction. Golden mice can breed throughout the year, but reproductive activity slows in the warmest and the coldest weather. Females are polyestrous. Gestation lasts 25 to 30 days. Litter size ranges from two to four (mean 2.6). Young are altricial and weigh 2 to 3 grams. Eyes open at 13 days of age and the young are weaned at three weeks. Longevity is greater than in many other small mammals, averaging six to seven months, with maximum longevity 30 months in the wild, eight years in the laboratory. There are a single maturational molt and two seasonal molts.

Suggested References. Linzey and Packard (1977); Packard (1969).

Onychomys leucogaster / Northern Grasshopper Mouse

Distribution. This mouse occurs on the Great Plains and in the Great Basin, ranging from Minnesota to California and from Saskatchewan to Tamaulipas, Mexico. That range encompasses most of the region of the plains states except extreme southeastern Nebraska, eastern Kansas, and eastern Oklahoma. See map 61.

Description. Readily distinguished by short tail. Upper parts brownish to reddish buff; venter white; tail white distally and below, brownish above. Total length, 135–165 mm; tail, 37–47 mm; hind foot, 20–22 mm; ear, 13–17 mm; weight, 35–40 g. See figure 85.

Habits and Habitat. Grasshopper mice live in grasslands and shrublands, generally on sandy to silty soils. They are commonly found on overgrazed rangelands and in abandoned fields and prairie dog towns, situations in which their insect food is abundant.

These are peculiar rodents. Although closely related to *Peromyscus*, *Onychomys* has adapted in structure and behavior to active predation. In the warmer months, more than 80 percent of the diet is animal matter, mostly insects. Grasshopper mice also kill and eat vertebrates up to three times their own size and take carrion.

Nest burrows are excavated by a mated pair. Such pair-bonding is rare in rodents, and, like other carnivorous mammals, these mice are strongly territorial. Territorial boundaries are scent-marked. Home ranges appear to be large, about six acres, and populations seldom appear to be particularly dense. Grasshopper mice fall prey to a variety of predators but are staple fare for none of them. Parasite loads are high (typical of mammals with a permanent nest burrow) and include mites, lice, fleas, ticks, worms, and protists.

Reproduction. Typical of carnivorous species, the courtship pattern is complex. Gestation lasts about four weeks (five for nursing females). Litter size is one to six (mean about 3.5). There is postpartum estrus and three to six litters per season are possible. Young are altricial but grow quickly and are weaned in about three weeks. The male provisions the lactating female with insects, another behavior reminiscent of true carnivores. The animals typically breed first as yearlings, and they may live two years or more. There are four distinct pelages—juvenile, subadult, adult, and senile, with intervening molts.

Suggested References. Engstrom and Choate (1979); McCarty (1978).

Sigmodon hispidus / Hispid Cotton Rat

Distribution. The hispid cotton rat is a neotropical species, ranging from Panama northward across most of Mexico to the southern United States, north to southern Nebraska. See map 62.

Description. Fur harsh to touch; grizzled brownish to blackish above, paling on sides; grayish below. Tail scaly, dark, sparsely haired. Total length, 200–275 mm; tail, 90–110 mm; hind foot, 30–35 mm; ear, 15–20 mm; weight, 50–150 g. See figure 86.

Habits and Habitat. Hispid cotton rats live in areas of dense herbaceous vegetation—highway rights-of-way, field margins, weedy ravines, and croplands provide suitable habitat. They may occupy marshlands but are less aquatic than are rice rats. Cotton rats clip vegetation (far more than is eaten) and build runways, like those of voles but larger. Thus they can become agricultural pests. They select a vegetable diet based on species and stage of growth. They also prey on insects, eggs and nestling birds, and young voles. These rats are primarily crepuscular and nocturnal.

Nests are spheres of plant fibers beneath rocks, logs, or debris. Use of burrows abandoned by other mammals, such as ground squirrels and skunks, has been noted. Such burrows allow cotton rats to den below the frost line and make make them less susceptible to inclement weather (which has been implicated in establishing their northern limits on the Great Plains). Numerous vertebrates prey on cotton rats, and helminth and arthropod parasites infest them.

These rodents are not territorial. They are mostly solitary in the warmer months, but they may huddle for warmth in winter. Home ranges average about an acre for males, half that for females. Populations as dense as 500 per acre have been reported, although densities usually are one-tenth to one-hundredth that size.

Reproduction. Breeding occurs throughout the warmer months. Gestation lasts 27 days and there is postpartum estrus. Litter size ranges as high as 12 and averages eight to 10. Neonates are rather precocial, well haired, and weigh 6 to 8 grams. Eyes open within a day and young venture outside the nest at four days of age. Females may breed when only six weeks old. Average longevity is less than one year.

Suggested References. Cameron and Spencer (1981).

Neotoma albigula / White-throated Woodrat

Distribution. This woodrat occurs from central Mexico northward to Colorado and Utah. It is known in the plains states only from the western end of the Oklahoma Panhandle (in Cimarron County). See map 63.

Description. A medium-sized woodrat, generally grayish buff in color; tail indistinctly bicolored; venter white; hairs of throat white at their bases (rather than gray as in *N. mexicana, N. micropus,* and *N. floridana*). Total length, 300–350 mm; tail, 125–150 mm; hind foot, 33–37 mm; ear, 26–30 mm; weight, 150–275 g. Males average larger than females. See figure 87.

Habits and Habitat. This wide-ranging species occupies a variety of habitats. In some places it uses rock shelters and rimrock (like the Mexican woodrat), and in other places it is found well away from rocks in shrubby country (building mound houses like the southern plains woodrat). A common denominator of these diverse habitats is cactus. Even when in a rock shelter, the living space is liberally strewn with cactus spines.

Houses may be of sticks or prickly pear pads and cholla joints. Cow chips and bones are also used. The nest chamber is lined with juniper bark, grass, fur, and yucca fibers. Food stores include cactus, juniper branches (with berries), yucca leaves, forbs, and woody cuttings of shrubs. Little grass is eaten. White-throated woodrats are active the year around. Densities along rimrock are nearly impossible to calculate, but mound houses in cactus have been reported at 20 per acre, which must be a maximal figure. The animals are solitary.

Predators include owls, coyotes, badgers, and snakes. Predator pressure, however, must be eased by the denning habit. The most vulnerable animals would be dispersing young in the initial phases of house building. Parasites include fleas, mites, ticks, cestodes, and nematodes. Commensals include the long-tailed, saxicolous species of *Peromyscus.* A variety of animals use the abandoned dens of these woodrats.

Reproduction. Females are seasonally polyestrous, with breeding spanning the warmer months. Mating is promiscuous. Average litter size is about two (range one to three) young, born moderately altricial after a gestation period of about one month. Lactation lasts another month. Most young probably disperse at two to three months and breed first as yearlings.

Suggested References. Finley (1958); Olsen (1973).

Neotoma cinerea / Bushy-tailed Woodrat

Distribution. This is a rodent of western North America, ranging from the Yukon southward to Nevada and Arizona and from California eastward to the Black Hills, the Pine Ridge, and the badlands of the Upper Missouri drainage area. Its distribution overlaps that of no other species of woodrat in the plains states. See map 63.

Description. Distinguished by large size and bushy tail. Dorsal color predominantly pale reddish buff, with blackish tinge on Black Hills; animals from badlands are paler. Total length, 330–420 mm; tail, 145–175 mm; hind foot, 38–46 mm; ear, 31–34 mm; weight, 250–325 g. Males larger than females and with bushier tails. See figure 88.

Habits and Habitat. The bushy-tailed woodrat is primarily a mammal of mountainous country, inhabiting rocky slopes and crevices, but it also occurs in the badlands of the Upper Missouri Basin. Large stick houses are built in crevices, among boulders, or on shelves in buildings or tunnels. Houses incorporate just about any object the rats can pack around—bones, cones, bits of trash and hardware, dung and owl pellets, fur, hide, carrion. The collecting instinct seems to be even better developed in this species than in other woodrats.

Inside the house is a cup-shaped nest of dry grass, soft bark, moss, lichen, and leaves. There the solitary, nocturnal "packrat" spends the daylight hours and passes inclement weather. Food is stored in the den for winter. The varied diet emphasizes woody plants (including shrubs and pine branches) but includes mushrooms, fruits, seeds, and herbage as well.

Predators are coyotes, weasels (which can follow the rats into their dens), bobcats, and owls, among others, although inaccessible habitat and a secure house protect the rats from undue predator pressure. Ectoparasites include ticks, fleas, and warbles, and among internal parasites are protozoans, flukes, tapeworms, and nematodes. Longevity in the wild may be three or four years for animals that survive dispersal and establish secure homes.

Reproduction. The breeding season extends through the warmer months. Females are polyestrous and may have two litters per season, breeding first as yearlings. Breeding is promiscuous. Gestation lasts about five weeks. A typical litter is three or four altricial young.

Suggested References. Escherich (1981); Finley (1958); Jones et al. (1983).

Neotoma floridana / Eastern Woodrat

Distribution. This is a species of the eastern and southern United States, ranging from Connecticut to Florida and westward to Colorado and Texas. In the plains states, this is the most widespread of woodrats, occurring from southwestern Nebraska across most of Kansas and the eastern two-thirds of Oklahoma. A relict outlying population occurs along the Niobrara River in north-central Nebraska. See map 64.

Description. Upper parts buffy brown to dark brownish, paling on sides; venter grayish to white, hairs dark gray at bases; tail indistinctly bicolored, brownish above, white below, sparsely haired but not scaly. Total length, 350–400 mm; tail, 135–180 mm; hind foot, 38–41 mm; ear, 25–30 mm; weight, 300–400 g. See figure 89.

Habits and Habitat. Eastern woodrats typically inhabit rocky ledges along ravines or river valleys, under fairly heavy cover. Large stick houses (to several cubic meters) are built, often over the course of several generations. They may be among rocks, under ledges, beneath down timber, or under roots. Bones, dung, rocks, leaves, and trash contribute to the house. Two or more spherical nests of plant fibers are formed in the center of the house. There the usually solitary animals pass daylight hours and inhospitable weather.

The diet includes a variety of plants, mostly forbs and shrubs, such as Osage-orange, acorns, and legumes. Food is stored for winter, but the rats do not hibernate. In the wild, water is obtained mostly from vegetation, but captives drink free water readily.

Known predators include owls, skunks, snakes, and weasels. Eastern woodrats harbor warbles as well as fleas, mites, ticks, and helminths. Several vertebrates (snakes, lizards, toads, mice) are commensals, using dens for shelter without interfering with the resident rat.

Reproduction. Females are polyestrous, breeding throughout the warmer months. Gestation takes about 35 days. Litter size ranges from one to seven, averaging two or three. Neonates are sparsely haired, have ears and eyes closed, and weigh 12 to 14 grams. Weaning takes place at about one month and the young are independent at two months. Some females may breed their first summer. Individuals may live three years or more.

Suggested References. Birney (1973); Jones et al. (1983); Wiley (1980).

Neotoma mexicana / Mexican Woodrat

Distribution. This rat is aptly named, ranging from Honduras northward through most of central and western Mexico into the southwestern United States, reaching its northern limits in Colorado. Like several other species of Mexican affinities, it occurs in the plains states only in the western Oklahoma Panhandle. See map 64.

Description. Grayish buff dorsally, well sprinkled with black; venter white to yellowish, hairs gray at their bases; tail distinctly bicolored. Average size slightly larger than *N. albigula* or *N. micropus;* total length, 360–380 mm; tail, 150–170 mm; hind foot, 32–38 mm; ear, 25–28 mm; weight, 230–260 g. See figure 90.

Habits and Habitat. Typical habitat is broken rimrock country, talus, and rocky canyons with open coniferous woodlands or brush. Like other wood-rats, these animals build houses of sticks, strewn with a wide variety of other items. At the center of the den is a cantaloupe-sized nest of shredded plant materials (mostly juniper bark but also including grasses, feathers, fur, and scrap paper). These rats are primarily solitary and are active the year around.

These and other woodrats are mainly herbivorous. Food is stored in the den, usually above the nest chamber, and outside the den, stuffed into cracks in the rocks. Young twigs of coniferous and deciduous trees and shrubs are eaten as are a variety of forbs, yucca, and some cacti. The animals may be fairly abundant in suitable habitat, with an active den every 100 feet or so along a rocky rim, but calculating home ranges and densities is difficult for a species with an essentially linear habitat.

Although fairly well protected by their rocky habitat and nearly impenetrable dens, Mexican woodrats fall prey to owls and coyotes, and snakes take nestling young. Inclement weather (especially flash floods) may be a major check on populations.

Reproduction. Females are seasonally polyestrous, producing two litters from March to May. Embryo counts average about 2.4 (range two to five). Gestation lasts 31 to 34 days. Young weigh about 10 grams at birth and development is rapid. Females of first litters may breed in their first summer, but males breed first as yearlings.

Suggested References. Armstrong (1982); Brown (1969); Finley (1958).

Neotoma micropus / Southern Plains Woodrat

Distribution. This species is closely related to the eastern woodrat and their distributions are allopatric except for a place along the Cimarron River in Major County, Oklahoma. See map 65. The southern plains woodrat occurs from southwestern Kansas and adjacent Colorado southward to San Luis Potosí in north-central Mexico.

Description. Upper parts clear steel gray; venter paler gray; chest and throat white, but hairs gray at bases. Tail bicolored, but less distinctly so than in *N. mexicana.* Total length, 320–360 mm; tail, 130–150 mm; hind foot, 34–42 mm; ear, 25–30 mm; weight, 180–290 g. Possible hybridization reported with *N. floridana* in Oklahoma and *N. albigula* in Colorado. See figure 91.

Habits and Habitat. This is a species of semiarid grasslands, typically areas with scattered shrubs or cholla. These woodrats build dens in depressions (such as abandoned coyote or badger burrows) filled with cactus pads, cholla joints, yucca stems, sticks, bones, dried dung, and other debris. The nest of shredded plant fibers is cup-shaped or globe-shaped and located near the center of the house.

Denning habits provide protection from most predators, but owls, coyotes, and large snakes capture these rats. Parasites include fleas, mites, ticks, and helminths. Desert shrews and deer mice are known commensals; there surely are others, because woodrat dens offer protection from perils both biotic and physical for these visitors.

These woodrats eat a variety of plant materials as available. Cacti are staples, as are yucca, juniper, and herbs; some grass is eaten. Water is obtained from food. Individuals forage by night along well-worn paths that radiate from the den. The animals are active year around; some food is stored in the den. There are two maturational molts and adults have one seasonal molt annually, in autumn.

Reproduction. Females are polyestrous and exhibit postpartum estrus. Breeding is promiscuous. Typical litters have two or three fairly altricial young, and females may have two or more litters per year. Breeding continues throughout the warmer months. Females born early in the year may breed late their first season; females of later litters and all males breed first as yearlings. Gestation takes 30 to 37 days.

Suggested References. Birney (1973); Finley (1958).

Clethrionomys gapperi / Southern Red-backed Vole

Distribution. This vole inhabits the transcontinental boreal forest of Canada and ranges southward on the Appalachians, around the upper Great Lakes, on the Rocky Mountains, and in the Pacific Northwest. It occurs in North Dakota generally north and east of the Missouri River and on the Killdeer Mountains, in northeastern South Dakota, and on the Black Hills. See map 66.

Description. Ears more conspicuous and tail relatively longer than in other voles on the Great Plains. Pelage with broad band of bright reddish to chestnut hairs extending dorsally from forehead to base of tail; underparts white; sides grayish. Total length, 119–152 mm; tail, 32–42 mm; hind foot, 17–19 mm; ear, 12–15 mm; weight, 19–35 g. See figure 92.

Habits and Habitat. The southern red-backed vole is most common in cool, moist forested areas but can be found in mesic prairie or relatively dry stands of pine where fallen logs or boulders provide a mesic microhabitat. Studies have revealed that this species requires 0.5 to 0.6 gram of water per gram of body weight per day. This requirement accounts for the fact that *C. gapperi* is generally restricted to habitats where free water is available.

Staple foods of this opportunistic vole include fruits, seeds, nuts, subterranean fungi, and occasionally insects. Roots and bark of small trees supplement the diet in winter. Seeds are cached in autumn, and caches of other species (such as the "middens" of red squirrels) may be raided.

Population densities of this vole are seldom high even though reproductive capacity is great. Predators, especially foxes, weasels, raptors, and snakes, consume many. Also, because the species is neither colonial nor gregarious, agonistic behavior among individuals may help limit populations. Finally, these voles harbor numerous parasites, including fleas, mites, ticks, chiggers, lice, tapeworms, lungworms, and intestinal roundworms. There are two seasonal molts. Summer pelage is attained by mid-May and is replaced by winter pelage in November.

Reproduction. The breeding season lasts about seven months, from late winter to late autumn. Gestation lasts 17 to 19 days, and litter size ranges from two to 10. Larger litters are produced at higher latitudes and higher elevations. This species is polyestrous and exhibits postpartum heat.

Suggested References. Merritt (1981).

0 ____ 100
MILES

Map 63. *(Left).* Distribution of the white-throated woodrat, *Neotoma albigula* (1), and the bushy-tailed woodrat, *Neotoma cinerea* (2).

Map 64. *(Right).* Distribution of the eastern woodrat, *Neotoma floridana* (1), and the Mexican woodrat, *Neotoma mexicana* (2).

Map 65. *(Left).* Distribution of the southern plains woodrat, *Neotoma micropus*.

Map 66. *(Right).* Distribution of the southern red-backed vole, *Clethrionomys gapperi*. The dot indicates an isolated population.

Map 67. *(Left).* Distribution of the prairie vole, *Microtus ochrogaster.*

Map 68. *(Right).* Distribution of the meadow vole, *Microtus pennsylvanicus.* The dot indicates an isolated population.

Map 69. *(Left).* Distribution of the long-tailed vole, *Microtus longicaudus* (1); the woodland vole, *Microtus pinetorum* (2); and the sagebrush vole, *Lemmiscus curtatus* (3).

Map 70. *(Right).* Distribution of the southern bog lemming, *Synaptomys cooperi.* Dots represent isolated relict populations.

Microtus longicaudus / Long-tailed Vole

Distribution. The long-tailed vole inhabits montane areas of western North America from east-central Alaska southward into Arizona and New Mexico. In the plains region, the species occurs only as an isolated population on the Black Hills. See map 69.

Description. Tail long, often nearly half as long as head and body; ears small. Dorsum brownish gray, sometimes with diffuse reddish tinge; venter grayish white. Total length, 148–191 mm; tail, 48–68 mm; hind foot, 20–22 mm; ear, 13–17 mm; weight, 30–45 g. See figure 93.

Habits and Habitat. The natural history of *M. longicaudus* is poorly known. Specimens have been collected at elevations ranging from sea level to 12,000 feet and in habitats ranging from coniferous forest to rocky alpine tundra and sagebrush flats. On the Black Hills, this vole ranges from 4,200 feet in the semiarid foothills up into boreal forest. At lower elevations it occurs with the meadow vole in mesic riparian habitats, and at higher elevations it inhabits aspen and spruce forest in company with the red-backed vole. It is subordinate to both of these competitors and may be displaced into shrubby or forest-edge habitats. Populations usually are low but occasionally reach 100 or more per acre.

Foods consist mostly of green vegetation, supplemented with seeds, berries, and subterranean fungi in autumn, and with the inner bark of shrubs and small trees in winter. These voles appear not to be colonial or gregarious, and they seldom make the well-defined runways characteristic of other microtines. Mortality is high in this and in other voles, with the result that few live longer than one year. Predators include hawks, owls, coyotes, foxes, bobcats, and weasels.

Reproduction. No comprehensive study of reproduction in this species has been undertaken. Breeding probably begins in late spring and continues through summer. Fifteen pregnant females from the Black Hills carried four to six fetuses, and litter size in Wyoming has been reported to range from two to seven. In related species, the number of young varies among litters produced at different times of the year. Reproductive maturity is acheived at three weeks of age, and up to four litters may be produced each year.

Suggested References. Conley (1976); Randall (1978); Turner (1974).

Microtus ochrogaster / Prairie Vole

Distribution. This vole inhabits the central grasslands of North America from the Rocky Mountains east to West Virginia and from Alberta south to Oklahoma and Arkansas. Populations formerly existed as far south as Louisiana and Texas. The species occurs throughout most of the plains region except parts of Oklahoma. See map 67.

Description. A stocky, short-tailed vole with grizzled grayish brown dorsum, paler sides, and ochraceous venter. Distinguished from *M. pennsylvanicus* by the salt-and-pepper appearance of its dorsal pelage and its brownish gray (rather than silver) ventral fur. Prairie voles from north and east of the Missouri River and from southwestern South Dakota and northwestern Nebraska are considerably smaller than specimens from elsewhere on the Great Plains. Total length, 110–188 mm; tail, 25–53 mm; hind foot, 15–23 mm; ear, 11–15 mm; weight, 35–70 g. See figure 94.

Habits and Habitat. Prairie voles inhabit primarily tall-grass communities. On the northern plains, they often are restricted to upland habitats by another vole, *M. pennsylvanicus,* which occupies lush lowlands and swales. In the south, they occur in both uplands and lowlands where grasses provide overhead cover; in the west, such cover is often available only along watercourses.

This vole is an opportunistic herbivore, feeding on green stems and leaves of grasses, sedges, and flowering plants in spring and summer. At other times it eats roots, tubers, fruits, seeds, and bark. Burrows and foraging areas are connected by well-maintained runways constructed by clipping grass stems along routes of travel. Litter often covers these runways and provides protection from raptors. Nevertheless, few prairie voles live as long as one year. Predators include snakes, raptors, short-tailed shrews, and several carnivores. Another potentially important cause of mortality is aggressive competition with other species, such as the hispid cotton rat. Parasites include arthropods, trematodes, cestodes, nematodes, and a protozoan.

Reproduction. Most breeding occurs in spring and autumn in the south and in summer in the north. Ovulation is induced by breeding, and gestation lasts about three weeks. Number of young per litter ranges from one to seven. Females produce several litters during the breeding season.

Suggested References. Choate and Williams (1978); Fleharty and Olson (1969); Gaines and Rose (1976); Jameson, (1947); Severinghaus (1977).

Microtus pennsylvanicus / Meadow Vole

Distribution. *Microtus pennsylvanicus* inhabits suitable habitats throughout the northern half of North America. On the Great Plains, it occurs as far south as northernmost Kansas. See map 68.

Description. A large, dark-colored vole with a tail averaging longer than that of other species except *M. longicaudus.* Dorsum dark chestnut brown, slightly grizzled but lacking salt-and-pepper appearance; sides pale brown; venter dusky gray to silver. Total length, 140–190 mm; tail, 32–52 mm; hind foot, 18–24 mm; ear, 11–16 mm; weight, 30–75 g. See figure 95.

Habits and Habitat. This vole requires water, and therefore it typically inhabits moist meadows, marshes, and other communities characterized by lush grasses, sedges, and rushes. On the northern and western plains, such communities are usually associated with streambanks and other riparian situations. *M. pennsylvanicus* displaces *M. ochrogaster* from the most luxuriant vegetation near water where the two species occur together.

Meadow voles eat most available species of grasses, sedges, and herbaceous plants plus subterranean fungi and occasional insects. During periods of high population density, they may girdle small trees or shrubs.

Unlike the prairie vole, which is social, somewhat colonial, and monogamous, the meadow vole exhibits little social organization. The high reproductive capacity of *M. pennsylvanicus* is counterbalanced by a high mortality rate; life expectancy at birth is less than one month, and life expectancy for voles that achieve sexual maturity is only an additional six to 10 weeks. Even so, both internal and external parasites are abundant.

Populations fluctuate cyclically in periods of two to five years. When populations are high, meadow voles are preyed upon by virtually all potential predators. Neither predation nor disease, however, seems to be responsible for population crashes, and the cause of fluctuations remains unknown.

Reproduction. Litters may be produced at any time of year, even beneath snow in winter. *M. pennsylvanicus* is promiscuous, and females in estrus breed with whatever males are attracted to them. Ovulation is induced by copulation, and pregnancy lasts 21 days. Litter size ranges from one to 11 (usually four to seven). Litters produced in summer, when food is plentiful and the voles are heaviest, average larger than litters produced in other seasons.

Suggested References. Reich (1981).

Microtus pinetorum / Woodland Vole

Distribution. The woodland vole occurs throughout the eastern United States, from the Great Lakes region and New England southward into Texas and Florida. In the five-state region, it has been found only in southeastern Nebraska, the eastern third of Kansas, and the eastern half of Oklahoma. See map 69.

Description. A slender, semifossorial vole with distinctive soft, dense pelage and a short tail, both adapted to fore and aft movement in burrows. Readily distinguished from other microtines by its dorsal coloration, which is dull reddish brown to chestnut brown, washed with dark-tipped guard hairs; sides paler; venter grayish buff. Total length, 120–140 mm; tail, 18–28 mm; hind foot, 15–20 mm; ear, 11–13 mm; weight, 25–45 g. See figure 96.

Habits and Habitat. Unlike most other North American voles, *M. pinetorum* dwells primarily in wooded areas and burrows beneath leaf litter and among the roots of trees. Well-drained wooded slopes seem to be the favored natural habitat, but woodland voles also become established in old fields or pastures containing successional woody vegetation. These microtines can become especially numerous in fruit orchards, where they do considerable damage by gnawing on trees just below ground level. The diet consists mostly of underground plant parts although nuts, seeds, and stems of grasses and forbs also are stored in underground chambers to supplement the diet during winter.

Woodland voles seem to be tolerant of other individuals of the same species. It has been suggested that they form monogamous pairs and share their burrows with their offspring. Home ranges average about a half acre and overlap broadly. The semifossorial habits of the species afford some protection from predators. Nevertheless, raptors, carnivorous mammals, and snakes exact a toll, and only about half of the individuals in a population survive from one year to the next.

Reproduction. In northern areas, most breeding occurs between winter and autumn; in Oklahoma, breeding is primarily between August and May. Estrus is induced by copulation after behavior interpreted as courtship has been initiated by the female. Gestation lasts 24 days, and the average interval between litters is about 25 days. Breeding females average two or three litters during their lifespans. Litter size ranges from one to six but averages about two.

Suggested References. Jones et al. (1983); Smolen (1981).

Lemmiscus curtatus / Sagebrush Vole

Distribution. This Great Basin species occurs from central Washington southward to eastern California and eastward to the northern plains (southern Canada to northern Colorado). In the five-state region, the sagebrush vole is known only from western North Dakota and northwesternmost South Dakota. See map 69.

Description. A small vole with long, lax, dense pelage. Distinguished from all other North American microtines by its short tail (seldom extending posteriorly much beyond the hind feet when pulled back) in combination with pale coloration (pale gray to pale buffy gray dorsally and silvery white to pale buff below). Total length, 103–142 mm; tail, 16–30 mm; hind foot, 14–18 mm; ear, 9–16 mm; weight, 17–39 g. See figure 97.

Habits and Habitat. The sagebrush vole usually inhabits temperate, arid, shrub-steppe habitats characterized by the presence of bunchgrasses and sagebrush or rabbitbrush. It constructs poorly defined runways and has the unusual habit of hollowing out "cow chips" to use as temporary shelters from inclement weather and predators or as feeding stations.

This strictly herbivorous vole feeds on the leaves, stems, flowers, and immature fruits of a wide variety of grasses and forbs. It favors the leaves of sagebrush and rabbitbrush, but it is not an accomplished climber and cannot readily obtain them; therefore, it steals terminal twigs and leaves clipped from these shrubs by deer mice.

Sagebrush voles are colonial, and the burrows and runways of a colony may be interconnected. Males and females of different ages share the same nests, and captive females have been observed to nurse young from another litter. In winter, colonies are concentrated in areas such as valleys, where snow provides the best shelter. In spring, the animals move to areas such as south-facing slopes, where the new growth of plants is most advanced.

Reproduction. Sagebrush voles breed throughout the year, although reproductive effort diminishes somewhat during severe summer drought or winter cold. The gestation period averages 25 days, and postpartum estrus occurs within 24 hours of parturtition. Litter size ranges from one to 13 and averages four to six. At least three litters may be produced in one year; a female in captivity produced eight litters in succession.

Suggested References. Carrol and Genoways (1980).

Ondatra zibethicus / Muskrat

Distribution. The muskrat occurs in permanent bodies of water from the tree line in Alaska and Canada south to the Gulf of Mexico. The species does not occur in Florida, central Texas, or certain areas of the Southwest and the Pacific Coast. It is found throughout the plains states. See map 71.

Description. Largest of voles. Aquatic specializations include large, partly webbed feet, laterally rotated ankles, laterally compressed tail, dense, waterproof underfur (for swimming), and lips that close behind front teeth (to permit grasping food underwater). Dorsal pelage pale, glossy brown to blackish brown; sides paler; venter silvery gray, becoming whitish on throat. Total length, 456–578 mm; tail, 200–254 mm; hind foot, 65–81 mm; ear, 20–25 mm; weight, 1.5–3.5 lb. See figure 98.

Habits and Habitat. This species is most common in marshes and other shallow water where emergent vegetation is abundant. Muskrats construct characteristic colonial houses of sticks, which provide secure lodging above the waterline, or they occupy bank dens. Both kinds of dens have several entrances to facilitate escape from predators, such as mink. Additionally, muskrats construct "feeding houses," which are less elaborate than the main dwelling, to provide access to air when they forage beneath the ice in winter.

Muskrats feed mostly on aquatic vegetation, including roots, stems, bulbs, and leaves of cattails, bulrushes, sedges, lilies, and pondweeds, but they also consume crayfish, clams, snails, fish, and frogs. Muskrats are social during winter, with several animals typically denning together. With the approach of the breeding season, they become aggressive and disperse to separate lodges.

Juveniles molt into subadult pelage and subadults into adult pelage; adults molt once annually. The muskrat is the most valuable semiaquatic furbearer in North America in total dollar volume.

Reproduction. Muskrats have been described as "loosely monogamous," and they may produce two or, more commonly, three litters per year. Breeding occurs throughout the year in the south, but is restricted to spring and summer in the north. On the northern plains, the first litter is usually born in April. The gestation period varies between 25 and 31 days, and litters range in size from four to eight (average six or seven). Females undergo postpartum estrus. Longevity may be three or four years.

Suggested References. Willner et al. (1980).

Synaptomys cooperi / Southern Bog Lemming

Distribution. This microtine occurs in the eastern United States and south-eastern Canada north of approximately 37° north latitude. In the plains states, this theoretically includes the eastern half of Kansas and Nebraska, and south-eastern South Dakota. The few scattered populations in all but the eastern parts of those states, however, appear to be Pleistocene relicts left behind as the species retreated to the north and east since the last glaciation. See map 70.

Description. Resembles *Microtus pinetorum* except has coarser, longer, and darker dorsal fur and long grayish or silvery hairs on the venter; dorsal color dull brown to golden brown with black- or gray-tipped hairs. Tail nearly same length as hind foot. Total length, 125–152 mm; tail, 17–25 mm; hind foot, 20–26 mm; ear, 10–13 mm; weight, 40–75 g. See figure 99.

Habits and Habitat. Southern bog lemmings can be found in a variety of mesic habitats. In otherwise dry regions, they commonly occur around bogs where plant stems and litter provide a canopy and dense cover. When they occur together with the prairie vole or the meadow vole, they typically are most abundant in communities even wetter than those inhabited by the other species. They burrow into soil just above the water table, or if the ground is saturated they construct nests on the surface under fallen logs or other shelters. They use runways maintained by voles or construct their own, which are less tidy than those of *Microtus.*

   Leaves and stems of sedges are finely ground before they are swallowed, resulting in the characteristic bright green feces that can be found in runways used by *Synaptomys.* Other foods include rootstocks of grasses and sedges, berries, bark, mosses, and fungi. Known predators include owls, coyotes, foxes, raccoons, and weasels. Parasites include ticks, lice, mites, fleas, and tapeworms.

Reproduction. Most of what is known about reproduction in this species is derived from a study conducted in New Jersey. Breeding may occur through-out the year, but most litters are produced from spring through autumn. Pregnancy lasts 21 to 23 days, and females experience postpartum estrus. Litter size ranges from one to seven, with three the most common number.

Suggested References. Connor (1959); Jones et al. (1983); Linzey (1983); Wetzel (1955).

Zapus hudsonius / Meadow Jumping Mouse

Distribution. This species inhabits northern coniferous forest across Canada from Alaska to Labrador. In the United States, its range extends southward in eastern deciduous forest and westward across the Great Plains. In the five-state region, the species occurs from northeastern Oklahoma northward across eastern Kansas and most of Nebraska and the Dakotas. See map 72.

Description. A colorful mouse characterized by a tapering, sparsely haired tail longer than head and body, large hind legs and feet adapted for hopping, and small forelegs and feet. Dorsal pelage coarse yellowish brown with black-tipped hairs forming dark dorsal stripe; sides yellowish orange; venter white. Total length, 187–230 mm; tail, 108–139 mm; hind foot, 28–31 mm; ear, 12–14 mm; weight, 15–22 g. See figure 100.

Habits and Habitat. This jumping mouse occurs in mesic habitats with herbaceous or grassy ground cover. These requirements are met by meadows, brushy abandoned fields, the edges of forested areas, and dense vegetation around marshes and along streams. There is reason to suspect that the range of the species in the southern part of our region is retreating northward and eastward.

These graceful rodents are omnivorous, feeding on insects, seeds, fruits, and fungi. Like other members of the genus *Zapus,* they are excellent swimmers and divers. They enter hibernation in late September or October and do not emerge for about seven months. While in torpor their body temperature drops to 35° to 40° F, and their heart and breathing rates drop appreciably. Jumping mice live through winter on energy obtained from fat stored in their bodies the previous summer. Males emerge before females in spring.

A post-juvenile molt occurs at the age of four weeks. Adults molt annually in August or September. Winter kill may be more important than predation in controlling populations.

Reproduction. Breeding occurs as soon as the females emerge from hibernation. Gestation lasts 18 to 19 days (20 to 21 days in lactating females), and the first litter is born in late May or June. Postpartum estrus has not been observed. As many as three litters may be produced during the breeding season. Litter size ranges from two to eight, probably depending on the age of the female and timing of the litter.

Suggested References. Whitaker (1972).

0 _____ 100
MILES

Map 71. *(Left).* Distribution of the muskrat, *Ondatra zibethicus.*

Map 72. *(Right).* Distribution of the meadow jumping mouse, *Zapus hudsonius.*

0 |___| 100
     MILES

Map 73. *(Left).* Distribution of the western jumping mouse, *Zapus princeps.*

Map 74. *(Right).* Distribution of the porcupine, *Erethizon dorsatum.*

Zapus princeps / Western Jumping Mouse

Distribution. This western mouse ranges from the southern Yukon south to Arizona and New Mexico. In the plains states, it occurs in northern and eastern North Dakota and northeasternmost South Dakota. See map 73.

Description. Closely resembles *Z. hudsonius,* from which it differs by its more grizzled dorsal pelage (resulting from grayish hairs in the dorsal stripe), less pronounced orange lines on sides, border of whitish hairs on the ears, and less distinctly bicolored tail. Total length, 204–230 mm; tail, 118–138 mm; hind foot, 27–30 mm; ear, 11–14 mm; weight, 18–24 g (as much as 35 just before hibernation). See figure 101.

Habits and Habitat. Zapus princeps, like *Z. hudsonius,* is most abundant in mesic areas where tall grasses and herbaceous vegetation provide dense cover. On the northern Great Plains, such habitats usually are associated with marshes and floodplains. Research is needed to determine differences in habitat preference between the two species.

The diet in spring consists of insects and other invertebrates, whereas in summer the diet shifts to seeds and fat begins to accumulate in preparation for the next hibernation. Western jumping mice apparently consume more seeds for a longer period of time (about four weeks) than do meadow jumping mice (which accumulate fat over a shorter period). At the onset of hibernation in September, as much as two-thirds of the body weight consists of stored fat to be metabolized during nine months of torpor.

Home ranges average about three-quarters of an acre for males and half an acre for females, and they are often elongate because they follow a stream. Raptors, weasels, and garter snakes prey on these mice. The incidence of parasitism is low, but these mice harbor tapeworms and roundworms.

Reproduction. Breeding occurs within one week after females emerge from hibernation, usually in June. Pregnancy lasts 18 days, and most young are born in late June or July. There may be only one litter per year, as opposed to two or three litters in *Z. hudsonius.* Litter size ranges from two to eight and averages about five. Young jumping mice are dependent upon their mother for a longer period of time (about one month) than most other small rodents.

Suggested References. Brown (1967); Clark (1971); Cranford (1978); Krutzsch (1954).

Erethizon dorsatum / Porcupine

Distribution. The range of the porcupine includes most of Canada, all but southern California and the Southeast in the United States, and northern Mexico. Porcupines occur throughout the plains states except in southeastern Kansas and eastern Oklahoma. See map 74.

Description. A large rodent with pelage specialized for defense from predators; underfur and guard hairs as in other mammals, but long hairs modified as quills present on the dorsum, sides, limbs, and tail. Total length, 727–872 mm; tail, 175–300 mm; hind foot, 95–120 mm; ear, 20–42 mm; weight, 8 to more than 30 lb. See figure 102.

Habits and Habitat. Porcupines are most abundant in coniferous forests but also inhabit deciduous woodlands. They occur on the plains (outside of conifer woodlands) most frequently in riparian habitats, but they are occasionally seen several miles from the nearest trees. The species can survive in shrubby habitats, and it has the reputation of feeding on fenceposts and other manmade objects of wood if no woody vegetation is available.

The diet is varied, depending on potential foods available. Herbaceous plants make up the bulk of the food during the growing season, whereas woody plants are eaten in winter. The cambium (just beneath the bark) of conifers is favored, but porcupines also gnaw on deciduous trees. Leaves, buds, twigs, roots, berries, seeds, and flowers may be eaten in addition to bark. The animals eat as much as one pound of vegetation each day, which is digested by bacteria in the intestine.

Dens may be located in any available cavity. Porcupines generally are solitary although two or more may den together, especially during cold weather. They repel predators by means of their quills, which cannot be projected from the body although the rapidly flailing tail may leave that impression. Nevertheless, they occasionally fall prey to coyotes, wolves, wolverines, fishers, mountain lions, lynx, bobcats, and other carnivores.

Reproduction. Porcupines breed once each year, in November or December. Females may come into estrus repeatedly if fertilization does not occur during the first ovulation. One young (rarely twins) is born after a gestation period of about seven months. Quills are soft until after birth but harden quickly upon exposure to air. The life span may exceed 10 years.

Suggested References. Costello (1966); Woods (1973).

Figure 92. Southern red-backed vole, *Clethrionomys gapperi* (E. C. Birney).

Figure 93. Long-tailed vole, *Microtus longicaudus* (R. W. Barbour).

Figure 94. Prairie vole, *Microtus ochrogaster* (D. C. Lovell and R. S. Mellott).

Figure 95. Meadow vole, *Microtus pennsylvanicus* (E. C. Birney).

Figure 96. Woodland vole, *Microtus pinetorum* (R. Altig).

Figure 97. Sagebrush vole, *Lemmiscus curtatus* (M. L. Johnson).

Figure 98. Muskrat, *Ondatra zibethicus* (R. Altig).

Figure 99. Southern bog lemming, *Synaptomys cooperi* (A. V. Linzey).

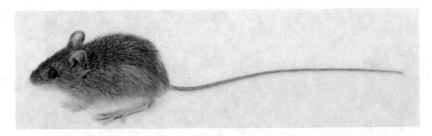

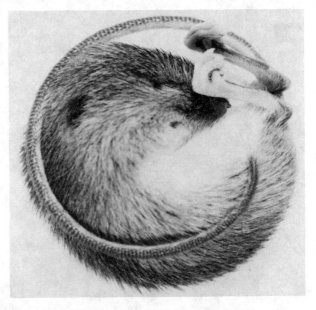

Figure 100. Meadow jumping mouse, *Zapus hudsonius* (W. H. Hamilton, Jr.).

Figure 101. Western jumping mouse, *Zapus princeps,* in hibernation (V. B. Scheffer).

Figure 102. Porcupine, *Erethizon dorsatum* (J. L. Tveten).

Figure 103. Coyote, *Canis latrans* (U.S. National Park Service).

Figure 104. Gray wolf, *Canis lupus* (U.S. Fish and Wildlife Service).

Figure 105. Red wolf, *Canis rufus* (Valan Photos, photograph by W. Lankinen).

Figure 106. Swift fox, *Vulpes velox* (Kansas Fish and Game Commission, photograph by K. Steibben).

Figure 107. Red fox, *Vulpes vulpes* (R. Altig).

Figure 108. Gray fox, *Urocyon cinereoargenteus* (Kansas Fish and Game Commission, photograph by K. Steibben).

Figure 109. Black bear, *Ursus americanus* (J. L. Tveten).

Order Carnivora

The order Carnivora has a long fossil history, dating back about 60 million years to early Paleocene times. Recent carnivores are represented by 12 families in which more than 100 genera and about 270 species generally are recognized. These mammals occur on all major land masses except Antarctica, although the wild dog (dingo) of Australia was carried there by early man; they are absent, however, from most oceanic islands except where introduced—principally domesticated dogs and cats and the mongoose—by humans.

As the ordinal name implies, carnivores typically are flesh-eaters, but species in many groups regularly take vegetable matter (usually fruit and nuts) and a variety of invertebrates, and some are truly omnivores. Terrestrial carnivores have well-developed canine teeth and a special pair of shearing teeth (the carnassials) formed by the last premolar in the upper jaw and the first molar below. Carnassials are best developed in the family Felidae (cats) and least developed (but still evident) in the omnivorous bears and procyonids (raccoons and allies); they are absent only in the African aardwolf.

Five families of wild carnivores, including 14 genera and 26 species, are native to the plains states, but several species have been driven to extinction there by human activity. As in the rodents, it is convenient to key out families initially before providing a key to species in each family.

Key to Families of Carnivores

1. Claws retractile, completely concealable in fur; molars 1/1, premolars 2/2 or 3/2 .... Felidae
1′. Claws not retractile, not concealed in fur; molars 1/2 or more; premolars never less than 3/3 2
2. Tail conspicuously ringed; molars 2/2 .... Procyonidae

2'. Tail not ringed; molars 1/2 or 2/3 3
3. Size small to medium (*Gulo* largest); molars 1/2; premolars 4/4 (*Gulo*, *Martes*), 4/3 (*Lutra*), or 3/3 .... Mustelidae
3'. Size medium to large (*Vulpes* smallest); molars 2/3; premolars always 4/4 4
4. Size large; feet plantigrade; large cheekteeth flattened, only slightly cuspidate, and lacking conspicuous cutting edges) .... Ursidae
4'. Size medium; feet digitigrade; large cheekteeth not flattened, cuspidate, and with conspicuous cutting edges .... Canidae

Key to Canids / Coyote, Wolves, and Foxes

1. Total length more than 1,050 mm; weight more than 20 lb 2
1'. Total length less than 1,050 mm; weight less than 20 lb 4
2. Total length usually more than 1,400 mm; length of first lower molar more than 25 mm .... *Canis lupus*
2'. Total length usually less than 1,400 mm; length of first lower molar less than 25 mm 3
3. Dorsal pelage usually brownish gray; orbits not rising abruptly above rostrum .... *Canis latrans*
3'. Dorsal pelage variable in color; orbits usually rising abruptly above rostrum .... *Canis familiaris**
4. Upper surface of skull flat from nares to orbits; temporal ridges prominent 5
4'. Upper surface of skull rising abruptly at orbits; temporal ridges usually not prominent .... *Canis familiaris**
5. Dorsal pelage reddish; ears with black tips; maxillary toothrow more than 55 mm .... *Vulpes vulpes*
5'. Dorsal pelage not reddish; ears without black tips; maxillary toothrow less than 55 mm 6
6. Dorsal pelage grizzled gray; cheeks reddish; temporal ridges lyre-shaped .... *Urocyon cinereoargenteus*
6'. Dorsal pelage yellowish brown; cheeks white; temporal ridges not lyre-shaped .... *Vulpes velox*

NOTES: *Canis rufus* is extinct and is not included in the key. It was approximately intermediate in size between *C. lupus* and *C. latrans*. The domestic dog, *Canis familiaris**, is included in the key because feral individuals occasionally are difficult to distinguish from coyotes (*C. latrans*).

Key to Ursids / Bears

1. Claws of front and hind feet of approximately equal length; face with flat profile; length of toothrow less than 110 mm . . . . *Ursus americanus*
1'. Claws of front feet markedly larger than those of hind feet; face with concave profile; length of toothrow greater than 100 mm . . *Ursus arctos*

Key to Procyonids / Raccoons and Allies

1. Tail longer than 310 mm, striped only on upper surface; weight less than 3 lb . . . . *Bassariscus astutus*
1'. Tail shorter than 300 mm, striped on both upper and lower surfaces; weight more than 10 lb . . . . *Procyon lotor*

Key to Mustelids / Weasels, Skunks, and Allies

1. Feet webbed between toes; tail thick at base, tapering toward tip; premolars 4/3 . . . . *Lutra canadensis*
1'. Feet not webbed between toes; tail not thickened at base and tapering toward tip; premolars 4/4 or 3/3 2
2. Length of hind foot 96 mm or more (rarely slightly less in *Taxidea taxus*); greatest length of skull 90 mm or more 3
2'. Length of hind foot 96 mm or less (rarely slightly more in *Martes americana*); greatest length of skull 85 mm or less 5
3. Dorsum yellowish gray, with white medial stripe from nose to neck or beyond; premolars 3/3 . . . . *Taxidea taxus*
3'. Dorsum brownish, lacking white stripe; premolars 4/4 4
4. Dorsum dark brown to blackish, with pale reddish stripes extending from shoulder to rump on each side; length of tail approximately 25 percent of total length . . . . *Gulo gulo*
4'. Dorsum grizzled dark brown to blackish, accentuated by pale head, neck, and shoulders, lacking stripes on sides; length of tail approximately 40 percent of total length . . . . *Martes pennanti*
5. Pelage black, with white stripes or spots on dorsum 6
5'. Pelage not black, lacking white stripes or spots on dorsum 8
6. Dorsum black, with two white stripes of variable length that merge with a white spot on the head and neck; greatest length of skull more than 65 mm . . . . *Mephitis mephitis*

6'. Dorsum black, with four to six white stripes, breaking up into spots posteriorly; greatest length of skull less than 65 mm 7

7. Total length 450 mm or more; dorsal stripes relatively narrow; white tip on tail usually not extensive . . . . *Spilogale putorius*

7'. Total length usually less than 450 mm; dorsal stripes relatively broad; tail with extensive white tip . . . . *Spilogale gracilis*

8. Length of hind foot more than 80 mm in males, more than 70 in females; premolars 4/4 . . . . *Martes americana*

8'. Length of hind foot less than 80 mm in males, less than 70 in females; premolars 3/3 9

9. Total length usually more than 475 mm; greatest length of skull more than 55 mm 10

9'. Total length usually less than 475 mm; greatest length of skull less than 55 mm 11

10. Pelage buff, with black legs, feet, tip of tail, and mask across eyes . . . . *Mustela nigripes*

10'. Pelage uniformly dark brown except for occasional white patches on venter . . . . *Mustela vison*

11. Total length less than 230 mm, usually less than 200; tail less than one-third length of body, lacking distinct black tip . . . . *Mustela nivalis*

11'. Total length more than 200 mm; tail at least one-third length of body, with distinct black tip 12

12. Length of tail more than 110 mm, more than 44 percent of length of body; summer pelage yellowish below, lacking white line connecting venter and toes . . . . *Mustela frenata*

12'. Length of tail less than 110 mm, less than 44 percent of length of body; summer pelage whitish below, with white line running down inside of hind legs to toes . . . . *Mustela erminea*

Key to Felids / Cats

1. Tail long, more than 500 mm; weight more than 75 lb . . . *Felis concolor*

1'. Tail short, less than 200 mm; weight less than 50 lb 2

2. Tail less than half length of hind foot, black at tip both above and below . . . . *Felis lynx*

2'. Tail more than half length of hind foot, black on upper surface of tip, white below . . . . *Felis rufus*

Canis latrans / Coyote

Distribution. The range of the coyote extends from northern Alaska to Costa Rica and from coast to coast. See map 75.

Description. A medium-sized canid, about the size of a small German shepherd. Coyotes can be distinguished from dogs by their longer upper canine teeth, relatively longer skull, and habit of running with the tail held low (almost between the legs). Pelage buffy to reddish or blackish above, whitish below. Total length, approximately 1,100–1,400 mm; tail, 320–380 mm; hind foot, 180–230 mm; ear, 90–110 mm; weight, 20–50 lb. See figure 103.

Habits and Habitat. More is known about the natural history of the coyote than that of any other wild carnivore. Coyotes are extremely adaptable and occur in nearly all available habitats within their extensive distribution. They have survived repeated attempts to exterminate or control them, and they seem to have benefited from agricultural development on the Great Plains. They are economically important furbearers.

The coyote is an opportunistic predator and will eat whatever foods are most readily available. Those commonly eaten include carrion, rabbits, rodents, ground-nesting birds and their eggs, amphibians, reptiles, fish, crayfish, insects, and any available fruit. Overall, about 90 percent of the diet consists of mammalian flesh. Coyotes occasionally kill and eat young, sick, or injured livestock, and they can cause financial losses by preying on lambs born on open rangeland. With this exception, however, most of the livestock they eat is in the form of carrion.

The mournful vocalizations of coyotes are well known to all who live on the Great Plains. They are regarded with disdain by some but with aesthetic admiration by others. Group vocalizations are heard most frequently in winter, when small packs (family groups) sometimes forage together.

Reproduction. The same individuals may mate in successive years, but not necessarily for life. Females come into heat once each year, sometime between January and March, after a period of courtship lasting as long as two or three months. Estrus lasts from two to five days. The gestation period is about 63 days, and the average litter contains six pups. Pups are weaned after six or seven weeks, during which time the male brings food to the nursing bitch. Longevity in the wild rarely exceeds 10 years.

Suggested References. Bekoff (1977).

Canis lupus / Gray Wolf

Distribution. The gray wolf once ranged through much of Eurasia and in North America from Alaska to southern Mexico. Areas south of Canada inhabited by the species today are in the northern Great Lakes region, Montana and Idaho, and perhaps certain areas of the Southwest. Dispersing wolves occasionally wander into the Dakotas from Minnesota, Montana, or Manitoba. The distribution is not mapped.

Description. Largest canid except for a few breeds of domestic dogs; fur long, ranging from white to black, usually pale gray mixed with buff and with black on the dorsum, tail, upper legs, and backs of ears. Distinguished from large domestic dogs by features of cranial anatomy. Total length, 1,350–2,050 mm; tail, 330–500 mm; hind foot, 250–300 mm; ear, 100–150 mm; weight, 45–175 lb. See figure 104.

Habits and Habitat. Gray wolves originally occurred in most habitats except deserts and mountaintops. They are predators of large mammals. Formerly, their most frequent prey on the Great Plains, where they were known as "buffalo wolves," was the bison. In Michigan, where the most frequent prey is moose, the average kill rate is one moose per wolf per 45 days.

Most gray wolves hunt in packs, which pursue prey over long distances and attack young, old, or infirm animals that cannot maintain the pace. The hunting territory of a pack ranges from 10 to 100 square miles, and neighboring territories mostly are mutually exclusive.

Packs frequently represent family groups and usually consist of five to eight members, but groups of up to 36 wolves have been reported. The pack is headed by an "alpha male" that dominates the adult female. The female in turn dominates the pups, which establish their own order of dominance by the age of about 30 days.

Reproduction. Copulation is preceded by courtship and occurs during estrus lasting from five to seven days. Gestation takes about 63 days, and litters begin to appear in March. The number of pups per litter ranges from one to 11 and averages six. The male and other pack members provide food for the bitch and help rear the pups, which are weaned in about five weeks.

Suggested References. Bogan and Mehlhop (1983); Mech (1974); Young (1944).

Canis rufus / Red Wolf

Distribution. The distribution of the red wolf originally encompassed most of the Southeast, including eastern Oklahoma and possibly southeastern Kansas. The species was extirpated over much of its range after settlement of the region, but it persisted in eastern Texas, eastern Oklahoma, Arkansas, and Louisiana. Hybridization between the abundant coyote and the rare red wolf began in Texas and perhaps Oklahoma, producing a hybrid population that interbred with red wolves farther east. By 1975, only a few "pure" red wolves survived in inaccessible swampland in southeasternmost Texas and southwestern Louisiana. Except for animals in captivity and a population experimentally established on an island off South Carolina, the species now is extinct and its distribution is not mapped.

Description. A medium-sized canid, approximately intermediate in size between *C. latrans* and *C. lupus*. Pelage sparsely haired, frequently reddish but often tawny, buffy, gray, or black. Distinguished from gray wolves, coyotes, and certain breeds of domestic dogs by analysis of characteristics of the skull and teeth. Total length, 1,295–1,650 mm; tail approximately 350–400 mm; hind foot approximately 220–230 mm; ear at least 114 mm; weight, 40–90 lb. See figure 105.

Habits and Habitat. This species dwelt in forests, both upland pine and bottomland hardwood, and coastal prairies and marshes. Wooded areas around bayous that traverse coastal prairies served as the last refuge. Red wolves preyed primarily on animals smaller than themselves. Cottontails and rodents are reported to have been eaten, and the abundance of muskrats and the introduced nutria, or coypu, in coastal marshes suggests they might have been staple foods. Social structure was not as highly developed as in *C. lupus*. Packs consisted of family groups of two to seven animals, and lone wolves were common. As in other wild canids, hookworms, heartworms, and distemper served to control populations.

Reproduction. Little is known of the reproductive biology of the red wolf in the wild. Pregnant females have been trapped from early March through mid-May, and gestation in captive animals lasts 60 to 63 days. Twenty-nine red wolves from Oklahoma, Arkansas, and Texas had two to 10 fetuses (average six to seven), whereas captive females give birth to two to six pups.

Suggested References. Carley (1979); Paradiso and Nowak (1972).

0 _____ 100
MILES

Map 75. *(Left).* Distribution of the coyote, *Canis latrans*.

Map 76. *(Right).* Distribution of the swift fox, *Vulpes velox*.

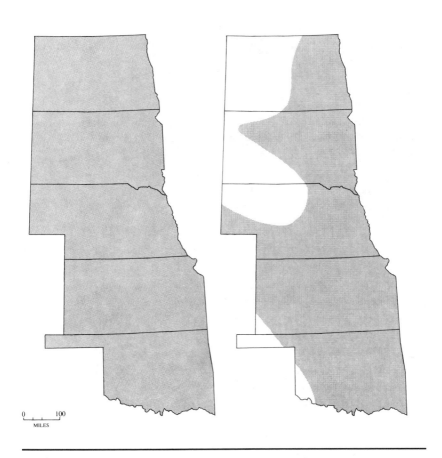

0 ⌞_,_,_⌟ 100
MILES

Map 77. *(Left).* Distribution of the red fox, *Vulpes vulpes.*

Map 78. *(Right).* Distribution of the gray fox, *Urocyon cinereoargenteus.*

Vulpes velox / Swift Fox

Distribution. This fox is a mammal of the Great Plains, ranging from the Prairie Provinces of central Canada southward through the High Plains of Texas. The species occurs, or occurred, throughout much of the five-state region except in the areas of tall-grass prairie in the eastern part, and most of Oklahoma. See map 76.

Description. A small, pale fox, distinguished from all other canids on the Great Plains by its small size, prominent black patches on each side of the muzzle, and black-tipped tail. Winter pelage long, dense, dark buffy gray above, with orangish sides, legs, and undersurface of tail; venter buff to white; summer pelage short and more reddish. Total length, 702–880 mm; tail, 240–350 mm; hind foot, 113–135 mm; ear, 56–75 mm; weight, 4–6.5 lb. See figure 106.

Habits and Habitat. Swift foxes are most abundant on short-grass prairies but are also found in mixed-grass prairie and sandhills prairie habitats. They dig dens in rangeland or cultivated fields, often on hilltops, sometimes within a few hundred yards of human habitation or roadways.

The diet consists mostly of small mammals. A study in Oklahoma revealed remains of 13 species of mammals (especially cottontails and jackrabbits), four birds, one reptile, one amphibian, and 30 invertebrates (especially grasshoppers) in stomachs and scats (feces) of these foxes. Some mammalian flesh consumed is carrion. A small amount of grass is also eaten.

Swift foxes readily enter traps and consume poisoned meat set to kill coyotes and wolves. As a result, they were nearly extirpated early in this century. Recovery was noted beginning in the 1950s, and these foxes are again becoming numerous over much of their former range. The swift fox is host to numerous ectoparasites. Intolerable populations of fleas may even result in the abandonment of certain dens.

Reproduction. These foxes may mate for life, although occasional trios of one male and two females have been reported. In Oklahoma, breeding occurs in late December or early January, and young are born about seven weeks later, in March or early April. Birth occurs about one month later on the northern plains. Litter size varies from three to six. Young foxes disperse in autumn and breed during their first winter.

Suggested References. Egoscue (1979).

Vulpes vulpes / Red Fox

Distribution. This species occurs in both the Old and New worlds. In North America, the distribution includes Canada and all but treeless regions of the United States. The species can be found throughout the plains states but usually is restricted in the West to the vicinity of watercourses or other wooded areas. See map 77.

Description. A small canid with long, bushy, reddish-yellow dorsal pelage; underparts pale, ranging from white to grayish; tail tipped with white; feet, nose, and backs of ears black. Other color phases of this species include the "silver fox" and the "cross fox." Total length, 890–1,150 mm; tail, 290–406 mm; hind foot, 138–172 mm; ear, 72–110 mm; weight, 6–13 lb. See figure 107.

Habits and Habitat. The red fox is most common in wooded areas but does not require forest habitat. Rather, this fox uses brushy cover at the forest edge for shelter and forages in brushy areas and thickets. This explains its extensive distribution in riparian habitats in otherwise essentially treeless regions of the Great Plains.

This opportunistic predator takes whatever animals are most abundant and easiest to catch. The diet typically consists of nearly 50 percent cottontails, with rodents and other small mammals, ground-nesting birds, insects, fruit, fish, and crayfish making up most of the remainder.

Red foxes forage over an area of one to three square miles. The boundaries of adjacent foraging areas tend not to overlap and probably are marked by scent. Dens are used only in severe winter weather and as nurseries for young. These canids seldom rest twice beneath the same bush, and thereby possibly avoid heavy accumulations of external parasites. Nevertheless, they harbor various ectoparasites and worms. Red foxes occasionally are preyed upon by coyotes, and are hunted by humans for sport and fur.

Reproduction. Females are receptive to their mates for less than one week in January or February. Pregnancy lasts 53 days, and most litters consist of three to six pups. The male provisions the vixen during lactation, and brings the pups their first solid food. The family breaks up in autumn, but the parents may mate again the next breeding season.

Suggested References. Allen (1984); Pils and Martin (1978); Stanley (1963).

Urocyon cinereoargenteus / Gray Fox

Distribution. The range of *U. cinereoargenteus* extends from South America northward through the eastern United States into Canada and through the desert Southwest to Washington state. In the plains region, this species is restricted mostly to eastern forests and riparian woodland. See map 78.

Description. Distinguished from other foxes by its grizzled salt-and-pepper dorsum of silver-gray to buff, cinnamon to buff neck and underparts, and black-tipped tail with dorsal mane of coarse, black-tipped hairs. Total length, 800–1,125 mm; tail, 275–400 mm; hind foot, 100–150 mm; ear, 70–85 mm; weight, 5–10 lb. See figure 108.

Habits and Habitat. In the eastern United States, this fox occurs almost exclusively in deciduous forest, whereas in the West it favors brushy vegetation associated with rugged, broken terrain. Historical records suggest that this species, like the red fox, has dispersed westward and northward on the plains during this century along the ribbons of riparian woodland associated with watercourses. The gray fox, however, is more closely associated with trees than the red fox, and it has not extended its distribution as far as the latter.

In contrast to other canids, gray foxes readily climb trees, where they rest in the security afforded by elevated perches or they search for squirrels, birds (and their eggs), and fruit. Other important items in the diet are rabbits, rodents, insects (especially grasshoppers), and vegetable matter.

Dens may be under rock piles, in thickets, in hollow logs, or even in abandoned beaver lodges. These foxes seldom excavate their own burrows. The home range may be up to two and one-half miles in diameter. Predators of the gray fox include the coyote and bobcat, and parasites include mites, ticks, fleas, lice, roundworms, tapeworms, and microbes. The probability of survival from the first to the second year of life is only 30 percent.

Reproduction. The pattern of reproduction is similar to that of the red fox. Breeding occurs sometime during the period of January to March, and litters of from one to seven (usually four) pups are born 53 to 63 days later. Nearly full grown young-of-the-year disperse in autumn and breed during their first winter.

Suggested References. Choate and Krause (1976); Fritzell and Haroldson (1982).

Ursus americanus / Black Bear

Distribution. Black bears once ranged throughout the wooded areas of North America, from coast to coast and from the Arctic Slope to central Mexico. Today, their range is greatly restricted within those limits. They persist in the plains states only on the Black Hills and in eastern Oklahoma, although individuals occasionally wander elsewhere in riparian woodland. The distribution is not mapped.

Description. A large, short-tailed, heavy-bodied carnivore. Color usually blackish, but sometimes pale cinnamon to chocolate brown. Smaller than grizzly bear, with flatter (not dished-in) face and shorter claws on front feet. Total length, 1,270–1,780 mm; tail, 80–125 mm; hind foot, 190–280 mm; ear usually 110–125 mm; weight, 225–500 lb. See figure 109.

Habits and Habitat. Black bears occur almost exclusively in forested areas or brushy habitats where caves or broken terrain provide den sites. By day they rest in a leaf-lined den in a hollow log or beneath a boulder or stump. In the evening they emerge to forage, covering a route several miles long in search of food. This omnivorous species eats virtually anything organic. Local and seasonal availability is a stronger factor of diet than choice. The greatest economic detriment of these bears is their depredation in bee yards.

Black bears generally are solitary and exhibit mutual avoidance, sometimes fighting noisily among themselves. They mark "register trees" with bites and clawmarks three to six feet above the ground. These are a sure sign of black bears, but their function is unknown. Home range varies from less than four to more than 80 square miles.

These bears are dormant in winter. Their body temperature decreases slightly and their breathing slows markedly, but they can arouse quickly. They have no habitual predators except armed humans. Parasites include flatworms, roundworms, and arthropods. Maximum longevity is 20 to 25 years.

Reproduction. Black bears are promiscuous and first breed at three or four years of age. The male plays no role in care of the young. Mating takes place in late June to July. Implantation of the embryos is delayed until November. The one to five tiny (250 grams), altricial young are born to the sleeping mother in the winter den.

Suggested References. Pelton (1982); Van Wormer (1966).

Ursus arctos / Grizzly Bear

Distribution. The former range of this Holarctic species included the western half of America from the subarctic to northern Mexico. Grizzly bears occurred throughout the plains states except, perhaps, in forested areas of eastern Kansas and Oklahoma. Dates of last reports of grizzly bears from four of the five states are North Dakota, 1889, South Dakota, 1890, Nebraska, 1858, and Kansas, 1880. The former distribution is not mapped.

Description. Largest carnivore in the contiguous United States; recognizable by its humped shoulders, shaggy brown coat (washed with yellowish or whitish on the shoulders and back), front legs conspicuously longer than hind legs, long claws on the forefeet, and concave face. Total length, 1,800 to as much as 2,800 mm; weight 300 to more than 600 lb (an old male in a zoo weighed 1,153 lb). See figure 110.

Habits and Habitat. This bear exhibits no particular habitat preference and once occurred in both open country and forests. On the plains, grizzly bears were most common where broken terrain provided den sites and facilitated approach to prey. These bears are omnivorous; they are powerful enough to kill any land mammal in North America but they rely primarily on carrion, fish, fruits, burrowing mammals, and other foods that are plentiful and easy to obtain, occasionally livestock. They typically are solitary, with a home range of 10 to more than 100 square miles. They are crepuscular to nocturnal, resting by day under the cover of boulders or windthrown trees.

Grizzly bears often dig their own winter dens, where they retreat from October or November until April or May. After the bears emerge from dormancy, wilderness hikers and fishermen are well advised to wear "bear bells" so as not to wander inadvertently too near a grizzly.

Reproduction. Grizzly bears, like black bears, are promiscuous. They breed in mid-July, and gestation (including delayed implantation of embryos) lasts 184 days. From one to four young, usually twins, are born during winter dormancy. Cubs nurse during their first summer, and remain with their mothers through two winters. They achieve sexual maturity in three and a half years, and females breed every two or three years thereafter.

Suggested References. Craighead and Mitchell (1982); Schoonmaker (1968).

Procyon lotor / Raccoon

Distribution. The range of *Procyon lotor* includes most of North America, from central Canada south to Panama. The species does not occur in high mountains, and in the plains states it is restricted primarily to wooded habitats near streams, lakes, and marshes but occasionally can be found several miles from trees. See map 79.

Description. Differs from other plains mammals by the combination of bulky body, masked face, and tail striped both above and below. Dorsum grizzled grayish and blackish, sometimes reddish, washed with yellow; venter dull brown washed with yellowish gray. Forefeet handlike for manipulation of food; tail well furred with five to seven alternating pale and dark rings. Total length, 650–960 mm; tail, 200–288 mm; hind foot, 105–132 mm; ear, 48–58 mm; weight, 13 to more than 25 lb (one weighed 62 lb). See figure 111.

Habits and Habitat. Raccoons prefer timbered habitats, where they occupy dens in hollow trees and old squirrel nests. They also inhabit caves and mines, abandoned buildings, haystacks, muskrat lodges, and occasionally ground dens. Several dens within the home range typically are used in a random pattern.

This opportunistic omnivore feeds on carrion, small mammals, birds, crayfish, insects, fruits, grains, nuts, and whatever else is available. Raccoons are selective in their diet only when food is abundant. Bottomland dwellers consume 70 to 80 percent animal foods, whereas inhabitants of uplands consume more plant materials. The sense of touch is highly developed in raccoons, and this may account for their well-known habit of washing or feeling foods.

The annual molt takes place in spring. New guard hairs appear in autumn, and the pelt of this economically valuable furbearer is prime in December.

Reproduction. The breeding season lasts from December until August, but most females are inseminated in February or March. Ovulation is spontaneous, and gestation lasts 63 to 65 days. Most litters consist of three or four young born in late April or May. Females that lose their first litter of the year often breed again in June or July. Males do not contribute to the rearing of young and do not associate with females that have young. Longevity probably averages two or three years.

Suggested References. Lotze and Anderson (1979).

Bassariscus astutus / Ringtail

Distribution. This southwestern species occurs from southern Mexico north-ward as far as Kansas, Wyoming, Utah, Nevada, and Oregon. In the five-state region, it occurs over much of Oklahoma and is known from three localities in Kansas. See map 80.

Description. A catlike carnivore distinguished from the closely related rac-coon by its smaller size, more slender body, and longer tail that is striped only on the upper surface. Dorsal pelage buff, washed with dark brown or black; eyes ringed with white, black, or dark brown; underparts whitish or buffy, including undersurface of tail. Total length, 616–811 mm; tail, 310–438 mm; hind foot, 57–78 mm; ear, 44–55 mm; weight, 1.7–2.5 lb. See figure 112.

Habits and Habitat. Ringtails live in a variety of habitats but seem to prefer canyons, rock-strewn hillsides, and talus slopes. They inhabit hollow trees and logs in wooded areas. A few have been found in abandoned buildings. Because of their secretive, noctural habits, they seldom are seen.

A study conducted in Texas revealed a diet consisting of, in descending order of abundance, insects and other invertebrates, small mammals, fruits, small birds, and snakes and lizards. Diet varies seasonally, which suggests that ringtails are opportunistic feeders.

These animals are best known for their climbing behavior and vocaliza-tions. Structural adaptations enable ringtails to rotate the hind feet at least 180 degrees, which facilitates rapid head-first descent of rocks, cliffs, and trees, often without the use of claws. Vocalizations include growls and barks (indi-cating aggressive behavior), screams or howls (in times of stress), and whis-tles, grunts, chitter, and mewing (in social contacts with other ringtails).

Reproduction. Little is known about reproduction in this species. A pregnant female trapped in Utah gave birth in May to three young. The kits (two females and one male) exhibited sexual activity (chasing, sniffing, and mount-ing) when only 13 weeks old, but one female did not become receptive until March of her fourth year. She apparently initiated breeding by means of vocal chirps, after which the pair copulated repeatedly over a period of two days. The gestation period is not known. Litter size reportedly ranges from two to four.

Suggested References. Bailey (1974); Trapp (1972); Willey and Richards (1981).

Martes americana / Marten

Distribution. This boreal species occurs from Alaska and Canada southward in montane habitats and, at least formerly, around the Great Lakes. The species is known from northeasternmost North Dakota and questionably from the Black Hills. It may no longer occur in the five-state region, although its numbers are increasing in adjacent Minnesota. See map 81.

Description. A cat-sized mustelid with a bushy tail about one-third the length of the head and body; legs proportionately longer than in other weasels. Upperparts yellowish brown; underparts darker except for orangish to whitish patch on chest; legs and tail also darker than dorsum. Total length, 460–760 mm; tail, 170–250 mm; hind foot, 78–98 mm; ear, 34–45 mm; weight 1.5 to more than 3 lb. As in most other mustelids, males average about 15 percent larger than females. See figure 113.

Habits and Habitat. In Canada, martens are most abundant in dense forests of fir, spruce, and hemlock, but they also occur around rocky slopes at and above timberline. They occasionally can be found in alpine meadows and on the tundra. Populations in North Dakota and adjacent Minnesota apparently inhabit, or inhabited, mixed coniferous and deciduous forest. The home range varies with habitat from less than one square mile to more than 10.

In a study of food habits in northwestern Wyoming, voles made up more than half of all items eaten. Red squirrels, flying squirrels, and snowshoe hares had been thought to be important food items; they were represented in only six of more than 500 scats, although at least the first of these species was especially abundant in the area. Observation revealed that martens frequently took over red squirrel dens whether or not they caught the occupants.

Reproduction. Martens are solitary animals, and males and females occur together only in midsummer, when the female is sexually receptive. The zygote divides several times but does not implant in the uterus until February or March. Subsequent development is rapid, and from two to five young are born 25 to 28 days later. The young are reared by the female in a hollow tree or other cavity. They disperse later that summer but do not achieve sexual maturity until two years old. Maximum longevity is about 15 years.

Suggested References. Jonkel and Weckwerth (1963); Murie (1961); Streeter and Braun (1968); Weckwerth and Hawley (1962).

Martes pennanti / Fisher

Distribution. The range of *M. pennanti* is similar to that of the marten. In the five-state region, the fisher reportedly occurred only in northeastern North Dakota. Between 1800 and 1940 the species was extirpated in most of the United States and much of Canada as a result of overtrapping and the destruction of habitat by logging. Subsequently, it has reoccupied some of its original range, although its current status in North Dakota is unknown. See map 81.

Description. Resembles the marten but much larger and lacks a pale patch on the chest. Tail, rump, and legs black; face, neck and shoulders hoary gold or silverish; underparts brown with pale patches on the lower abdomen. Total length, 750–1,200 mm; tail, 340–400 mm; hind foot, 103–155 mm; ear, 45–50 mm; weight, 4.5–12.5 lb. See figure 114.

Habits and Habitat. The fisher prefers habitat with continuous forest canopy. This species is most abundant in dense lowland forests and spruce-fir forests. Fishers occupy several temporary sleeping sites in hollow trees, stumps, and other protected areas, and have no permanent dens except for females with young.

This carnivore feeds on carrion and small- to medium-sized mammals and birds. Common food items include snowshoe hares, squirrels, mice, shrews, and the flesh of dead deer and moose. It is best known for its predilection for porcupines, which it kills by means of bites to the unprotected face. This requires that the fisher circle the porcupine, awaiting opportunities to lunge at the head. It also limits such predation mostly to times when porcupines are found on the ground.

Fishers harbor fleas, ticks, and the usual complement of internal parasites. Longevity may be 10 years or more.

Reproduction. Time of breeding varies geographically but is within the period March through May. Implantation of the embryo is delayed for 10 to 11 months, and subsequent development requires an additional 30 days. Birth occurs as early as February or as late as May. Litters of as many as six young have been reported, but the average litter size is three. Males achieve reproductive maturity at one year of age, whereas females do not produce their first litters until they are two years old.

Suggested References. Powell (1981, 1982).

Figure 110. Grizzly bear, *Ursus arctos* (R. S. Palmer).

Figure 111. Raccoon, *Procyon lotor* (Kansas Fish and Game Commission, photograph by K. Steibben).

Figure 112. Ringtail, *Bassariscus astutus* (J. L. Tveten).

Figure 113. Marten, *Martes americana* (D. Randall).

Figure 114. Fisher, *Martes pennanti* (R. Altig).

Figure 115. Ermine, *Mustela erminea* (L. E. Bingaman).

Figure 116. Long-tailed weasel, *Mustela frenata* (U.S. Fish and Wildlife Service, photograph by C. N. Hillman).

Figure 117. Black-footed ferret, *Mustela nigripes* (photographer unknown).

Figure 118. Least weasel, *Mustela nivalis* (Bruce Coleman, Inc., H. Reinhard).

Figure 119. Mink, *Mustela vison* (W. D. Zehr).

Figure 120. Wolverine, *Gulo gulo* (San Diego Zoological Society).

Figure 121. Badger, *Taxidea taxus* (D. Randall).

Figure 122. Striped skunk, *Mephitis mephitis* (J. L. Tveten).

Mustela erminea / Ermine

Distribution. The ermine has a circumboreal distribution that extends south-ward to about 35° north latitude. In the plains region, the species occurs in northeastern North Dakota and on the Black Hills in South Dakota. See map 80.

Description. Long body, short legs, long but muscular neck, and flat, triangular-shaped head, as in other weasels. Tail approximately one-third of total length, and always black at tip. Pelage in winter completely white except for black-tipped tail; pelage in summer dark brown above and white below, with white extending down inner side of hind legs to ankles. Total length, 290–340 mm in North Dakota, 200–243 mm on the Black Hills; tail, 70–100 mm, 28–40 mm; hind foot, 40–44 mm, 20–31 mm; ear, 15–20 mm, 13–16 mm; weight, 40–170 g. Males are larger than females. See figure 115.

Habits and Habitat. This species occurs in habitats ranging from arctic tundra to coniferous forest, deciduous forest, marshy grassland, and agricultural areas. It is most abundant in boreal, montane, and Pacific Coast coniferous forests.

Ermines prey primarily on small mammals and birds up to the size of a cottontail, which they kill with an accurately delivered bite to the neck. Excess food may be cached for later use. In winter, they forage extensively beneath the snow and feed almost exclusively on rodents. The long, slender, small body of this and other weasels is not conducive to the maintenance of body temperature in cold climates, but *M. erminea* uses snow as insulation from subfreezing weather conditions.

The dense, white winter pelage of this furbearer is economically valuable. Raptors and mammalian predators prey on the ermine.

Reproduction. Ermines breed from May until July, while females are still nursing their previous litters. Ovulation occurs after copulation. Implantation of embryos is delayed until the following March or April, after which gestation lasts from three to four weeks. Litter size ranges from four to 12, usually six to nine. Young females often are bred before they are weaned, sometimes before their eyes open, by the same male that breeds with their mother. There is no pair bond in this species, however, so there is little likelihood the adult male that mates with young females is their father.

Suggested References. King (1983).

Mustela frenata / Long-tailed Weasel

Distribution. The long-tailed weasel has no close relatives in the Old World. In the New World, it occurs from southwestern Canada, the Great Lakes region, and New England southward through much of the United States (including the entire Great Plains) to South America. See map 82.

Description. As in other weasels, males much larger than females. Tail more than 44 percent of length of head and body, and with short black tip; pelage white in winter (except for black tip on tail) as far south as Kansas, sometimes mottled or brown in Kansas and Oklahoma; summer pelage brown dorsally, with white lips and chin and yellowish venter. Populations in southwestern Kansas and western Oklahoma frequently with dark facial masks highlighted by patches of white. Total length, 350–460 mm; tail, 125–175 mm; hind foot, 40–54 mm; ear, 18–27 mm; weight, 150–315 g. See figure 116.

Habits and Habitat. This weasel occurs in a variety of forest and grassland habitats. On the plains, it typically is most abundant around marshes but can be found almost anywhere, often near a source of water. Probably this secretive animal is more common throughout the five-state region than most professional trappers and naturalists suspect.

Males prey on mammals as large as cottontails, snowshoe hares, and tree squirrels, whereas the smaller females feed mostly on mouse-sized rodents. Solitary individuals forage both day and night and pursue their prey down into burrows or up into trees. In addition to mammals, they eat birds, snakes, frogs, and insects.

The autumn molt begins in October. The yellow ventral pelage is replaced with white pelage first, and the dorsum molts as long as two months later. Molt in spring begins in March and procedes in the reverse direction.

Reproduction. Females experience their first estrus in July or August at the age of three to four months. Implantation is delayed for about seven and one-half months after fertilization. Subsequent embryonic development lasts 23 or 24 days, and litters of from four to nine young are born in April or May. Young males do not become sexually mature until they are 14 or 15 months old.

Suggested References. Hall (1951); Jones et al. (1983).

Mustela nigripes / Black-footed Ferret

Distribution. This ferret once occurred in intermontane basins and semiarid grasslands from southern Canada south to Arizona and Texas, including all the plains states except subhumid areas in the east. No individuals of this endangered species have been taken in the plains region for more than a decade and it is known to persist for certain only in northwestern Wyoming. However, *M. nigripes* still may occur in some places within its original distribution (shown on map 81) on the plains.

Description. About the size of a mink. Pelage yellowish buff, paler around face, with black facial marks, black-tipped tail, and black feet. Distinguished from *M. frenata* by its larger size (in animals of the same sex) and black feet; distinguished from the European (domestic) ferret by the latter's bushier pelage and blacker appearance. Total length in males, 490–572 mm; tail, 100–150 mm; hind foot, 59–73 mm; ear, 29–32 mm; weight, 530–590 g; females average about 10 percent smaller. See figure 117.

Habits and Habitat. The historical geographic distribution of this little-known species nearly coincided with that of prairie dogs. More than 90 percent of ferret scats contain remains of prairie dogs, and ferrets use abandoned prairie dog burrows as shelter. Accordingly, this mustelid has the narrowest range of ecological tolerance of any predatory mammal in North America.

Dependence on prairie dogs became a liability for the ferret when the Great Plains and surrounding areas were settled. Prairie dogs prefer deep, relatively level soils, and these soils also are preferred for agriculture. Agricultural development fragmented most large prairie dog towns in which ferrets lived, and subsequent attempts to exterminate remaining prairie dogs by means of poisons also affected *M. nigripes.* The presence of ferrets is indicated by their characteristic trenches, which may be as long as 10 feet.

Reproduction. Captive females came into heat in late February or early March and remained in breeding condition for 21 to 28 days. Copulation occurred in late March and early April, and gestation in one female in two consecutive years lasted 42 and 45 days. Litter size in the wild ranges from one to five. Young ferrets remain below ground until July.

Suggested References. Choate, Boggess, and Henderson (1982); Henderson, Springer, and Adrian (1969); Hillman and Clark (1980).

Mustela nivalis / Least Weasel

Distribution. The distribution of this circumboreal weasel in the New World includes most of Canada, the north-central United States, and the Appalachian Mountains. In the plains states, it can be found in nearly all of North Dakota, the eastern three-fourths of South Dakota and Nebraska, and northern Kansas. The range of the species apparently has expanded southward since 1960. See map 83.

Description. Smallest of the weasels that occur in the plains region, although its measurements overlap with those of *M. erminea* (distinguished from the latter by its uniformly brown tail, which is one-fourth or less the length of the head and body). Summer pelage chocolate brown above and white with occasional brown spots below; winter pelage pure white as far south as southern Nebraska, mottled or indistinguishable from summer pelage in certain specimens from Kansas. Total length, 158–227 mm; tail, 26–44 mm; hind foot, 20–29 mm; ear, 9–15 mm; weight, 32–65 g. See figure 118.

Habits and Habitat. The least weasel occurs in habitats ranging from tundra to prairie. It is most abundant around marshes and other permanent bodies of water and least abundant in northern forests inhabited by *M. erminea*. Southward dispersal of this species into Kansas apparently followed watercourses.

The diet consists mostly of small rodents, insects, and ground-nesting birds. Least weasels reportedly require from one-third to one-half their body weight in food each day, and they adjust the size of the area in which they forage to compensate for fluctuations in the density of prey species. They pursue mice into their burrows and may occupy the burrows for a time after they consume the occupants. Least weasels are preyed upon by hawks, owls, foxes, and larger mustelids.

Reproduction. Unlike most other weasels, *M. nivalis* breeds throughout the year and does not exhibit delayed implantation. Females may produce as many as three litters per year, although one or two litters probably are more common. Gestation lasts from 34 to 37 days, and litter size ranges from one to 10 (usually four or five). Young females become sexually mature at three to four months of age, and young males somewhat later.

Suggested References. Choate, Engstrom, and Wilhelm (1979); Hall (1951); Jones et al. (1983).

Mustela vison / Mink

Distribution. The range of the mink in North America extends from Alaska and Canada southward to the Gulf of Mexico. The species does not occur in the desert Southwest where stream flow is irregular, but it can be found around permanent water all through the plains states. See map 84.

Description. A large, semiaquatic mustelid. Pelage dense, soft, glossy, and water-repellent; dorsum brown to nearly black with paler underfur; venter similar, often with white patches. Ears short and rounded; feet partially webbed. Total length, 490–686 mm; tail, 154–217 mm; hind foot, 57–76 mm; ear, 22–27 mm; weight, 1.5–3.5 lb. See figure 119.

Habits and Habitat. This species is found only around water except when dispersing overland from one body of water to another. In the plains region, it is common near lakes, watercourses, and marshes, especially where stumps, driftwood, or muskrat lodges break the surface.

Mink prey heavily on muskrats but also consume crayfish, fish, rodents, and waterfowl. They are agile swimmers and can catch rough fish (such as carp) without difficulty. Opportunistic feeders, especially in winter, they occasionally catch cottontails or tree squirrels. Excess food is cached.

Dens are near water in hollow logs, bank cavities, or old muskrat lodges or burrows. Males and females den separately except during the breeding season. Males may have numerous dens, whereas females with litters restrict their activities to the vicinity of natal dens; after the young are weaned, the female and her offspring occupy several dens. The linear home ranges of females vary from 20 to 50 acres, whereas those of males are much larger. Besides man (*M. vison* is a valuable furbearer), the greatest cause of mortality may be conflict with other mink. Parasites include cestodes, nematodes, trematodes, mites, fleas, and lice.

Reproduction. Mink breed as early as January in Kansas and as late as March in the Dakotas. Females in heat are promiscuous and breed with any available males. Implantation is delayed; the total period of gestation is 40 to 75 days, but actual fetal development occurs in about one month. Litters of from three to six young are born in April or May. Young mink become sexually mature about the time of the first breeding period after their birth.

Suggested References. Jackson (1961); Jones et al. (1983).

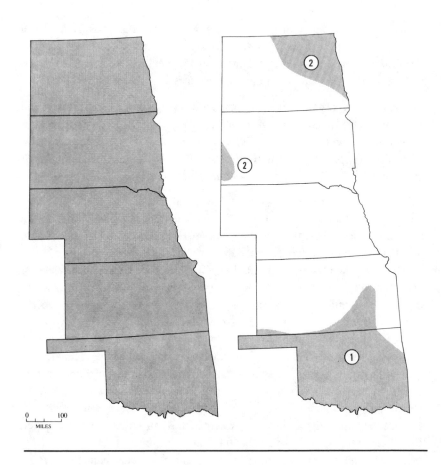

Map 79. *(Left).* Distribution of the raccoon, *Procyon lotor.*

Map 80. *(Right).* Distribution of the ringtail, *Bassariscus astutus* (1), and the ermine, *Mustela erminea* (2).

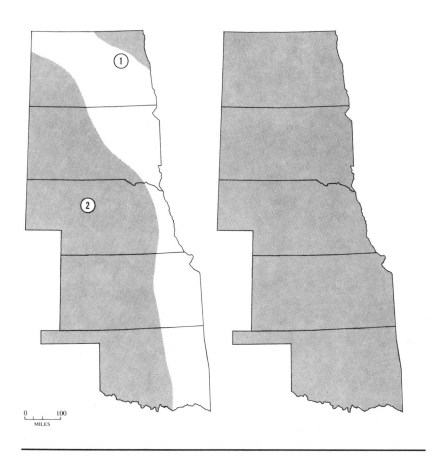

Map 81. *(Left).* Distribution of the marten, *Martes americana* (1); the fisher, *Martes pennanti* (1); and the black-footed ferret, *Mustela nigripes* (2).

Map 82. *(Right).* Distribution of the long-tailed weasel, *Mustela frenata.*

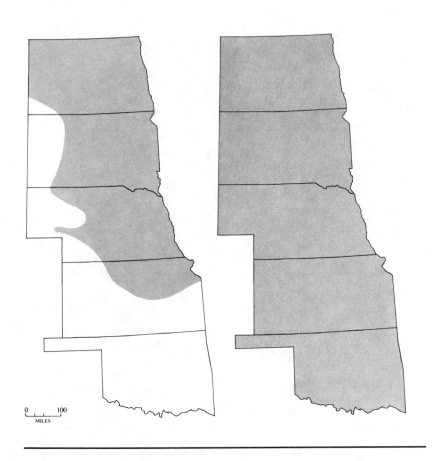

Map 83. *(Left).* Distribution of the least weasel, *Mustela nivalis.*

Map 84. *(Right).* Distribution of the mink, *Mustela vison.*

Map 85. *(Left).* Distribution of the badger, *Taxidea taxus*.

Map 86. *(Right).* Distribution of the western spotted skunk, *Spilogale gracilis* (1), and the eastern spotted skunk, *Spilogale putorius* (2).

Gulo gulo / Wolverine

Distribution. This circumboreal species was once found in North America southward to about the 38th parallel, and farther south on western mountains. It occurred in northern North Dakota and ranged southward, at least sporadically, to western Nebraska. Wolverines declined in number during the late 1800s, and today they are restricted to relatively inaccessible areas. The former distribution in the plains states is not mapped.

Description. Largest of mustelids known from the plains region; superficially resembles an elongate bear cub more than a weasel. Body heavy with powerful legs. Shaggy pelage ranging in color from black to brown, and with reddish stripes extending from shoulders to rump. Total length, 720–1,310 mm; tail, 170–260 mm; hind foot, 150–185 mm; ear, 50–60 mm; weight, 30 to more than 60 lb. See figure 120.

Habits and Habitat. Wolverines occur primarily in boreal forests, but they also wander both north and south, and above and below (in mountains), of the tree line. They are most abundant in marshy areas where deep snow covers the ground for long periods. Deep snow restricts the movement of large herbivores and thereby facilitates predation by wolverines.

A comprehensive study of diet in Norway revealed the following foods, in descending order: reindeer, moose, deer, foxes, rabbits, rodents, birds, and plants. In North America, wolverines also eat beaver, squirrels, carrion (including that of walrus, seals, and whales), marmots, gophers, and wasps. Wolverines frequently feed on kills made by other animals and are reported to cache excess food.

These are solitary animals that hunt over large areas. Territories of males are as large as 800 square miles, whereas those of females seldom exceed 175 square miles. Within these areas, any available shelter, such as windfalls or rock overhangs, may be used as dens. Wolverines typically are nocturnal, but they may be active at any time of day.

Reproduction. This species breeds in summer. Implantation is delayed until the following January, after which fetuses develop in 30 to 40 days. Litter size ranges from one to six and averages two or three. Maternal care sometimes lasts longer than a year, in which case females breed every other year.

Suggested References. Rausch and Pearson (1972); Wilson (1982); Wright and Rausch (1955).

Taxidea taxus / Badger

Distribution. The range of the badger includes arid and semiarid regions of the central and western United States and adjacent Canada and Mexico. The species occurs throughout the plains states except in southeastern Oklahoma. See map 85.

Description. A large, broad-bodied mustelid with short, strong legs and large claws adapted for digging. Characterized by a white patch on each cheek and a white stripe on the dorsum extending from the nose at least to the shoulders. Pelage bushy, variable in color, consisting of stiff hairs with gray bases, brown or black bands, and gray tips; tail bushy and not much longer than hind foot. Total length, 600–785 mm; tail, 100–150 mm; hind foot, 95–128 mm; ear, 47–64 mm; weight, 12–25 lb. See figure 121.

Habits and Habitat. Badgers are typical inhabitants of grassland communities but also inhabit the edges of forests. They are most common where deep soil facilitates burrowing. In agricultural areas, they commonly forage in roadside ditches and along fencerows. Badgers prey mostly on small mammals by locating their burrows and digging them out. They are opportunistic feeders, utilizing whatever animals are most easily obtained. Common foods include ground squirrels, pocket gophers, mice, cottontails, insects, birds, snakes, prairie dogs, and crayfish.

Burrows dug by badgers have ellipsoid rather than round openings. The burrows may extend six to eight feet below the surface of the ground and have several chambers. Badgers are solitary, and typically only one individual is associated with a burrow except when females have young. Burrows frequently are abandoned and become inhabited by rodents, cottontails, or snakes. Subsequently, the badger may return and feed on the new occupants.

Molt occurs annually in summer or autumn. It begins on the head, and progresses first posteriorly then ventrally. Parasites include various worms and arthropods.

Reproduction. Breeding takes place in late summer or early autumn. Implantation is delayed until sometime between December and February. Litters of one to five young are born in April, May, or June. Young badgers are weaned at the age of two months and disperse from the natal burrow in autumn. Most males and occasional females are reproductively active as yearlings.

Suggested References. Lampe (1976); Long (1973).

Spilogale gracilis / Western Spotted Skunk

Distribution. This spotted skunk occurs from southwestern British Columbia through much of the western United States and southward into Latin America. In the five-state region, it has been reported only from the western tip of the Oklahoma Panhandle. See map 86.

Description. As *S. putorius,* smaller and more weasel-like than other skunks. Pelage black, with four to six whitish stripes on back and sides, breaking into spots posteriorly. Distinguished from the eastern spotted skunk by smaller size, broader dorsal stripes, and more extensive white tip on tail. Total length, 330–460 mm; tail, 100–180 mm; hind foot, 34–53 mm; ear, 25–33 mm; weight averages about 530 g in males and 300 g in females. See figure 122.

Habits and Habitat. Most of the distribution of this species is west of the Continental Divide, where it commonly dwells in rocky, brushy habitats associated with broken terrain. In Colorado, it seldom is found above 8,000 feet. East of the Continental Divide this skunk occupies dissected terrain associated with the foothills of the Rocky Mountains and mesas and canyons. The one locality of record for the species in the plains states is on the Black Mesa.

This opportunistic predator eats primarily rodents and insects. When threatened, spotted skunks retreat to cover if possible; if not, they raise their tails and stomp their front feet while facing the intruder. They often raise the hind part of the body, stand on their forefeet, and arch their back so both the head and the anal glands located beneath the tail are directed toward the intruder. The odoriferous spray from those glands can temporarily blind or otherwise repel all but the most persistent of intruders. Accordingly, spotted skunks have few enemies other than humans and domestic dogs, and an occasional venturesome wild carnivore.

Reproduction. Copulation occurs in September or October, at which time both juvenile and adult females are bred. Implantation of the blastocyst is delayed for 180 to 200 days, and most births occur in May. Litter size averages about four. Adult males become fertile as early as May, and some juvenile males are capable of breeding in September at the age of four or five months. Male reproductive organs regress at other times.

Suggested References. Mead (1968); Van Gelder (1959).

Spilogale putorius / Eastern Spotted Skunk

Distribution. This mustelid ranges northward from Mexico to the Canadian border (in Minnesota) between the Rocky Mountains and the Mississippi River and to Pennsylvania east of the Mississippi. Historical records suggest that it did not occur on the northern and western Great Plains until early in this century, when it dispersed westward into Colorado and Wyoming and northward as far as North Dakota. See map 86.

Description. Larger than the western spotted skunk, with narrower dorsal stripes and usually with less extensive white tip on tail. Total length, 450–540 mm; tail, 165–225 mm; hind foot, 41–51 mm; ear, 24–30 mm; weight about 600 g in males and 425 g in females. See figure 123.

Habits and Habitat. This skunk seems to prefer forest edge habitats and seldom is found in dense forest or marshy areas. In the plains states, it frequents riparian woodland, fencerows, and shelterbelts and is commensal with man around farms. Mammalian flesh, especially rodents and carrion, is the principal food. This skunk is an agile predator, and its consumption of mice and rats around barns and other buildings is a service to farmers. Other foods include corn, fruit, insects (mostly beetles, grasshoppers, and crickets), birds and their eggs, and sometimes poultry. Excess food is not cached.

Dens may be located in any dry, dark place that affords protection from enemies such as dogs. Typical den sites are beneath haystacks or outbuildings, among exposed tree roots, beneath overhanging creekbanks, and in fallen timber or woodpiles. Several skunks may occupy the same den in winter, but at other times these animals are solitary.

The home range is an area of about one-fourth square mile and often contains two or three dens; that of promiscuous males increases to two to four square miles during the breeding season. Most mortality in this species is caused by humans and their pets, or by great horned owls; like other skunks, many are killed on roadways.

Reproduction. Unlike *S. gracilis,* this species breeds in March and implantation is delayed for only two weeks. Gestation lasts 50 to 65 days, and litters of from four to nine young (average about five) are born in late May or June.

Suggested References. Choate, Fleharty, and Little (1974); Jones et al. (1983); Van Gelder (1959).

Mephitis mephitis / Striped Skunk

Distribution. The range of this skunk includes all of the United States and adjacent areas of Canada and Mexico, except coastal marshes and the most arid southwestern deserts. The species is abundant and conspicuous throughout the five-state region. See map 87.

Description. Larger and less weasel-like than spotted skunks. Pelage black, with narrow white stripe from nose to forehead; broad white stripe on head and shoulders, splitting into two lateral stripes on the back and sometimes down the tail. Total length, 560–795 mm; tail, 225–295 mm; hind foot, 68–85 mm; ear, 26–35 mm; weight, 5–10 lb in males, 4–9 lb in females. See figure 🐾. ⌐ 122.

Habits and Habitat. This species exhibits no obvious habitat preference but apparently avoids dense forests and marshy areas where dry den sites are unavailable. It is commensal with man around farmsteads, and regularly occurs in cities and towns. This skunk is an opportunistic omnivore. Diet in summer emphasizes insects (especially beetles and grasshoppers) because of their abundance. Other foods include carrion, small mammals, frogs, lizards, birds, eggs, fruit, worms, spiders, grubs, and garbage. Unlike spotted skunks, the striped skunk is a poor climber and forages only on the ground.

The odoriferous chemical in the musk of all skunks is butylmercaptan, which temporarily affects the central nervous system of animals that are sprayed by them. Skunks seem instinctively to recognize their defensive power, and they have an indifferent attitude toward humans, other animals, and automobiles.

The first annual molt occurs when adults are about 11 months of age. The underfur is shed first, followed by the guard hairs beginning anteriorly and progressing posteriorly. The molt process is completed by autumn.

Skunks are nocturnal. They excavate in banks or brushy areas, in hollow stumps, or beneath buildings, rockpiles, or other debris. *M. mephitis* does not hibernate; rather, individuals are inactive during severe winter weather, at which time they may congregate in a communal den for as long as a month.

Reproduction. Breeding occurs from mid-February to mid-March. Gestation lasts about 63 days, and litters of four to 11 (average about seven) young are born in April or May.

Suggested References. Storm (1972); Wade-Smith and Verts (1982).

Lutra canadensis / River Otter

Distribution. Otters originally occurred in permanent bodies of water from Alaska and northern Canada southward through most of the United States. They were found in riparian habitats throughout the plains states until the late 1800s. *L. canadensis* was extirpated over much of its range, but apparently the species is becoming reestablished in certain areas of the five-state region. See map 88.

Description. A slender, aquatic mustelid with webbed feet. Pelage water-repellent with dense underfur; color lustrous brown dorsally, slightly paler or grayish ventrally. Total length, 1,020–1,350 mm; tail, 350–475 mm; hind foot, 110–135 mm; ear about 16 mm; weight (in Minnesota), 15–25 lb. See figure 125.

Habits and Habitat. This species swims by means of an undulating movement of the body and tail coupled with paddling by the hind feet. Otters can remain submerged up to two minutes and use pockets of air for breathing when they swim under ice in winter. Molting occurs in spring and autumn when the insulating qualities of the pelage are not critical for survival.

Otters are opportunistic carnivores. They eat crayfish whenever available and dig them, together with turtles and frogs, from the bottom mud during winter. Rough fish, such as carp and suckers, are eaten throughout the year. Insects and earthworms are available in summer, as are young muskrats and beaver. Abandoned lodges of beaver or muskrat are often used as dens.

Movement by otters on land, hindered by short legs, is hastened by sliding in the mud, ice, wet grass, or snow. Established slides down riverbanks are used repeatedly in the same manner as a child uses a sled, although the otter can vary its play by sliding headfirst, feetfirst, on its back, or on its belly. Vocalization is varied, consisting of chirps, chuckles, and screams.

Reproduction. In New York, river otters breed in March and April. Blastocysts do not implant in the uterus until January or early February; actual gestation lasts until March or April. Litter size ranges from one to four (usually two) young. Adult females breed again while still lactating, and young otters breed when they are one or two years old.

Suggested References. Hamilton and Eadie (1964); Knudsen and Hale (1968); van Zyll de Jong (1972).

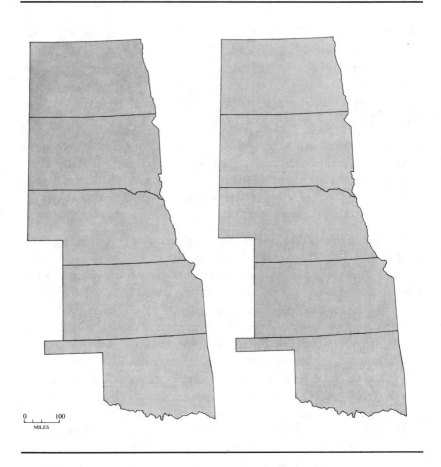

0 — 100
MILES

Map 87. *(Left).* Distribution of the striped skunk, *Mephitis mephitis.*

Map 88. *(Right).* Distribution of the river otter, *Lutra canadensis.*

Map 89. *(Left).* Distribution of the lynx, *Felis lynx.*

Map 90. *(Right).* Distribution of the bobcat, *Felis rufus.*

Felis concolor / Mountain Lion

Distribution. The mountain lion, known in much of the plains region as the puma, historically occurred from British Columbia southward to Argentina. The species disappeared over much of its range in the late 1800s but persisted in areas remote from human habitation. Recent sightings suggest that it now occurs sporadically in all five plains states. The distribution is not mapped.

Description. A large cat with a long, black-tipped tail. Pelage pale brown or buffy above, somewhat paler below. Measurements of a male from Colorado, a female from Kansas, and a series of adults from Wisconsin: total length, 2,105 mm, 1,962 mm, 1,700–2,590 mm; tail, 803 mm, 713 mm, 700–900 mm; hind foot, 292 mm, — , 254–295 mm; weight, — , 88 lb, 80–210 lb. Ear 95–100 mm or more. See figure 126.

Habits and Habitat. This magnificent predator depends on stealth and surprise to catch its prey. Therefore, it is most common in areas where rugged terrain, trees, or brushy vegetation provide cover. In the five-state region, this species was the "top carnivore" in such habitats, and it seldom preyed on grazing animals of the open prairie, such as bison and pronghorn.

Solitary mountain lions are somewhat nomadic and do not occupy a permanent den. It takes about one deer a week to sustain a lion, and individuals move on after a deer has been eaten. Dawn and dusk are the times when most hunting is done, although these animals may be active at any time both in summer and winter. Because they neither feed on carrion nor have an established den, *F. concolor* has few parasites.

This species has few enemies other than humans, who have been primarily responsible for the disappearance of its principal prey (deer), resulting in a reduction in numbers of the predators dependent upon deer. Preservation and management of deer apparently has had the unexpected consequence of the reestablishment of mountain lions in certain areas.

Reproduction. *F. concolor* breeds promiscuously throughout the year. Males do not remain with females after breeding. Gestation lasts about 96 days; birth may occur in any month although there is a peak of births in summer. Young animals remain with their mother for as long as two years. Captive lions have lived longer than 20 years.

Suggested References. Anderson (1983); Currier (1983); Young and Goldman (1946).

Felis lynx / Lynx

Distribution. The distribution in the New World of this circumboreal species includes most of northern North America south to approximately 40° north latitude. Its occurrence in the southern part of this range, including the northern Great Plains, is sporadic. See map 89.

Description. A cat with a short, black-tipped tail and pronounced ear tufts. Distinguished from the bobcat by its larger size, more grayish pelage, larger ear tufts, and more distinctive black tip on tail. Measurements of adults from Wisconsin are: total length, 875–1,000 mm; tail, 100–120 mm; hind foot, 215–250 mm; ear usually about 75 mm; weight, 16–35 lb. See figure 127.

Habits and Habitat. This cat is a characteristic inhabitant of boreal and montane forests. During periods of high population density, "irruptions" occur in which lynx are found in atypical habitats, such as prairie, far to the south of the boreal forests. Some of the historic records of lynx on the northern plains possibly are the result of such irruptions.

The relationship of the lynx and its staple prey, the snowshoe hare, is one of the most fascinating phenomena in ecology. Populations of snowshoe hares cycle in density, with nine to 10 years between population peaks. Populations of lynx also cycle but lag about two years behind those of hares. When hares are abundant, lynx enjoy considerable reproductive success. When hares are scarce, reproduction by yearling lynx females is suppressed, and most lynx kittens produced do not survive to become reproductive adults.

In addition to snowshoe hares, which constitute about 70 percent of the diet, this species also eats carrion (15 percent), ruffed grouse (10 percent), and other birds and small mammals (5 percent). Lynx typically hunt by lying in wait along a game trail and pouncing on unsuspecting prey. An adult lynx requires about one and a third pounds of food per day. Lynx molt annually in spring. They harbor few parasites.

Reproduction. *F. lynx* breeds in February or March. The gestation period is about 63 days, and litters are born in April or May. Litters consist of one to four kittens, or rarely five. Young females often achieve sexual maturity the winter after they are born.

Suggested References. Brand, Keith, and Fischer (1976); Gunderson (1978); Nellis, Wetmore, and Keith (1972).

Felis rufus / Bobcat

Distribution. The range of the bobcat potentially includes all of the conterminous United States plus adjacent areas of Canada and most of Mexico. The species occurs throughout the five-state region. See map 90.

Description. Slightly smaller than the lynx, with markedly shorter hind foot, less pronounced ear tufts, and less distinctive black tip on tail. Pelage reddish with well-defined spots, bands of black hairs on the front legs. Total length, 770–940 mm; tail, 144–162 mm; hind foot, 156–190 mm; ear, 64–80 mm; weight, 12–30 lb. See figure 128.

Habits and Habitat. This species, unlike the closely related lynx, occurs in a variety of habitats and is widely distributed in the plains states. Like other American felids, bobcats depend on surprise rather than speed to capture prey. Therefore, they are most abundant in forested regions or in areas where broken terrain provides cover. In Kansas, population densities of bobcats have been estimated at one per 2.48 square miles in rugged terrain associated with the Flint Hills, Chautauqua Hills, and Red Hills, one per 10.25 square miles in eastern forests and wooded river valleys, and one per 31.42 square miles on featureless plains.

Bobcats prey primarily on rabbits, but they also eat rodents (ranging from mice and rats to porcupines and beaver) and ground-nesting birds. They sometimes eat carrion, especially in winter. These cats forage throughout the night, but are most active at dawn and dusk. A night's travels may cover three to seven miles. A bobcat requires the equivalent of one rabbit every other day to remain in good physical condition.

Bobcats molt each autumn. Pelage in winter is long, dense, and grayish. By summer the worn pelage becomes shorter, coarser, and more reddish. Maximum longevity in nature is approximately 12 years, at which time the teeth are too abraded to facilitate effective predation.

Reproduction. Females have only one litter per year, but they experience estrus repeatedly if not successfully mated. The breeding season extends from January through June, and gestation lasts about 10 weeks. Litter size ranges from one to seven and averages about three. Females may breed as yearlings, whereas males achieve sexual maturity in the second year of life.

Suggested References. Mahan (1980); Young (1958).

Figure 123. Western spotted skunk, *Spilogale gracilis* (Texas Parks and Wildlife Department, photograph by R. D. Porter).

Figure 124. Eastern spotted skunk, *Spilogale putorius* (New York Zoological Society).

Figure 125. River otter, *Lutra canadensis* (Michigan Department of Natural Resources).

Figure 126. Mountain lion, *Felis concolor* (J. L. Tveten).

Figure 127. Lynx, *Felis lynx* (L. E. Bingaman).

Figure 128. Bobcat, *Felis rufus* (D. C. Lovell and R. S. Mellott).

Figure 129. Wapiti, *Cervus elaphus* (U.S. Fish and Wildlife Service).

Figure 130. Mule deer, *Odocoileus hemionus* (U.S. Fish and Wildlife Service, photograph by E. P. Haddon).

Figure 131. White-tailed deer, *Odocoileus virginianus* (Texas Parks and Wildlife Department).

Figure 132. Moose, *Alces alces* (Montana Fish and Game Department).

Figure 133. Caribou, *Rangifer tarandus* (U.S. Fish and Wildlife Service).

Figure 134. Pronghorn, *Antilocapra americana* (D. Randall).

Figure 135. Bison, *Bison bison* (J. L. Tveten).

Figure 136. Mountain goat, *Oreamnos americanus* (C. B. Rideout).

Figure 137. Mountain sheep, *Ovis canadensis* (R. Altig).

Order Artiodactyla

Artiodactyls, or even-toed ungulates as they sometimes are termed, have an extensive fossil record extending back to early Eocene times. The order comprises nine modern families encompassing about 80 Recent genera and 185 species. These generally large and conspicuous mammals are native to all continents except Australia (where they have been introduced) and Antarctica. Three families—Antilocapridae (pronghorn), Bovidae (bison, sheep, and allies), and Cervidae (deer and allies)—occur in the plains states.

Eleven species are known from the five-state region. Of these, eight are native and three (mountain goat, wild pig, and fallow deer) have been introduced. Four native species were extirpated by man, but three of them (bison, mountain sheep, and wapiti) have been reintroduced. The caribou, which apparently once occurred sparingly in North Dakota, no longer inhabits the plains region. The pronghorn and two species of deer, which were driven to near extinction in the area covered by this guidebook at the turn of the century, now occur in fair to good numbers in appropriate habitat in all five states, and the moose is found sparingly in eastern North Dakota southward to extreme northeastern South Dakota.

Key to Artiodactyls / Deer, Bison, and Allies

1. Animals horned (both sexes); if horns shed, horn-cores permanent ... 2
1'. Animals antlered (males only, except in *Rangifer*); antlers shed
    annually 5
2. Horns with one prong (prong lacking in many females), tip somewhat
    recurved, sheath shed annually; striped brown or black markings on
    neck . . . . *Antilocapra americana*
2'. Horns unbranched, not shed; neck lacking distinctive markings 3

3. Horns brown, heavily ridged and curving backward, forming a massive spiral in adult males; color grayish brown; rump, backs of legs, and muzzle white . . . . *Ovis canadensis*

3'. Horns black, not forming a spiral; color uniformly whitish or brown 4

4. Horns curving backward, quite slender and slightly ridged; color uniformly white or white tinged with yellowish. .*Oreamnos americanus**

4'. Horns completely smooth, curving upward and toward each other; color uniformly dark brown . . . . *Bison bison*

5. Antlers palmate, at least in part 6

5'. Antlers not palmate 8

6. Antlers palmate on most of the main beam; greatest length of skull more than 500 mm . . . . *Alces alces*

6'. Antlers palmate distally; greatest length of skull less than 500 mm . . . 7

7. Antlers palmate distally on both the main beam and one or more brow tines; canines 1/1 . . . . *Rangifer tarandus*

7'. Antlers palmate distally only on main beam; brow tines not palmate; canines 0/1 . . . . *Cervus dama**

8. Underparts brownish, similar in color to back; upper canine teeth present; larger than typical deer . . . . *Cervus elaphus*

8'. Underparts paler than back; no upper canines; smaller than wapiti (*C. elaphus*) 9

9. Hindquarters mostly white; tail large and white below, often held high while running; antlers with single main beam that gives rise to a series of simple tines . . . . *Odocoileus virginianus*

9'. Hindquarters mostly grayish; tail smaller and tipped with black, held down while running; antlers with main beam forked, forming two secondary branches, each of which bears tines . . . *Odocoileus hemionus*

Cervus elaphus / Wapiti

Distribution. Historically, the wapiti (also termed American elk) ranged across much of the Northern Hemisphere, including the plains states. The species was extirpated over most of its range in the late 1800s. It has been reestablished in several areas on the Great Plains, but free-ranging individuals are seen infrequently. The distribution is not mapped.

Description. A large cervid with a dark mane that hangs to the brisket. Rump yellowish, bordered with dark brown or black. After spring molt, in May or June, entire pelage sleek reddish brown. After autumnal molt, in September or October, back and sides grayish brown; head, neck, and legs dark brown. Bulls larger than cows, with heavy antlers. Total length, 2,135–2,745 mm; tail, 114–157 mm; hind foot, 580–710 mm; ear about 210 mm; weight, 500–825 lb. See figure 129.

Habits and Habitat. Although presently restricted primarily to forested areas, the wapiti is a forest edge species and was abundant near riparian habitats on the Great Plains. In spring and summer, this species grazes on grasses and forbs; in winter it feeds mostly on browse.

Wapiti are gregarious, forming small herds in summer and larger herds in winter. Rut and bugling (mating call of male) begin in September, when dominant bulls accumulate harems of 15 to 30 cows. Young bulls follow the harems and occasionally breed with cows while the dominant bull chases away other interlopers. After breeding is completed, bulls become solitary.

This species is nomadic, constantly moving to obtain food and water and to avoid predators (such as mountain lions and grizzly bears). These cervids typically feed moving upslope during morning, rest at midday, and feed moving downslope in the afternoon. They avoid summer heat by bedding down in snowbanks or by remaining on north slopes or in dense forest. To avoid flies, they move to high, breezy areas.

Reproduction. The breeding season extends through September and October. Gestation lasts about eight and one-half months. One calf (or rarely twins) usually is born in early June. Young cows breed in their third year. Young bulls become sexually mature at two years of age but seldom breed before their fourth year.

Suggested References. Jones et al. (1983); Murie (1951); Varland, Lovaas, and Dahlgren (1978).

Odocoileus hemionus / Mule Deer

Distribution. This deer is distributed from Alaska through western Canada and the western United States into central Mexico. It occurs throughout the plains states except in southeastern Nebraska, the eastern third of Kansas, and the eastern two-thirds of Oklahoma. See map 91.

Description. A long-eared cervid, smaller than the wapiti, with a small, white tail tipped with black. Dorsal pelage reddish brown after molt to summer pelage, grayish brown in winter. Bucks have antlers with main beams divided into equal-sized, branched tines. Typically runs with a stiff-legged bounce, with tail held down. Total length, 1,160–1,800 mm; tail, 110–230 mm; hind foot, 325–590 mm; ear, 120–250 mm; weight in males to about 470 lb, to about 160 lb in females. See figure 130.

Habits and Habitat. Mule deer are common in open country, but they rest in brushy or wooded habitats if available. In Nebraska, their diet consists of about 40 percent agricultural crops, 30 percent browse, and the remainder grasses, forbs, and sedges. Populations that occur in the plains region reportedly consume parts of more than 600 species of plants.

Antlers begin to grow in April or May, and the first fork has developed by June. New antler growth is covered with vascular skin known as velvet, which nourishes the growing tissue. Bucks rub off velvet against trees or other stationary objects in August or September, just before breeding begins. The antlers fall off in late December or early January.

Mule deer are most active at dawn and dusk. They tend to remain within an area of a few square miles if food, water, and cover are plentiful, but they may travel distances up to 150 miles when food is scarce. Populations of mule deer in the five-state region are not migratory, but the deer may move several miles seasonally. *O. hemionus* contracts epizootic hemorrhagic disease, brucellosis, and other maladies, and is parasitized by a variety of organisms. The major cause of mortality is starvation.

Reproduction. These deer breed from late October through December. The gestation period is variable, generally about 203 days, and from one to three (most often two) fawns are born in early summer. Known longevity in the wild is 20 years.

Suggested References. Anderson and Wallmo (1984); Wallmo (1981).

Odocoileus virginianus / White-tailed Deer

Distribution. The white-tailed deer ranges throughout most of the United States (including all the plains states), northward into Canada, and southward as far as 15° south latitude in South America. See map 92.

Description. Differs from the mule deer as follows: ears smaller; tail larger, fringed with white; antlers with main beams having upright, unbranched tines. Gracefully lopes rather than bounces, the white tail held high, waving from side to side. Total length, 1,500–2,150 mm; tail, 250–360 mm; hind foot, 480–530 mm; ear, 140–230 mm; weight up to 490 lb in males, as much as 240 lb in females. See figure 131.

Habits and Habitat. The white-tailed deer occurs in a variety of habitats but is most common in forest edge. In the plains states, this species frequently inhabits riparian communities and forages in adjacent cropland or rangeland. The animals browse opportunistically on leaves, stems, buds, and bark; they also consume corn, soybeans, forbs, grasses, and fungi.

White-tailed deer are most likely to be seen when they feed in the morning and evening, although they may move from one place to another at any time of the day or night. The distances traveled are related to the availability of food. On the northern plains, these deer sometimes congregate in areas termed "yards" in autumn and winter. Such areas provide adequate food and shelter for the deer to survive long periods of winter weather.

Rut begins after the antlers are fully developed and the velvet is shed, usually in October. At that time bucks, previously indifferent, begin to court the does and to attempt to drive away other bucks. Combat between bucks seldom is fatal. The species is prey to a number of large predators and harbors a wide range of parasites.

Reproduction. The breeding season extends from October to January. Estrus lasts about 24 hours, and unbred does come into estrus again after 28 days. The gestation period ranges from 195 to 212 days, and most fawns are born in late May or June. Litter size ranges from one to three. Does may breed in their first year of life, but most bucks are a year and a half old when they first participate in rut.

Suggested References. Jones et al. (1983); Taylor (1956).

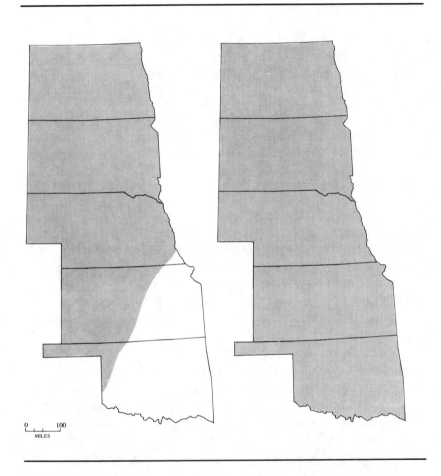

Map 91. *(Left).* Distribution of the mule deer, *Odocoileus hemionus.*

Map 92. *(Right).* Distribution of the white-tailed deer, *Odocoileus virginianus.*

0 _____ 100
MILES

Map 93. *(Left).* Distribution of the moose, *Alces alces*.

Map 94. *(Right).* Present distribution of the pronghorn, *Antilocapra americana*.

Alces alces / Moose

Distribution. This species has a circumboreal distribution in coniferous forests. The range in the United States extends southward on the Central Rocky Mountains, in the Great Lakes region, and in the Northeast, and individuals occasionally wander as far south as Missouri. In the five-state region, moose are found southward to northeastern South Dakota. See map 93.

Description. Largest member of the family Cervidae. Head long and narrow; body heavy, with short tail and long, slender legs; males with large, palmate antlers. Pelage variable in color, ranging from blackish to pale reddish brown or gray. Pendulous dewlap, or "bell," hanging from throat. Total length, 2,040–2,900 mm; tail, 65–120 mm; hind foot, 725–840 mm; ear, 250–275 mm; weight to about 1,200 lb in males and 850 lb in females. See figure 132.

Habits and Habitat. Although a forest species, the moose is most common in areas that have been burned, logged, or otherwise disturbed. Habitat selection is influenced by food preference; moose prefer to browse on plant species that become established after the forest canopy is disrupted, such as aspen and birch. They also browse on conifers and, in summer, eat grasses, sedges, and aquatic vegetation. Moose ordinarily do not occur where temperatures long exceed 75° F and shade or access to lakes or rivers are lacking.

These generally solitary animals occupy separate home ranges in summer and winter that seldom exceed eight to 15 square miles. They are adept at walking and foraging in snow but are subject to predation (by wolves) and starvation when the snow is especially deep. Other causes of mortality are sport hunting, accidents, and disease. The population of moose in North America totals about one million.

Reproduction. Rut extends from early September to November. Cows are receptive for seven to 12 days, during which time estrus lasts about 24 hours. The interval between successive periods of heat is about three weeks. Gestation lasts approximately eight months, until May or June. Most cows produce only one calf, but twins are not uncommon and triplets have been reported. Females may breed when only a year and a half old, whereas males usually are much older; longevity is 20 years or more.

Suggested References. Bédard (1975); Franzmann (1981).

Rangifer tarandus / Caribou

Distribution. The caribou has a circumpolar distribution. It has been domesticated in the Old World, where it is referred to as the "reindeer." The North American range includes much of Canada and Alaska and formerly extended into the northern United States, including northernmost North Dakota. Populations in the contiguous United States have been extirpated, and the former distribution of the species in the plains states is not mapped.

Description. A large cervid in which both sexes have antlers; brow tine of antlers modified as shovel-like structure above face. Pelage grayish white to grayish brown with white rump patch. Total length, 1,370–2,535 mm; tail, 100–218 mm; hind foot, 380–700 mm; ear, 110–150 mm; weight to about 600 lb in males, and as much as 300 lb in females. See figure 133.

Habits and Habitat. Suitable habitats for this gregarious species must provide food during periods of deep snow and relief from flying insects in summer. Herds are nomadic, and travel extensively to satisfy these habitat requirements. Foods of this opportunistic feeder include lichens and mosses, newly emergent green vegetation, and browse. In winter, caribou congregate in areas with little snow cover where they can browse or dig with their hooves for food. In summer, they seem to follow the receding snow to feed on new plant growth.

Both caribou and moose are subject to a fatal neurological disease caused by a roundworm that also commonly occurs in white-tailed deer (but does not harm them). Where forest edge habitats are established by logging or other activities, white-tailed deer may contact caribou and moose and spread the disease to those species. Starvation during severe winter weather and predation on calves by wolves, lynx, and grizzly bears serve as additional population controls.

Reproduction. The period of rut is usually in October, when females come into heat at intervals of 10 to 12 days. Bulls fight fiercely for cows, and one male typically services 10 to 15 females. Calving occurs in May or June after a gestation period of 227 to 230 days. Most cows bear only one calf per year, but twins occasionally are produced.

Suggested References. Banfield (1962); Bergerud (1978); Jones et al. (1983); Skoog (1968).

Antilocapra americana / Pronghorn

Distribution. About 35 million pronghorn once inhabited the arid and semi-arid grasslands of western North America from Alberta and Saskatchewan to the Mexican Plateau. Only some 17,000 remained by 1900, but subsequent protection and reintroductions have resulted in recovery over much of the original range. In Kansas, for example, there were only 37 animals in 1962, but by 1983 there were more than 2,500. The present distribution is mapped (see map 94).

Description. A small (about three feet tall at shoulder), mostly tan-colored artiodactyl with white underparts, two white bands across the throat, and pronged horns (in both sexes) composed of fused hairs. Measurements of adults from Alberta: total length, 1,360–1,495 mm; tail, 70–145 mm; hind foot, 380–440 mm; ear, 132–160 mm; weight, 91–155 lb (males). See figure 134.

Habits and Habitat. This denizen of rangeland usually occurs in areas where the featureless terrain prevents predation by stealth. It uses its great speed (up to 60 miles per hour for short distances) to outdistance most predators. The diet emphasizes forbs, especially sagebrush and prickly pear, in late spring, summer, and autumn. Sagebrush is also eaten in winter except in agricultural areas, where winter wheat and alfalfa make up a substantial part of the diet during the part of the year when green forbs are not available.

Pronghorn herd together in winter, usually in groups of fewer than 100 individuals, but they separate into bachelor herds and female-kid groups from spring until the onset of rut. In rut, bucks defend territories against interloping males and scent-mark all tall vegetation within their territories. Threatening displays usually suffice to expel intruders, but sometimes fights ensue. Combat may last two minutes or less but often results in injury to one or both of the combatants.

Pelage is shed continuously, but molt is most obvious from March through May when the heavy winter coat is shed. Disease and starvation during periods of deep snow are the principal natural controls on populations.

Reproduction. Rut begins in September, and most females are bred in October. Gestation lasts 230 to 250 days, and young (usually twins) are born in mid-June. The normal life span is about five years.

Suggested References. O'Gara (1978); Sexson and Choate (1981); Sexson, Choate, and Nicholson (1981).

Bison bison / Bison

Distribution. The range of the bison formerly reached from Alaska to Mexico and included all but southwestern deserts and coastal areas of the United States. Within this range there were approximately 70 million bison when Europeans first arrived, but fewer than 1,000 remained by 1889. Today, the species occurs only in herds maintained by public and private organizations and individual ranchers. The distribution is not mapped.

Description. A bovid with massive forequarters and a large head. Front half of body covered with longer hairs than remainder of body; pelage yellowish- or reddish-brown to black. Horns present in both sexes. Total length, 1,980–3,800 mm; tail, 430–815 mm; hind foot, 460–660 mm; ear about 120 mm in females and up to 150 mm in males; weight up to 1,100 lb in females and up to 2,000 lb in males. See figure 135.

Habits and Habitat. This ungulate grazes extensively on grasses and is especially adapted for short-grass species, such as buffalograss and the gramas, typical of the High Plains. When grass is unpalatable, bison consume forbs or browse on woody plants. They paw the ground or push snow out of the way with their heads to uncover vegetation in winter.

Bison are highly gregarious. One herd in southwestern Kansas in 1871 was estimated to include more than four million animals. More typical today are herds of 11 to 20 animals, consisting of cows, bull calves, and heifers; breeding bulls are solitary or form small bachelor herds. Beginning in July, bulls intermix with cow-calf herds for the purpose of breeding. Bulls do not establish harems; rather, they are polygynous in that they breed sequentially with several females as they come into heat.

Cows sometimes produce calves until they are about 28 years old, whereas bulls seldom live longer than 20 years. Tuberculosis, brucellosis, and anthrax were once natural population controls.

Reproduction. Heifers first breed at about three years of age, whereas most breeding bulls are seven years old or more. Copulation occurs in August or September and calves are born nine and a half months later, usually in May. A cow typically bears one calf per year, but twins are not uncommon.

Suggested References. Allen (1877); McDonald (1981); Roe (1970).

Oreamnos americanus / Mountain Goat

Distribution. This species occupies a native range from the Rocky Mountains and Cascades northward through the mountains of western Canada to the Yukon and southeastern Alaska. It was introduced on the Black Hills in 1924. The current population there, numbering about 300 to 400 individuals, resides in the highest, most rugged parts of the region, around Harney Peak and the adjacent Needles. The distribution is not mapped.

Description. Only artiodactyl in North America with scent glands behind bases of horns (which are curved slightly outward and backward in both sexes), and the only one in the 48 contiguous states that is whitish in color. Adults have tuft of hair beneath throat. Horns black. Total length of males, 1,245–1,785 mm; tail, 85–200 mm; hind foot, 300–365 mm; ear, 110–140 mm; weight to 300 lb; females are up to 30 percent smaller. See figure 136.

Habits and Habitat. As implied by the vernacular name, mountain goats inhabit high, rocky areas with cliffs and steep slopes. In the Northern Rockies, the range includes alpine tundra and subalpine areas—places characterized by low temperatures, high winds, and heavy snowfall in winter. These goats are excellent climbers and frequent terrain that is mostly inaccessible to other large mammals, which indirectly results in protection from predators and lack of competition for food. They seek the shelter of caves and overhanging ledges in severe winter weather.

O. americanus consumes a variety of plants, both by grazing and browsing. On the Black Hills, the diet in winter consists of 60 percent mosses and lichens, 20 percent bearberry, 10 percent pine twigs and needles, and 10 percent miscellaneous browse, grasses, and forbs.

Mountain goats occur in groups of two to four in summer, but larger groups form in winter. Principal predators are mountain lions and eagles; the latter take small kids and occasionally knock animals from ledges. Maximum longevity is about 15 years.

Reproduction. Breeding can begin when these goats are two years of age. Mating takes place in November and December. The gestation period lasts 147 to 178 days, and kids are born in late May and early June. A single offspring is most common, but twins occur frequently and triplets rarely.

Suggested References. Cowan and McCrory (1970); Rideout (1978); Rideout and Hoffmann (1975).

Ovis canadensis / Mountain Sheep

Distribution. The former range of this bovid included much of western North America from southwestern Canada to northwestern Mexico. In the five-state region, mountain sheep occurred in the western Dakotas and northwestern Nebraska. These populations were extirpated by the early 1920s, and today the species occurs in the plains states only where reestablished and protected. The distribution is not mapped.

Description. A brownish sheep with a gray muzzle and a white rump. Curved, ridged horns present in both sexes, massive in adult males. Total length, 1,370–1,950 mm; tail, 80–150 mm; hind foot, 370–482 mm; ear, 112–130 mm; weight 160 to more than 265 lb in males, 115–200 lb in females. See figure 137.

Habits and Habitat. Before settlement of western North America, mountain sheep were as common in foothills and even river valleys as on mountains. They moved downslope to winter in protected lowland habitats and returned upslope in summer. The so-called desert bighorn of the southwestern deserts are nothing more than mountain sheep living in remote desert habitats.

This ungulate obtains food by both browsing and grazing; feeding seems to be opportunistic—whatever nutritious vegetation is readily available. A study conducted in Idaho showed the diet to consist mostly of grasses supplemented with browse and forbs. In North Dakota, however, the diet reportedly consists of 90 percent browse in both summer and winter. Mountain sheep use their hooves to locate food beneath snow, or they move into areas with less snow-cover.

During rut, large rams use their curved horns both in combat and as a visual display to establish dominance over other rams. Dominant rams do not establish harems or defend territories; rather, a ram associates with a ewe as it comes into estrus and attempts to repel other rams that approach the ewe.

Reproduction. Ewes first breed when two or three years of age, but social behavior prevents most young rams from breeding until considerably older. The breeding season is in November and December, and gestation lasts about 180 days. Lambs, usually one per litter, are born in late May or June.

Suggested References. Cowan (1940); Geist (1971); Wishart (1978).

Introduced Species and Species of Possible Occurrence

Seven species of mammals not native to North America and introduced there have been found in the Plains States. A North American native species, the mountain goat, was introduced on the Black Hills some years ago from the Northern Rockies. The nonnative, introduced taxa are briefly treated in this section. Users of this guidebook should also be aware of the final category of mammals discussed, ten native species that naturally occur near enough to the borders of the plains region that they may someday be found there.

Introduced Species

Oryctolagus cuniculus, European Rabbit (Lagomorpha, Leporidae). Although there is one record of a specimen of this rabbit in wild pelage that was taken in northeastern Nebraska in 1958, the species probably does not regularly occur in the wild in the region. Domesticated animals, widely raised both for food and fur, may escape or be released from time to time, and thus the presence of this lagomorph in the plains fauna is always possible.

In key characters, *Oryctolagus* resembles *Sylvilagus,* but *O. cuniculus* is larger than all native rabbits save for *S. aquaticus.* The specimen from Nebraska had the following external dimensions: total length, 514 mm; length of tail, 52 mm; length of hind foot, 110 mm; length of ear, 79 mm; weight, 5 lb.

Mus musculus, House Mouse (Rodentia, Muridae). This Eurasian native was introduced into the Americas by early immigrants to the New World and now occurs over much of the temperate and tropical parts of the two continents. In the plains states, it is a common, frequently abundant, inhabitant of the environs of man. Additionally, feral populations are sometimes encountered in the eastern parts of the region.

House mice may be confused with native species of *Reithrodontomys* and *Peromyscus,* especially when immature. *M. musculus* differs from these native cricetids as follows: ears nearly naked; tail scantily haired and bearing conspicuous scaly annulations; venter grayish (usually) or dark buffy rather than white; molars with three longitudinal rows of tubercles; and a distinct notch (best seen in lateral view) on the occlusal surface of the upper incisors. It differs also from *Reithrodontomys* in having a smooth (rather than grooved) face on the upper incisors.

Ranges in measurements of a series from western Nebraska are: total length, 166–178 mm; tail, 80–87 mm; hind foot, 18–20 mm; ear, 13–15 mm. Adults generally weigh 20–25 g.

Rattus norvegicus, Norway Rat (Rodentia, Muridae). This rat was introduced along the eastern seaboard of the United States about the time of the American Revolution and subsequently spread across the country in the wake of European colonization and through additional introductions at coastal ports. It occurs widely in the plains states but is mostly limited to urban areas or other human habitations such as farm buildings. Feral populations are rare, but this rat can live in the wild some distance from dwellings.

Both species of introduced *Rattus* are likely to be confused only with the five kinds of native woodrats (*Neotoma*) known from the plains region, from which they can be distinguished as follows: tail scantily haired with scaly annulations clearly evident; crowns of molar teeth cuspidate and more or less cuboid, not elongate and semiprismatic; underparts usually some color other than white; skull with well-developed temporal ridges.

Upperparts grayish brown, pelage coarse with black guard hairs; venter usually pale grayish. Ears large and nearly hairless. Total length, 295–440 mm; tail, 125–200 mm; hind foot, 35–44 mm; ear, 21–24 mm; weight usually 250–400 g.

Rattus rattus, Black Rat (Rodentia, Muridae). Originally a native of Asia like the Norway rat, this species spread to Europe and North Africa and was introduced into the New World with colonization. It tends to be restricted more to southern regions of North America than the Norway rat. *R. rattus* is known in the plains states only from as far north as Wichita, Kansas, and apparently is strictly limited to urban environments, mostly large cities. In such places it frequently occupies the upper parts of buildings and thus is often termed the "roof rat," especially when in direct competition with *R. norvegicus*. It differs from the Norway rat as follows: tail longer, rather than shorter, than head and body; ears larger; females normally with 10 mammae instead of 12; temporal ridges on skull bowed outward posteriorly rather than essentially parallel.

Dorsal color brownish to dark reddish brown (although considerable individual variation is possible), usually with a darkened middorsal band; underparts whitish tinged with yellow; tail tending to be somewhat bicolored (darker above) in contrast to *R. norvegicus*. Ears large, relatively broad, and naked. Measurements of the only specimen known from Kansas: total length, 381 mm; tail, 230 mm; hind foot, 38 mm; ear, 24 mm; weight 155 g.

Myocastor coypus, Coypu or Nutria (Rodentia, Myocastoridae). This large, semiaquatic rodent is a native of temperate South America. It was first introduced in the western United States at the turn of the century as a potentially valuable furbearer. Later, it was introduced in the Southeast. Currently, *M. coypus* is well established in the wild in most Gulf Coast states, and it occurs northward to southeastern Oklahoma. There are records of individuals taken in the wild both from Kansas and Nebraska, but these probably represent animals released from captivity because none has been taken recently in the two states and no wild populations are known there.

The coypu is most likely to be confused with the beaver, from which it can be distinguished as indicated in the key to rodent families. Also, it tends to be more yellowish in color, with a white patch around the nose and mouth, and the pelage is not as soft as that of the beaver. Measurements of a series from Louisiana are: total length, 837–1,010 mm; tail, 300–450 mm; hind foot, 100–150 mm; ear, 21–30 mm. Adults generally weigh 10–20 lb.

Sus scrofa, Wild Pig (Artiodactyla, Suidae). A few individuals of this feral counterpart of the familiar domesticated pig have been reported as occurring in eastern Oklahoma. This species is not listed in the key to artiodactyls.

Cervus dama, Fallow Deer (Artiodactyla, Cervidae). The fallow deer was introduced in the Loup River drainage of central Nebraska just before the Second World War, and by the early 1960s the total population there was estimated at 500. This had declined, however, to fewer than 50 in 1978, and it is uncertain whether the species can survive there. A few fallow deer have also been reported from the area around the Black Hills in South Dakota and adjacent Wyoming, but the current status of that population is unknown. There is said to be a small herd on the McAlester Army Depot in Oklahoma also.

C. *dama* most closely resembles the native deer of the plains states, *Odocoileus,* from which it differs most conspicuously in several characteristics: antlers of males palmate (flattened) distally on main beam; internal nares not completely divided by inner bone and premaxillary bones distinctly separate for a third or more of their length (as viewed from below); dorsal pelage spotted in summer; tarsal glands lacking. The general size is much the same as in *O. hemionus* and *O. virginianus.*

Small numbers of another introduced cervid, the sika deer (*Cervus nippon*), may still be present in Kansas and Oklahoma. This deer has a spotted coat the year around and lacks the palmate antlers of *C. dama.*

Species of Probable or Possible Occurrence

Sorex longirostris, Southeastern Shrew (Insectivora, Soricidae). This shrew is known from southern Missouri and western Arkansas; almost certainly it will be found on the Ozark Plateau and in the Ouachita Mountains of eastern Oklahoma and possibly also in extreme southeastern Kansas. In that geographic region, the southeastern shrew would be the only member of the genus *Sorex,* and thus would differ from other local shrews in the same characters used in the key to distinguish other species of that genus.

Sorex preblei, Preble's Shrew (Insectivora, Soricidae). This small shrew, which somewhat resembles *S. cinereus,* has been recorded from eastern Montana and is to be looked for in the western Dakotas. It has a shorter (condylobasal length 14.6 mm or less) and flatter skull than the masked shrew.

Condylura cristata, Star-nosed Mole (Insectivora, Talpidae). This unique mole is known certainly to occur as far west as south-central Manitoba and west-central Minnesota. There is an old report of the species from Towner, North Dakota, based on hearsay, but no specimens have been taken in that state. It is possible that *C. cristata* will be found to occupy parts of eastern North Dakota.

Euderma maculatum, Spotted Bat (Chiroptera, Vespertilionidae). This large-eared, distinctively colored (white spots on black background dorsally) bat has been recorded from Colorado, New Mexico, and Wyoming. It is to be looked for in the western parts of the five states, where its occurrence is possible but doubtful.

Peromyscus boylii, Brush Mouse (Rodentia, Cricetidae). The brush mouse is known from southeastern Colorado, just north of the Oklahoma Panhandle, and may be found in the latter area and possibly also in extreme southwestern Kansas. See account of *P. attwateri.*

Baiomys taylori, Northern Pygmy Mouse (Rodentia, Cricetidae). This small mouse has been taken in recent years in northern Texas. If it continues to expand its range northward, and if the Red River does not prove to be a barrier, *B. taylori* soon may be found in southern Oklahoma. This mouse most closely resembles species of the genus *Peromyscus,* but it is smaller, has a shorter tail, and is grayish rather than buffy or brownish dorsally.

Synaptomys borealis, Northern Bog Lemming (Rodentia, Cricetidae). This bog lemming is known from northwestern Minnesota and southern Manitoba and possibly will be found to occur in the northeastern part of North Dakota. It differs from the southern bog lemming (*S. cooperi*) in cranial and dental details, and in having eight (rather than six) mammae.

Conepatus mesoleucus, Hog-nosed Skunk (Carnivora, Mustelidae). This interesting skunk is known from as far east as Baca County, southeastern Colorado, and may occur in the Oklahoma Panhandle and possibly also in extreme southwestern Kansas. It is about the size of *Mephitis mephitis,* differing most conspicuously from the latter in having a broad white dorsal band and white tail, and two (rather than three) upper premolars.

Felis pardalis, Ocelot (Carnivora, Felidae). There is a record of this spotted cat from northwestern Texas, not far from the Oklahoma boundary, but it probably does not occur there now and doubtfully will be found in Oklahoma.

Tayassu tajacu, Collared Peccary (Artiodactyla, Tayassuidae). Same distribution comment as for *F. pardalis* above.

Glossary

The following terms, adapted from Jones et al. (1983), are frequently used in descriptions or discussions of mammals. Many, but not all, have been used in the foregoing text. Some that appear on one or more of the three figures in the Glossary are not otherwise defined. Where a term listed has two or more meanings in the English language, only the one (or rarely two) applying to mammalian biology is given.

abdomen. Ventral part of body, lying between thorax (rib cage) and pelvis.

aestivation. Torpidity (dormancy) in summer.

agouti hair. Hair with alternate pale and dark bands of color.

albinism. Lacking external pigmentation; albino (may be only partial).

allopatric. Pertaining to two or more populations that occupy disjunct or nonoverlapping geographic areas.

altricial. Pertaining to young that are blind, frequently naked, and entirely dependent on parental care at birth.

alveolus. Socket in jawbone that receives root(s) of tooth.

angular process. Posterior projection of dentary ventral to condyloid (articular) process; evident but not labeled on figure 139.

annelid. Any member of invertebrate phylum Annelida, which includes earthworms.

annulation. Circular or ringlike formation as in dermal scales on tail of a mammal, or in dentine of a tooth.

anterior. Pertaining to or toward front end.

antler. Branched (usually), bony head ornament found on cervids, covered with skin (velvet) during growth; shed annually.

apposable. Capable of being brought together (as thumb with other digits of hand).

arboreal. Pertaining to activity in trees.

arthropod. Any member of the invertebrate phylum Arthropoda, such as insects and spiders.

articular condyle. Surface of condyloid (articular) process (fig. 139), articulating lower jaw with skull.

auditory bulla. Bony capsule enclosing middle ear; when formed by tympanic bone, termed tympanic bulla (see fig. 140).

auditory meatus. Opening leading from external ear to eardrum (see fig. 139).

avian. Of, relating to, or characteristic of birds.

baculum. Sesamoid bone (os penis) in penis of males of certain mammalian groups.

basal. Pertaining to base.

baubellum. See os clitoridis.

beam. Main trunk of antler.

bez tine. First tine above brow tine of antler.

bifid. Divided into two more-or-less equal lobes.

bifurcate. Divided into two branches.

bipedal. Pertaining to locomotion on two legs.

blastocyst. In embryonic development of mammals, a ball of cells produced by repeated division (cleavage) of fertilized egg; stage of implantation in uterine wall.

boreal. Northern, as in boreal coniferous forest.

braincase. Posterior portion of skull; part that encloses and protects brain.

breech birth. Birth in which posterior part of body emerges first.

brisket. Breast or lower part of chest.

brow tine. First tine above base of antler.

browse. Leaf and twig growth of woody vegetation available for animal consumption.

buccal. Pertaining to cheek.

bunodont. Low-crowned, rectangular, grinding teeth, typical of omnivores.

calcar. Spur of cartilage or bone that projects medially from ankle of many species of bats and helps support uropatagium.

canine. One of four basic kinds of mammalian teeth; anteriormost tooth in maxilla (and counterpart in dentary), frequently elongate, unicuspid, and single-rooted; never more than one per quadrant (see figs. 138–139). Also a term pertaining to dogs or to Canidae.

carnassials. Pair of large, bladelike teeth (last upper premolar and first lower molar) that occlude with scissorlike action; possessed by most modern members of order Carnivora.

carnivore. Animal that consumes meat as primary component of diet.

carpal. Any one of group of bones in wrist region, distal to radius and ulna, and proximal to metacarpals.

caudal. Pertaining to tail or toward tail (caudad).

cavernicolous. Living in caves (or mines).

centimeter (cm). Unit of linear measure in metric system equal to 10 millimeters; 2.54 cm equal one inch.

cestode. Any member of invertebrate class Cestoda (tapeworms).

cheekteeth. Collectively, postcanine teeth (premolars and molars).

circumboreal. In a distributional sense, around the northern part of the world.

cingulum. Enamel shelf bordering margin(s) of a tooth (cingulid used for those of teeth in lower jaw).

claw. Sheath of keratin on digits; usually long, curved, and sharply pointed.

cline. Gradual change in morphological character through a series of interbreeding populations; character gradient.

cloaca. A common chamber into which digestive, reproductive, and urinary systems empty and from which products of these systems leave the body.

commensal. An organism that receives food, protection, or other benefits from another organism without damage or benefit to it.

condylobasal length. See figure 138.

coprophagy. Feeding upon feces.

coronoid process. Projection of posterior portion of dentary dorsal to mandibular condyle (see fig. 139).

cosmopolitan. Common to all the world; not local or limited, but widely distributed.

cranial breadth. Measurement of cranium taken across its broadest point perpendicular to long axis of skull; frequently used for insectivores.

crepuscular. Pertaining to periods of dusk and dawn (twilight); active by twilight.

Cretaceous. See geologic time.

cursorial. Pertaining to running; running locomotion.

cusp. Point, projection, or bump on crown of a tooth.

cuspidate. Presence of cusp or cusps on a tooth.

deciduous dentition. Juvenile or milk teeth, those that appear first in lifetime of a mammal, consisting (if complete) of incisors, canines, and premolars; generally replaced by adult (permanent) dentition.

delayed implantation. Postponement of embedding of blastocyst (embryo) in uterine epithelium for several days, weeks, or months; typical of some carnivores.

dental formula. Convenient way of designating number and arrangement of

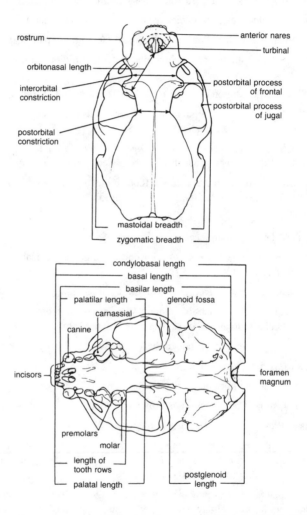

Figure 138. Dorsal and ventral views of skull of a river otter, showing cranial features and measurements (after Hall 1955).

mammalian teeth (for example, i 3/3, c 1/1, p 4/4, m 3/3); letters indicate incisors, canines, premolars, and molars, respectively; numbers before slashes (or above line) indicate number of teeth on one side of upper jaw, whereas those following (or below) line indicate number on one side of lower jaw.

dentary. One of pair of bones that constitute entire lower jaw (mandible) of mammals.

dentine. Hard, generally acellular material between pulp and enamel of tooth; sometimes exposed on surface of crown.

dentition. Teeth of mammal considered collectively.

dewclaw. Vestigial digit on foot.

dewlap. Pendulous fold of skin under neck.

diastema. Space between adjacent teeth; for example, space between incisors and cheekteeth in species lacking canines.

dichromatism. Having two distinct color phases.

digit. Finger or toe.

digitigrade. Pertaining to walking on digits, with wrist and heel bones held off ground.

diploid chromosome number. Total number of chromosomes in normal body cell (twice the number found in egg and sperm).

dissected. In a geographical sense, rough, broken country consisting of hills and ridges cut by breaks and valleys.

distal. Away from base or point of attachment, or from any named reference point (as opposed to proximal).

distichous. Arranged alternately in two vertical rows on opposite sides of an axis, as in hairs on tail of some rodents.

diurnal. Pertaining to daylight hours; active by day.

dorsal. Pertaining to back or upper surface (dorsum).

dorsum. Back or upper surface.

ecotone. Transition zone between two adjacent communities.

ectoparasite. Parasite living on, and feeding from, external surface of an animal (for example, fleas, lice, ticks, mites).

enamel. Hard outer layer of tooth, usually white, consisting of calcareous compounds and small amount of organic matrix.

endemic. Native to a particular region and occurring nowhere else.

endoparasite. Parasite living within host (for example, flukes, tapeworms).

Eocene. See geologic time.

epiphysis. Secondary growth center near end of long bone.

estrous cycle. Recurring growth and development of uterine endometrium, culminating in time when female is receptive to male.

estrus. Stage of reproductive receptivity of female for male; "heat."

excrescence. Dermal projection, as on face and ears of bats.

extirpation. Extinction, usually referring to a specified geographic area.

familial name. Name applying to a group of organisms of family rank among animals, ending in -idae (names of subfamilies end in -inae).

feces. Excrement.

fecundity. Rate of producing offspring; fertility.

femoral. Of, relating to, or located near the femur.

femur. Single bone of upper (proximal) part of each hind (pelvic) limb.

fenestrate. Having openings.

feral. Pertaining to a domestic animal that has reverted to a wild state.

fetal membranes. Tissue layers that surround, or attach to, the growing mammalian embryo (chorion, amnion, allantois).

fetus. Embryo in later stages of development (still in uterus).

fibula. Smaller of two bones in lower part of hind (pelvic) limb.

flank. Sides of animal between ribs and hips.

foramen. Any opening, oriface, or perforation, especially through bone.

foramen magnum. Large opening at posterior of skull through which spinal cord emerges from braincase (see figs. 138, 140).

forb. Any herbaceous plant other than grasses, rushes, and sedges.

fossa. Pit or depression in bone; frequently site of bone articulation or muscle attachment.

fossorial. Pertaining to life under surface of ground.

frontal bone. See figures 139–140.

fusiform. Compact, tapered; pertaining to body form with shortened projections and no abrupt constrictions.

geologic time. Mammals arose in the *Mesozoic* era, which began some 230 million years ago. Periods of the Mesozoic (from oldest to youngest) are: *Triassic; Jurassic,* which began about 180 million years ago; and *Cretaceous,* which began about 135 million years ago. The following *Cenozoic* era, the "Age of Mammals," was the time of evolution and radiation of major modern groups. The Cenozoic is divided into two periods, *Tertiary* (beginning about 63 million years ago and continuing until two million years ago) and *Quaternary* (two million years ago to present). Subdivisions of the Tertiary (termed epochs) are (oldest to youngest): *Paleocene; Eocene,* which began about 58 million years ago; *Oligocene,* which began about 36 million years ago; *Miocene,* which began about

25 million years ago; and *Pliocene*, which began about 12 million years ago. The Quarternary has only two epochs, *Pleistocene* (two million years ago to 10,000 years ago) and *Holocene* or *Recent* (10,000 years before the present until now).

gestation period. Period of embryonic development during which developing zygote is in uterus; period between fertilization and parturition.

gram (g). Unit of weight in metric system; there are about 28.3 grams in an ounce (or 454 g per pound).

granivorous. Subsisting on diet of grains, seeds from cereal grasses.

gravid. Pregnant.

greatest length of skull. Measurement encompassing overall length of skull, including teeth that may project anterior to premaxilla; frequently recorded instead of condylobasal length in some kinds of mammals.

guano. Excrement of bats or birds; sometimes sold commercially as fertilizer.

guard hairs. Outer coat of coarse protective hairs found in most mammals.

hallux. First (most medial) digit of hind foot (pes).

hamular process. Hooklike projection, such as hamular process of pterygoid bone.

hardpan. A cemented, or compacted, and often clayey layer in soil.

hectare. Unit of land area in metric system equal to 10,000 square meters or 2.47 acres.

heifer. A bovid that has not produced a calf and is less than three years old.

herbivore. Animal that consumes plant material as primary component of diet.

helminth. Generalized term for any member of invertebrate phylum Platyhelminthes, such as tapeworms and flukes.

hibernaculum. Shelter in which animal hibernates.

hibernation. Torpidity (dormancy) in winter.

home range. Area in which an animal lives, contains all necessities of life; generally is not entirely defended and, therefore, can overlap with those of other individuals.

horn. Structure projecting from head of mammal and generally used for offense, defense, or social interaction; members of family Bovidae have horns formed by permanent hollow keratin sheaths growing over bony cores (see also pronghorn).

humerus. Single bone in upper (proximal) portion of each front (pectoral) limb.

hypsodont. Pertaining to a particularly high crowned tooth; such teeth have shallow roots.

imbricate. Overlapping, as shingles of a roof.

implantation. Process by which blastocyst (embryo) embeds in uterine lining.

incisive foramen. See figure 140.

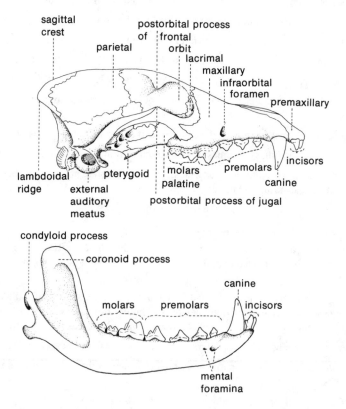

Figure 139. Lateral views of skull and lower jaw of a coyote, showing cranial and mandibular features (after Bekoff 1977).

incisor. One of four basic kinds of teeth in mammals, usually chisel-shaped; anteriormost of teeth; always rooted in premaxilla in upper jaw. (see figs. 138–139).

infraorbital canal. Canal through zygomatic process of maxilla, from anterior wall of orbit to side of rostrum (see fig. 139).

infraorbital foramen. Foramen through zygomatic process of maxilla (see fig. 139 and above).

inguinal. Pertaining to region of groin.

insectivorous. Preying on insects.

interfemoral membrane. See uropatagium.

intermontane. Situated between mountains.

interorbital. Referring to region of skull between eye sockets.

interparietal. Unpaired bone on dorsal part of braincase between parietals and just anterior to supraoccipital (see fig. 140).

interspecific. Between or among species (interspecific competition, for example).

intraspecific. Within a species (intraspecific variation, for example).

irruption. A sudden entry, as in irruption of teeth; also a sudden sharp increase in relative numbers of a natural population.

jugal bone. Bone connecting maxillary and squamosal bones to form midpart of zygomatic arch (see fig. 140).

juvenile pelage. Pelage characteristic of juvenile (young) mammals.

karyotype. Morphological description of chromosomes of cell, including size, shape, position of centromere, and number.

keel. Ridge that provides expanded surface for attachment.

keratin. Tough, fibrous protein especially abundant in epidermis and epidermal derivatives.

kilogram (kg). Unit of weight in metric system (frequently shortened to "kilo") equal to 1,000 grams or 2.2 pounds.

kilometer (km). Unit of linear measure in metric system equal to 1,000 meters, slightly more than six-tenths of a mile.

labial. Pertaining to lips; for example, labial side of a tooth is side nearer lips (as opposed to lingual side, which is nearer tongue).

lactating. Secreting milk.

lacrimal ridge. Ridge on lacrimal bone (see fig. 140).

lateral. Located away from midline; at or near sides.

lingual. Pertaining to tongue; lingual side of a tooth is side nearer tongue.

live trap. Any one of several kinds of traps designed to catch mammals alive.

loph. Ridge on occlusal surface of tooth formed by elongation and fusion of cusps.

malar process. Projection of maxillary that makes contact with jugal bone and forms base of zygomatic arch.

mammae. Milk producing glands unique to mammals; growth and activity governed by hormones of ovary, uterus, and pituitary; present in both sexes but degenerate in males.

mandible. Lower jaw; in mammals composed of single pair of bones, the dentaries.

marsupium. External pouch formed by fold of skin in abdominal wall and supported by epipubic bones; found in most marsupials and some monotremes; encloses mammary glands and serves as incubation chamber.

masticate. To chew.

mastoid. Bone bounded by squamosal, exoccipital, and tympanic bones.

mastoid process. Exposed portion of petromastoid bone; situated anterior or lateral to auditory bulla (evident but not labeled in ventral view, fig. 140).

maturational molt. Molt from juvenile or subadult pelage.

maxilla. Either of pair of relatively large bones that form major portion of side and ventral part of rostrum; contribute to hard palate, form anterior root of zygomatic arch, and bear all upper teeth except incisors; also termed maxillary (see figs. 139–140).

maxillary toothrow. That part of toothrow in cranium of a mammal seated in maxilla; length includes all postincisor teeth and generally is taken parallel to long axis of skull (measurement shown in fig. 138 is of total upper toothrow).

maxillovomerine notch. Notch on ventral surface of skull, between incisive foramina, separating nasal septum from anterior spine of bony palate.

medial. Pertaining to middle, as of a bone or other structure.

melanism. Unusual darkening of coloration owing to deposition of abnormally large amounts of melanins in integument (skin).

mesic. Area or habitat characterized by moderate amount of moisture—the environmental condition between xeric and hydric.

mesopterygoid fossa. Space between pterygoid bones on ventral surface of skull.

Mesozoic. See geologic time.

metabolic water. Water formed biochemically as end product of carbohydrate metabolism in body of animal.

metacarpals. Bones of the hand except digits.

metatarsals. Bones of the foot except digits.

meter (m). Unit of linear measure in metric system equal to 100 centimeters or 39.37 inches.

milk dentition. See deciduous dentition.

millimeter (mm). Unit of linear measure in metric system; 25.4 mm equal one inch.

Miocene. See geologic time.

mist net. Net of fine mesh used to capture birds and bats; usually two meters high and ranging from six to 30 meters wide.

molar. One of four basic kinds of mammalian teeth; any cheektooth situated posterior to premolars and having no deciduous precursor; normally not exceeding three per quadrant, four in some marsupials (see figs. 138–139).

molariform. Pertaining to teeth the form of which is molarlike.

molt. Process by which hair is shed and replaced.

monestrous. Having a single estrous cycle per year.

monotypic. Pertaining to taxon that contains only one immediately subordinate taxon; for example, genus that contains only one species.

montane. Mountainous.

musk gland. One of several kinds of glands in mammals with secretions that have a musky odor.

muzzle. Projecting snout.

nail. Flat, keratinized, translucent, epidermal growth protecting upper portion of tips of digits in some mammals; a modified claw.

nape. Back of neck.

nares. Openings of nose.

nasal septum. Thin sheet of bone, sometimes flared anteriorly, separating paired nasal cavities (also separating the incisive foramina—see fig. 140).

natal. Pertaining to birth.

nematode. Any member of invertebrate class Nematoda (roundworms).

neonate. Newborn.

nictitating membrane. Thin membrane at inner angle of eye in some species, which can be drawn over surface of eyeball; a "third" eyelid.

nocturnal. Pertaining to night (hours without daylight); active by night.

nomadic. Wandering.

occipital bone. Bone surrounding foramen magnum and bearing occipital condyles (see occiput on fig. 140); formed from four embryonic elements, a ventral basioccipital, a dorsal supraoccipital, and two lateral exoccipitals.

occiput. General term for posterior portion of skull (see fig. 140).

occlusal. Pertaining to contact surfaces of upper (cranial) and lower (mandibular) teeth.

ochraceous. Color of ocher, generally yellowish brown.

Oligocene. See geologic time.

omnivore. Animal that eats both animal and vegetable food.

orbit. Bony socket in skull in which eyeball is situated (see fig. 139).

ordinal name. Name applying to an order of organisms.

os clitoridis. Small sesamoid bone present in clitoris of females of some mammalian species; homologous to baculum in males.

ossicles. Bones (incus, malleus, and stapes) of the mammalian middle ear.

ossify. To become bony or hardened and bonelike.

palate. Bony plate formed by palatine bones and palatal branches of maxillae and premaxillae (see fig. 140).

Paleocene. See geologic time.

palmate. Pertaining to presence of webbing between digits or to flattening of tines of antler.

papilla. Any blunt, rounded, or nipple-shaped projection.

parapatric. Pertaining to two or more populations that occupy locally contiguous geographic areas, in which they are ecologically isolated.

parietal. Either of pair of bones contributing to roof of cranium posterior to frontals and anterior to occipital (see figs. 139–140).

parturition. Process by which fetus of mammals separates from uterine wall of mother and is born; birth.

patagium. Web of skin; in bats, the wing membrane.

patronym. Scientific name based on name of a person or persons.

pectoral. Pertaining to chest.

pectoral girdle. Shoulder girdle, composed in most mammals of clavicle and scapula or scapula alone.

pelage. Collectively, all the hairs on a mammal.

pelvic girdle. Hip girdle, composed of ischium, ilium, and pubis.

penicillate. Ending in tuft of fine hairs.

phalangeal epiphyses. Growth centers just proximal to articular surfaces of phalanges; fusion of epiphyses to shafts of phalanges used as a means of determining age in bats.

phalanges. Bones of fingers and toes, distal to metacarpals and metatarsals.

pigment. Minute granules that impart color to an organism; such granules are usually metabolic wastes and may be shades of black, brown, red, or yellow.

pinna. Externally projecting part of ear.

placenta. Composite structure formed by maternal and fetal tissues across which gases, nutrients, and wastes are exchanged.

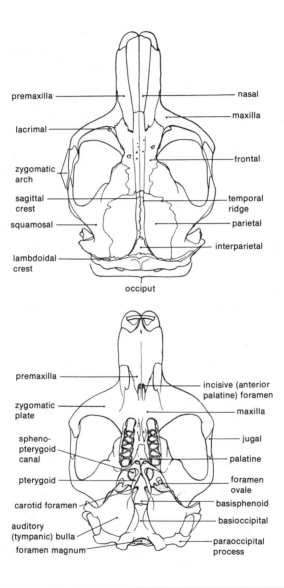

premaxilla

nasal

maxilla

lacrimal

frontal

zygomatic
arch

sagittal
crest

temporal
ridge

squamosal

parietal

interparietal

lambdoidal
crest

occiput

premaxilla

incisive (anterior
palatine) foramen

zygomatic
plate

maxilla

spheno-
pterygoid
canal

jugal

palatine

pterygoid

foramen
ovale

carotid foramen

basisphenoid

auditory
(tympanic) bulla

basioccipital

foramen magnum

paraoccipital
process

Figure 140. Dorsal and ventral views of skull of a pocket gopher (*Thomomys*), showing cranial features (after Hall 1955).

placental mammals. Collectively, all mammalian groups of which a true placenta is characteristic (includes all orders treated in this book except Marsupialia).

placental scar. Scar that remains on uterine wall after deciduate placenta detaches at parturition.

plantar pad (tubercle). Cutaneous pad or tubercle on sole of foot.

plantigrade. Foot structure in which phalanges and metatarsals or metacarpals touch ground; basic structure for ambulatory (walking) locomotion.

Pleistocene. See geologic time.

Pliocene. See geologic time.

pollex. Thumb; first (most medial) digit on hand (manus).

polyestrous. Having more than one estrous cycle each year.

polygynous. Male mating with several females.

postauricular. Pertaining to behind the ear.

posterior. Pertaining to or toward rear end.

postorbital process. Projection of frontal bone that marks posterior margin of orbit (see figs. 138–139).

postpartum estrus. Ability of female to become receptive to male directly after giving birth.

precocial. Pertaining to young that are born at relatively advanced stage, capable of moving about shortly after birth and usually able to do some feeding without parental assistance.

prehensile. Adapted for grasping by curling or wrapping around.

premaxilla. One of paired bones at anterior end of rostrum (see figs. 139–140); also termed premaxillary.

premolar. One of four basic kinds of teeth in mammals; situated anterior to molars and posterior to canines; only cheekteeth usually present in both permanent and milk dentitions; normally not exceeding four per quadrant, three in marsupials (see figs. 138–139).

primitive. Of, relating to, or characteristic of ancestral type or condition.

progeny. Offspring.

pronghorn. Modified horn (in both sexes of Antilocapridae) that grows over permanent bony cores and is shed annually; each is slightly curved, with one anterolateral prong in males and some females.

protist. Any member of kingdom Protista, which includes single-celled organisms such as protozoans.

proximal. Situated toward or near a point of reference or attachment (as opposed to distal).

pterygoid. Either of paired bones in ventral wall of braincase, posterior to palatines (see fig. 140).

pubic symphysis. Midventral plane of contact between two halves of pelvic girdle.

quadrupedal. Pertaining to use of all four limbs for locomotion.

race. Informal term for subspecies (which see).

radius. Medial of two bones in lower part of front (pectoral) limb.

ramus. Horizontal portion of dentary, that part in which teeth are rooted.

range. Geographic area inhabited by a particular taxon.

raptor. Bird of prey, such as hawk or owl.

Recent. See geologic time.

recurved. Curved downward and backward.

reentrant angle. Inward infolding of enamel layer on side, front, or back of cheektooth.

refugium. Geographic area to which species retreats in time of stress, such as glacial episode.

relict population. A population isolated from the main range of a species and indicative of a once broader (or different) distribution of that species.

retractile. Capable of being drawn back or in (as retractile claws of felids).

riparian. Referring to floodplains or valleys of watercourses.

root. Portion of tooth that lies below gum line and fills alveolus.

rooted tooth. Tooth with definitive growth; not evergrowing.

rootless tooth. Tooth that is ever growing, having continuously open root canal.

rostrum. Facial region of skull anterior to plane drawn through anterior margin of orbits (see fig. 138).

rugose. Wrinkled.

rumen. First "stomach" of ruminant mammals; modification of esophagus.

ruminant. Any of the Artiodactyla (including all those occurring in the plains states) that possess a rumen; cud chewing.

runway. Worn or otherwise detectable pathway caused by repeated usage.

rutting season. Season of sexual activity when mating occurs; particularly applied to deer and other artiodactyls.

sagittal crest. Medial dorsal ridge on braincase, often formed by coalescence of temporal ridges (see fig. 140).

saltatory. Adapted for leaping; usually with elongate and unusually well-developed hind legs.

saxicolous. Living among rocks.

scansorial. Pertaining to arboreal animals that climb by means of sharp, curved claws.

scapula. Shoulder blade.

scent glands. Sweat or sebaceous glands, or combination of these two, modified for production of odoriferous secretions.

scrotum. Pouch of skin in which testes are contained outside the abdominal cavity; permanently present in some species, seasonally present in some, and lacking in others.

scute. Thin plate or scale.

sebaceous glands. Epidermal glands that secrete fatty substance and usually open into hair follicle.

septum. A dividing wall, such as one formed by membrane or thin bone.

sexual dimorphism. Difference in sexual features or other features such as size between males and females of species.

snap trap. Kill trap that usually consists of wooden base, with wire bail, spring, and trigger mechanism; designed primarily to catch rodents and insectivores.

snout. Nose, muzzle.

species. Group of naturally or potentially interbreeding populations reproductively isolated (or mostly so) from other such groups.

squamosal. Either of pair of bones contributing to side of cranium (see fig. 140), and forming posterior part of zygomatic arch.

subspecies. Relatively uniform and genetically distinctive population of a species that represents a separately or recently evolved lineage, with its own evolutionary tendencies, definite geographic range, and actual or potential zone of intergradation (interbreeding) with another such group or groups.

superciliary. Pertaining to eyebrow.

supraorbital process. Projection of frontal bone on superior rim of orbit, as in hares and rabbits.

sweat gland. Tubular epidermal gland that extends into dermis and secretes sweat or perspiration and also various scents.

sympatric. Pertaining to two or more populations that occupy overlapping geographic areas.

symphysis. Relatively immovable articulation between bones.

tarsal. Any one of group of bones in ankle region, distal to fibula and proximal to metatarsals.

taxon. Any group (in this case, of mammals) distinctive from other groups at same taxonomic level.

teat. Protruberance of mammary gland in which numerous small ducts empty into common collecting structure that in turn opens to exterior through one or a few pores.

temporal ridges. Pair of ridges atop braincase of many mammals; usually originating on frontal bones near postorbital processes and converging posteriorly to form middorsal sagittal crest (see fig. 140).

territory. Portion of home range that individual defends against members of same (and sometimes different) species.

tibia. Larger of two bones in lower part of hind (pelvic) limb.

tine. Spike on an antler.

torpor. Dormancy; body temperature approximates that of surroundings; rate of respiration and heartbeat ordinarily much slower than in active animal.

tragus. Fleshy projection from lower medial margin of ear of most microchiropteran bats.

trematode. Any member of invertebrate class Trematoda (flukes).

tricolored. Having three colors.

trifid. Divided into three more-or-less equal lobes.

trifurcate. Having three branches.

tubercle. See plantar pad; also any prominence, such as on the crown of a tooth.

tularemia. Bacterial disease contracted by man through bite of tick harbored principally by hares and rabbits, but also by rodents and birds; also may be transmitted by direct contact with infected animal.

tympanic bulla. See auditory bulla and figure 140.

tympanum. Eardrum; thin membranous structure that receives external vibrations from air and transmits them to middle ear ossicles.

type specimen. Specimen (holotype) on which a species or subspecies name is based.

ulna. Outermost of two bones in lower part of front (pectoral) limb.

underfur. Short hairs of mammal that serve primarily as insulation.

ungulate. Hoofed mammals of extant orders Perissodactyla (horses, rhinos, tapirs) and Artiodactyla; term has no formal taxonomic status, but refers to a broad group of herbivorous mammals.

unguligrade. Foot structure in which only the unguis (hoof) is in contact with ground.

unicuspid. Single-cusped tooth in shrews posterior to large, anteriormost tooth (an incisor), and anterior to fourth premolar in upper jaw and first true molar in lower jaw.

uropatagium. Web of skin between hind legs of bats, frequently enclosing tail; interfemoral membrane.

valvular. Capable of being closed, like a valve.

venter. Under or lower surface.

ventral. Pertaining to under or lower surface (venter).

vernacular name. Common (as opposed to scientific) name.

vernal. Pertaining to the season spring.

vibrissae. Long, stiff hairs that serve primarily as tactile receptors.

volant. Able to fly.

vomer. Unpaired bone that forms septum between nasal passages.

vulva. External genitalia of female.

warble. Larval stage of bot fly, which develops in subcutaneous tissue of mammals from egg laid in wound or lesion by female fly.

wool. Underhair with angora growth, serves primarily for insulation.

xeric. Area or habitat characterized as being dry or deficient in moisture.

zygomatic arch. Arch of bone enclosing orbit and temporal fossa formed by jugal bone and parts of maxilla (malar process) and squamosal (see fig. 140).

zygomatic breadth. See figure 8.

zygomatic plate. Bony plate, part of zygomatic process of maxilla, forming anterior face of zygomatic arch (see fig. 140).

Literature Cited

Alcoze, T. M., and E. G. Zimmerman. 1973. Food habits and dietary overlap of two heteromyid rodents from the Mesquite Plains of Texas. J. Mamm., 54:900–908.

Aldous, C. M. 1937. Notes on the life history of the snowshoe hare. J. Mamm., 18:46–57.

Allen, D. L. 1943. Michigan fox squirrel management. Game Div. Publ., Michigan Dept. Conserv., 100:1–404.

Allen, J. A. 1877. History of the American bison, *Bison americanus*. Ann. Rept. U.S. Geol. Geogr. Surv. Territories, 9:443–587.

Allen, S. H. 1984. Some aspects of reproductive performance in female red fox in North Dakota. J. Mamm., 65:246–255.

Andersen, D. C. 1978. Observations on reproduction, growth, and behavior of the northern pocket gopher (*Thomomys talpoides*). J. Mamm., 59:418–422.

Anderson, A. E. 1983. A critical review of literature on puma (*Felis concolor*). Spec. Rept. Colorado Div. Wildlife, 54:1–91.

Anderson, A. E., and O. C. Wallmo. 1984. Odocoileus hemionus. Mamm. Species, 219:1–9.

Armstrong, D. M. 1972. Distribution of mammals in Colorado. Monogr. Mus. Nat. Hist., Univ. Kansas, 3:x + 1–415.

———. 1975. Rocky Mountain mammals. Rocky Mountain Nature Assoc., Estes Park, viii + 174 pp.

———. 1982. Mammals of the Canyon Country. Canyonlands Nat. Hist. Assoc., Moab, Utah, 273 pp.

Armstrong, D. M., and J. K. Jones, Jr. 1971. Sorex merriami. Mamm. Species, 2:1–2.

———. 1972. Notiosorex crawfordi. Mamm. Species, 17:1–5.

Baar, S. L., and E. D. Fleharty. 1976. A model of the daily energy budget and energy flow through a population of the white-footed mouse. Acta Theriol., 12:179–193.

Bailey, E. P. 1974. Notes on the development, mating behavior, and vocalization of captive ringtails. Southwestern Nat., 19:117–119.

Bailey, V. 1927. A biological survey of North Dakota. N. Amer. Fauna, 49:vi + 1–226.

Baird, D. D., R. M. Timm, and G. E. Nordquist. 1983. Reproduction in the arctic shrew, *Sorex arcticus*. J. Mamm., 64:298–301.

Baker, R. H. 1983. Michigan mammals. Michigan State Univ. Press, East Lansing, xx + 642 pp.

Banfield, A. W. F. 1962. A revision of the reindeer and caribou, genus *Rangifer*. Bull. Nat. Mus. Canada, 177:vi + 1–137.

———. 1974. The mammals of Canada. Univ. Toronto Press, xxv + 438 pp.

Barbour, R. W., and W. H. Davis. 1969. Bats of America. Univ. Press Kentucky, Lexington, 286 pp.

Bear, G. H., and R. M. Hansen. 1966. Food habits, growth and reproduction of white-tailed jackrabbits in southern Colorado. Tech. Bull. Agric. Exper. Sta., Colorado State Univ., 90:viii + 1–59.

Beck, W. H. 1958. A guide to Saskatchewan mammals. Spec. Publ. Saskatchewan Nat. Hist. Soc., 1:1–52.

Bédard, J. (ed.). 1975. Alces moose ecology. Les presses de l'Université Laval, Canada, (8) + 741 pp.

Bee, J. W., G. E. Glass, R. S. Hoffmann, and R. R. Patterson. 1981. Mammals in Kansas. Pub. Ed. Ser., Mus. Nat. Hist., Univ. Kansas, 7:ix + 1–300.

Beer, J. R. 1961. Hibernation in *Perognathus flavenscens*. J. Mamm., 42:103.

Bekoff, M. 1977. Canis latrans. Mamm. Species, 79:1–9.

Bergerud, A. T. 1978. Caribou. Pp. 83–101, *in* Big Game of North America (J. L. Schmidt and D. L. Gilbert, eds.), Stackpole Books, Harrisburg, Pennsylvania, xv + 494 pp.

Birney, E. C. 1973. Systematics of three species of woodrats (genus *Neotoma*) in central North America. Misc. Publ. Mus. Nat. Hist., Univ. Kansas, 58:1–173.

Birney, E. C., J. K. Jones, Jr., and D. M. Mortimer. 1971. The yellow-faced pocket gopher, Pappogeomys castanops, in Kansas. Trans. Kansas Acad. Sci., 73:368–375.

Blair, W. F. 1937. Burrows and food of the prairie pocket mouse. J. Mamm., 18:188–191.

———. 1939. Faunal relationships and geographic distribution of mammals in Oklahoma. Amer. Midland Nat., 22:85–133.

Bogan, M. A., and P. Mehlhop. 1983. Systematic relationships of gray wolves (*Canis lupus*) in southwestern North America. Occas. Papers Mus. Southwestern Biol., Univ. New Mexico, 1:1–21.

Bohlin, R. G., and E. G. Zimmerman. 1982. Genic differentiation of two chromosomal races of the *Geomys bursarius* complex. J. Mamm., 63:218–228.

Bowles, J. B. 1975. Distribution and biogeography of mammals of Iowa. Spec. Publ. Mus., Texas Tech Univ., 9:1–184.

Brand, C. J., L. B. Keith, and C. A. Fischer. 1976. Lynx responses to changing snowshoe hare densities in central Alberta. J. Wildlife Manag., 40:416–428.

Brown, L. N. 1967. Seasonal activity patterns and breeding of the western jumping mouse (Zapus princeps) in Wyoming. Amer. Midland Nat., 78:460–470.

———. 1969. Reproductive characteristics of the Mexican woodrat at the northern limit of its range in Colorado. J. Mamm., 50:536–541.

Cameron, G. N., and S. R. Spencer. 1981. Sigmodon hispidus. Mamm. Species, 158:1–9.

Carleton, W. M. 1966. Food habits of two sympatric Colorado sciurids. J. Mamm., 47:91–103.

Carley, C. J. 1979. Status summary: the red wolf (*Canis rufus*). U.S. Fish Wildlife Serv. Endangered Species Rept., 7:iv + 1–36.

Carroll, L. E., and H. H. Genoways. 1980. Lagurus curtatus. Mamm. Species, 124:1–6.

Chapman, B. R. 1972. Food habits of Loring's kangaroo rat, *Dipodomys elator*. J. Mamm., 53:877–880.

Chapman, J. A. 1975. Sylvilagus nuttallii. Mamm. Species, 56:1–3.

Chapman, J. A., and G. A. Feldhamer. 1981. Sylvilagus aquaticus. Mamm. Species, 151:1–4.

Chapman, J. A., J. G. Hockman, and W. R. Edwards. 1982. Cottontails. Pp. 83–123, *in* Wild mammals of North America: biology, management, and economics (J. A. Chapman and G. A. Feldhamer, eds.), Johns Hopkins Univ. Press, Baltimore, xiii + 1147 pp.

Chapman, J. A., J. G. Hockman, and M. M. Ojeda C. 1980. Sylvilagus floridanus. Mamm. Species, 136:1–8.

Chapman, J. A., and G. R. Willner. 1978. Sylvilagus audubonii. Mamm. Species, 106:1–4.

Choate, J. R., E. K. Boggess, and F. R. Henderson. 1982. History and status of the black-footed ferret in Kansas. Trans. Kansas Acad. Sci., 85:121–132.

Choate, J. R., M. D. Engstrom, and R. B. Wilhelm. 1979. Historical biogeography of the least weasel in Kansas. Trans. Kansas Acad. Sci., 82:231–234.

Choate, J. R., E. D. Fleharty, and R. J. Little. 1974. Status of the spotted skunk, *Spilogale putorius,* in Kansas. Trans. Kansas Acad. Sci., 76:226–233.

Choate, J. R., and J. K. Jones, Jr. 1982. Provisional checklist of South Dakota mammals. Prairie Nat., 13:65–77.

Choate, J. R., and J. E. Krause. 1976. Historical biogeography of the gray fox (*Urocyon cinereoargenteus*) in Kansas. Trans. Kansas Acad. Sci., 77:231–235.

Choate, J. R., and S. L. Williams. 1978. Biogeographic interpretation of variation within and among populations of the prairie vole, Microtus ochrogaster. Occas. Papers Mus., Texas Tech Univ., 49:1–25.

Cinq-Mars, R. J., and L. N. Brown. 1969. Reproduction and ecological distribution of the rockmouse, Peromyscus difficilis, in northern Colorado. Amer. Midland Nat., 81:205–217.

Clark, T. W. 1971. Ecology of the western jumping mouse in Grand Teton National Park, Wyoming. Northwest Sci., 45:229–238.

Cockrum, E. L. 1952. Mammals of Kansas. Univ. Kansas Publ., Mus. Nat. Hist., 7:1–303.

Conaway, C. H. 1952. Life history of the water shrew (Sorex palustris navigator). Amer. Midland Nat., 48:219–248.

Conley, W. 1976. Competition between *Microtus:* a behavioral hypothesis. Ecology, 57:224–237.

Connor, P. F. 1959. The bog lemming Synaptomys cooperi in southern New Jersey. Publ. Mus. Michigan State Univ., Biol. Ser., 1:161–248.

Costello, D. F. 1966. The world of the porcupine. J. R. Lippincott Co., Philadelphia, 157 pp.

Cowan, I. M. 1940. Distribution and variation in the native sheep of North America. Amer. Midland Nat., 24:505–580.

Cowan, I. M., and W. McCrory. 1970. Variation in the mountain goat, *Oreamnos americanus* (Blainville). J. Mamm., 51:60–73.

Craighead, J. J., and J. A. Mitchell. 1982. Grizzly bear. Pp. 515–556, *in* Wild mammals of North America: biology, management, and economics (J. A. Chapman and G. A. Feldhamer, eds.), Johns Hopkins Univ. Press, Baltimore, xiii + 1147 pp.

Cranford, J. A. 1978. Hibernation in the western jumping mouse (*Zapus princeps*). J. Mamm., 59:496–509.

Currier, M. J. P. 1983. Felis concolor. Mamm. Species, 200:1–7.

Czaplewski, N. J. 1976. Vertebrate remains in great horned owl pellets in Nebraska. Nebraska Bird Rev., 44:12–15.

Dalquest, W. W., and G. Collier. 1964. Notes on Dipodomys elator, a rare kangaroo rat. Southwestern Nat., 9:146–150.

Dapson, R. W. 1968. Reproduction and age structure in a population of short-tailed shrews, *Blarina brevicauda*. J. Mamm., 49:205–214.

Davis, W. B. 1940. Distribution and variation of pocket gophers (genus *Geomys*) in the southwestern United States. Bull. Texas Agric. Exper. Sta., 590:4–38.

———. 1974. The mammals of Texas. Bull. Texas Parks and Wildlife Dept., 41:1–294.

de Vos, A., and D. I. Gillespie. 1960. A study of woodchucks on an Ontario farm. Canadian Field-Nat., 74:130–145.

Diersing, V. E. 1980. Systematics and evolution of the pygmy shrews (subgenus *Microsorex*) of North America. J. Mamm., 61:76–101.

Diersing, V. E., and D. F. Hoffmeister. 1977. Revision of the shrews *Sorex merriami* and a description of a new species of the subgenus *Sorex*. J. Mamm., 58:321–333.

Dolan, P. G., and D. C. Carter. 1977. Glaucomys volans. Mamm. Species, 78:1–6.

Downhower, J. F., and E. R. Hall. 1966. The pocket gopher in Kansas. Misc. Publ. Mus. Nat. Hist., Univ. Kansas, 44:1–32.

Dunaway, P. B. 1968. Life history and populational aspects of the eastern harvest mouse. Amer. Midland Nat., 79:48–67.

Easterla, D. A. 1973. Ecology of the 18 species of Chiroptera at Big Bend National Park, Texas. Northwest Missouri St. Univ. Stud., 34(2–3):1–165.

Escherich, P. C. 1981. Social biology of the bushy-tailed woodrat, *Neotoma cinerea*. Univ. California Publ. Zool., 110:xiv + 1–132.

Egoscue, H. J. 1979. Vulpes velox. Mamm. Species, 122:1–5.

Engstrom, M. D., and J. R. Choate. 1979. Systematics of the northern grasshopper mouse (*Onychomys leucogaster*) on the Central Great Plains. J. Mamm., 60:723–739.

Fenneman, N. M. 1931. Physiography of western United States. McGraw-Hill Book Co., New York, xiii + 534 pp.

————. 1938. Physiography of eastern United States. McGraw-Hill Book Co., New York, xiii + 691 pp.

Fenton, M. B., and R. M. R. Barclay. 1980. Myotis lucifugus. Mamm. Species, 142:1–8.

Findley, J. S., A. H. Harris, D. E. Wilson, and C. Jones. 1975. Mammals of New Mexico. Univ. New Mexico Press, Albuquerque, xxii + 360 pp.

Findley, J. S., and G. L. Traut. 1970. Geographic variation in *Pipistrellus hesperus*. J. Mamm., 51:741–765.

Finley, R. B., Jr. 1958. The wood rats of Colorado: distribution and ecology. Univ. Kansas Publ., Mus. Nat. Hist., 10:213–552.

————. 1969. Cone caches and middens of Tamiasciurus in the Rocky Mountain Region. Misc. Publ. Mus. Nat. Hist., Univ. Kansas, 51:233–273.

Fitch, J. H., and K. A. Shump, Jr. 1979. Myotis keenii. Mamm. Species, 121:1–3.

Fitch, J. H., K. A. Shump, Jr., and A. U. Shump. 1981. Myotis velifer. Mamm. Species, 149:1–5.

Fleharty, E. D., and L. E. Olson. 1969. Summer food habits of *Microtus ochrogaster* and *Sigmodon hispidus*. J. Mamm., 50:475–486.

Forbes, R. B. 1964. Some aspects of the life history of the silky pocket mouse, Perognathus flavus. Amer. Midland Nat., 72:438–443.

————. 1966. Studies of the biology of Minnesotan chipmunks. Amer. Midland Nat., 76:290–308.

Franzmann, A. W. 1981. Alces alces. Mamm. Species, 154:1–7.

Frase, B. A., and R. S. Hoffmann. 1980. Marmota flaviventris. Mamm. Species, 135:1–8.

Fritzell, E. K., and K. J. Haroldson. 1982. Urocyon cinereoargenteus. Mamm. Species, 189:1–8.

Fujita, M. S., and T. H. Kunz. 1984. Pipistrellus subflavus. Mamm. Species, 228:1–6.

Gaines, M. S., and R. K. Rose. 1976. Population dynamics of *Microtus ochrogaster* in eastern Kansas. Ecology, 57:1145–1161.

Gardner, A. L. 1973. The systematics of the genus Didelphis (Marsupialia: Didelphidae) in North and Middle America. Spec. Publ. Mus., Texas Tech Univ., 4:1–81.

————. 1982. Virginia opossum. Pp. 3–36, *in* Wild mammals of North America: biology, management, and economics (J. A. Chapman and G. A. Feldhamer, eds.), Johns Hopkins Univ. Press, Baltimore, xiii + 1147 pp.

Geist, V. 1971. Mountain sheep. Univ. Chicago Press, xv + 383 pp.

George, S. B., J. R. Choate, and H. H. Genoways. 1981. Distribution and taxonomic status of *Blarina hylophaga* Elliot (Insectivora: Soricidae). Ann. Carnegie Mus., 50:493–513.

George, S. B., H. H. Genoways, J. R. Choate, and R. J. Baker. 1982. Karyotypic relationships within the short-tailed shrews, genus *Blarina*, J. Mamm., 63:639–645.

Gettinger, R. D. 1975. Metabolism and thermoregulation of a fossorial rodent, the northern pocket gopher (*Thomomys talpoides*). Physiol. Zool. 48:311–322.

Glass, B. P. 1947. Geographic variation in Perognathus hispidus. J. Mamm., 28:174–179.

Glass, B. P., and R. C. Morse. 1959. A new pipistrelle from Oklahoma and Texas. J. Mamm., 40:531–534.

Glass, B. P., and C. M. Ward. 1959. Bats of the genus *Myotis* from Oklahoma. J. Mamm., 40:194–201.

Goertz, J. W. 1963. Some biological notes on the plains harvest mouse. Proc. Oklahoma Acad. Sci., 43:123–125.

Grizzell, R. A. 1955. A study of the southern woodchuck, Marmota monax monax. Amer. Midland Nat., 53:257–293.

Gunderson, H. L. 1978. A mid-continent irruption of Canada lynx, 1962–63. Prairie Nat., 10:71–80.

Haberman, C. G., and E. D. Fleharty. 1972. Natural history notes on Franklin's ground squirrel in Boone County, Nebraska. Trans. Kansas Acad. Sci., 74:76–80.

Hall, E. R. 1951. American weasels. Univ. Kansas Publ., Mus. Nat. Hist., 4:1–466.

————. 1955. Handbook of mammals of Kansas. Misc. Publ. Mus. Nat. Hist., Univ. Kansas, 7:1–303.

————. 1981. The mammals of North America. John Wiley and Sons, New York, 2d ed., 1:xv + 1–600 + *90* and 2:vi + 601–1181 + *90*.

Hamilton, W. J., Jr., and W. R. Eadie. 1964. Reproduction in the otter, *Lutra canadensis*. J. Mamm., 45:242–252.

Hamilton, W. J., Jr., and J. O. Whitaker, Jr. 1980. Mammals of the eastern United States. Comstock, Ithaca, New York, 2d ed., 346 pp.

Hansen, C. M., and E. D. Fleharty. 1974. Structural ecological parameters of a population of *Peromyscus maniculatus* in west-central Kansas. Southwestern Nat., 19:293–303.

Hansen, R. M., and J. T. Flinders. 1969. Food habits of North American hares. Sci. Ser. Range Sci. Dept., Colorado State Univ., 1:ii + 1–18.

Hansen, R. M., and A. L. Ward. 1966. Some relations of pocket gophers to rangelands on Grand Mesa, Colorado. Tech. Bull. Colorado Agric. Exper. Sta., 88:1–22.

Harris, A. H., and J. S. Findley. 1962. Status of *Myotis lucifugus phasma* and comments on variation in *Myotis yumanensis*. J. Mamm., 43:192–199.

Hart, E. B. 1978. Karyology and evolution of the plains pocket gopher, *Geomys bursarius*. Occas. Papers Mus. Nat. Hist., Univ. Kansas, 71:1–20.

Hayward, B. J. 1970. The natural history of the cave bat *Myotis velifer*. WRI-SCI, 1:(4) + 1–74.

Hayward, B. J., and S. P. Cross. 1979. The natural history of *Pipistrellus hesperus* (Chiroptera: Vespertilionidae). Publ. Office Res., Western New Mexico Univ., 3:(4) + 1–36.

Hazard, E. B. 1982. The mammals of Minnesota. Univ. Minnesota Press, Minneapolis, xii+ 280 pp.

Heaney, L. R., and R. M. Timm. 1983. Relationships of pocket gophers of the genus *Geomys* from the central and northern Great Plains. Misc. Publ. Mus. Nat. Hist., Univ. Kansas, 74:1–59.

Henderson, F. R. 1960. Beaver in Kansas. Misc. Publ. Mus. Nat. Hist., Univ. Kansas, 26:1–85.

Henderson, F. R., P. F. Springer, and R. Adrian. 1969. The black-footed ferret in South Dakota. Tech. Bull. South Dakota Dept. Game, Fish and Parks, 4:vi + 1–37.

Hendrickson, R. L. 1972. Variation in the plains pocket gopher (Geomys bursarius) along a transect across Kansas and eastern Colorado. Trans. Kansas Acad. Sci., 75:322–368.

Hermanson, J. W., and T. J. O'Shea. 1983. Antrozous pallidus. Mamm. Species, 213:1–8.

Hibbard, C. W. 1938. Distribution of the genus Reithrodontomys in Kansas. Univ. Kansas Sci. Bull., 25:173–179.

Hill, J. E., and C. W. Hibbard. 1943. Ecological differentiation between two harvest mice (Reithrodontomys) in western Kansas. J. Mamm., 24:22–25.

Hillman, C. N., and T. W. Clark. 1980. Mustela nigripes. Mamm. Species, 126:1–3.

Hoditschek, B., and T. L. Best. 1983. Reproductive biology of Ord's kangaroo rat (Dipodomys ordii) in Oklahoma. J. Mamm., 64:121–127.

Hoffmann, R. S., and J. G. Owen. 1980. Sorex tenellus and Sorex nanus. Mamm. Species, 131:1–4.

Hoffmann, R. S., and D. L. Pattie. 1968. A guide to Montana mammals . . . . Univ. Montana, Missoula, x + 133 pp.

Hoffmeister, D. F. 1981. Peromyscus truei. Mamm. Species, 161:1–5.

Honeycutt, R. L., and D. J. Schmidly. 1979. Chromosomal and morphological variation in the plains pocket gopher, Geomys bursarius, in Texas and adjacent states. Occas. Papers Mus., Texas Tech. Univ., 58:1–54.

Honeycutt, R. L., and S. L. Williams. 1982. Genic differentiation in pocket gophers of the genus Pappogeomys, with comments on intergeneric relationships in the subfamily Geomyinae. J. Mamm., 63:208–217.

Humphrey, S. R., and T. H. Kunz. 1976. Ecology of a Pleistocene relict, the western big-eared bat (Plecotus townsendii), in the Southern Great Plains. J. Mamm., 57:470–494.

Iverson, S. L., and B. N. Turner. 1972. Natural history of a Manitoba population of Franklin's ground squirrels. Canadian Field-Nat., 86:145–149.

Jackson, H. H. T. 1928. A taxonomic review of the American long-tailed shrews (genera Sorex and Microsorex). N. Amer. Fauna, 51:vi + 1–238.

_____. 1961. Mammals of Wisconsin. Univ. Wisconsin Press, Madison, xiii + 504 pp.

James, T. R., and R. W. Seabloom. 1969a. Reproductive biology of the white-tailed jack rabbit in North Dakota. J. Wildlife Manag., 33:558–568.

_____. 1969b. Aspects of growth in the white-tailed jackrabbit. Proc. North Dakota Acad. Sci., 23:7–14.

Jameson, E. W., Jr. 1947. Natural history of the prairie vole (mammalian genus Microtus). Univ. Kansas Publ., Mus. Nat. Hist., 1:125–151.

Jenkins, S. H., and P. E. Busher. 1979. Castor canadensis. Mamm. Species, 120:1–8.

Johnson, K. 1981. Social organization in a colony of rock squirrels (*Spermophilus variegatus,* Sciuridae). Southwestern Nat., 26:237–242.

Jones, C. 1977. Plecotus rafinesquii. Mamm. Species, 69:1–4.

Jones, C.; and J. Pagels. 1968. Notes on a population of *Pipistrellus subflavus* in southern Louisiana. J. Mamm., 49:134–139.

Jones, J. K., Jr. 1964. Distribution and taxonomy of mammals of Nebraska. Univ. Kansas Publ., Mus. Nat. Hist., 16:1–356.

Jones, J. K., Jr., D. M. Armstrong, R. S. Hoffmann, and C. Jones. 1983. Mammals of the Northern Great Plains. Univ. Nebraska Press, Lincoln, xii + 379 pp.

Jones, J. K., Jr., D. C. Carter, H. H. Genoways, R. S. Hoffmann, and D. W. Rice. 1982. Revised checklist of North American mammals north of Mexico, 1982. Occas. Papers Mus., Texas Tech Univ., 80:1–22.

Jones, J. K., Jr., and J. R. Choate. 1980. Annotated checklist of mammals of Nebraska. Prairie Nat., 12:43–53.

Jonkel, C. J., and R. P. Weckwerth. 1963. Sexual maturity and implantation of blastocysts in the wild pine marten. J. Wildlife Manag., 27:93–98.

Kaufman, D. W,, and E. D. Fleharty. 1974. Habitat selection by nine species of rodents in north-central Kansas. Southwestern Nat., 18:443–451.

Kaye, S. V. 1961. Laboratory life history of the eastern harvest mouse. Amer. Midland Nat., 66:439–451.

Keith, L. B., and L. A. Windberg. 1978. A demographic analysis of the snowshoe hare cycle. Wildlife Monogr., 58:1–70.

Kennedy, M. L., and G. D. Schnell. 1978. Geographic variation and sexual dimorphism in Ord's kangaroo rat, *Dipodomys ordii.* J. Mamm., 59:45–59.

Kennerly, T. E., Jr. 1964. Microenvironmental conditions of the pocket gopher burrow. Texas Jour. Sci., 16:395–441.

Kilpatrick, C. W., and W. Caire. 1973. First record of the encinal mouse, *Peromyscus pectoralis,* for Oklahoma, and additional records for north-central Texas. Southwestern Nat., 18:351.

King, C. M. 1983. Mustela erminea. Mamm. Species, 195:1–8.

King, J. A. 1955. Social behavior, social organization, and population dynamics of a black-tailed prairiedog town in the Black Hills of South Dakota. Contrib. Lab. Vert. Biol., Univ. Michigan, 67:1–123.

———— (ed.). 1968. Biology of Peromyscus (Rodentia). Spec. Publ., Amer. Soc. Mammal., 2:xiii + 1–593.

Knudsen, G. J., and J. B. Hale. 1968. Food habits of otters in the Great Lakes region. J. Wildlife Manag., 32:89–93.

Koeppl, J. W., and R. S. Hoffmann. 1981. Comparative postnatal growth of four ground squirrel species. J. Mamm., 62:41–57.

Koford, C. B. 1958. Prairie dogs, whitefaces, and blue grama. Wildlife Mongr., 3:1–78.

Krutzsch, P. H. 1954. North American jumping mice (genus Zapus). Univ. Kansas Publ., Mus. Nat. Hist., 7:349–472.

Kunz, T. H. 1973. Population studies of the cave bat (*Myotis velifer*): reproduction, growth, and development. Occas. Papers Mus. Nat. Hist., Univ. Kansas, 15:1–43.

———. 1974a. Reproduction, growth, and mortality of the vespertilionid bat, *Eptesicus fuscus,* in Kansas. J. Mamm., 55:1–13.

———. 1974b. Feeding ecology of a temperate insectivorous bat (*Myotis velifer*). Ecology, 55:693–711.

———. 1982. Lasionycteris noctivagans. Mamm. Species, 172:1–5.

Kunz, T. H., and R. A. Martin. 1982. Plecotus townsendii. Mamm. Species, 175:1–6.

Lampe, R. P. 1976. Aspects of the predatory strategy of the North American badger, *Taxidea taxus.* Unpublished Ph.D. dissertation, Univ. Minnesota, 106 pp.

LaVal, R. K. 1970. Intraspecific relationships of bats of the species *Myotis austroriparius.* J. Mamm., 51:542–552.

Layne, J. N. 1954. The biology of the red squirrel, *Tamiasciurus hudsonicus loquax* (Bangs) in central New York. Ecol. Monogr., 24:227–267.

———. 1959. Growth and development of the eastern harvest mouse, *Reithrodontomys humulis.* Bull. Florida State Mus., 4:61–82.

Leraas, H. J. 1938. Observations on growth and behavior of harvest mice. J. Mamm., 19:441–444.

Linzey, A. V. 1983. Synaptomys cooperi. Mamm. Species, 210:1–5.

Linzey, D. W., and R. L. Packard. 1977. Ochrotomys nuttalli. Mamm. Species, 75:1–6.

Long, C. A. 1965. The mammals of Wyoming. Univ. Kansas Publ., Mus. Nat. Hist., 14:493–758.

———. 1973. Taxidea taxus. Mamm. Species, 26:1–4.

———. 1974. Microsorex hoyi and Microsorex thompsoni. Mamm. Species, 33:1–4.

Longley, W. H. 1963. Minnesota gray and fox squirrels. Amer. Midland Nat., 69:82–98.

Lotze, J.-H., and S. Anderson. 1979. Procyon lotor. Mamm. Species, 119:1–8.

Lowery, G. H., Jr. 1974. The mammals of Louisiana and its adjacent waters. Louisiana State Univ. Press, Baton Rouge, xxii + 565 pp.

McBee, K., and R. J. Baker. 1982. Dasypus novemcinctus. Mamm. Species, 162:1–9.

McCarty, R. 1978. Onychomys leucogaster. Mamm. Species, 87:1–6.

McDonald, J. N. 1981. North American bison: their classification and evolution. Univ. California Press, Berkeley, 316 pp.

McManus, J. J. 1974. Didelphis virginiana. Mamm. Species, 40:1–6.

Mahan, C. J. 1980. Winter food habits of Nebraska bobcats (*Felis rufus*). Prairie Nat., 12:59–63.

Martin, C. O., and D. J. Schmidly. 1982. Taxonomic review of the pallid bat, Antrozous pallidus (Le Conte). Spec. Publ. Mus., Texas Tech Univ., 18:1–48.

Martin, R. E., and K. G. Matocha. 1972. Distributional status of the kangaroo rat, *Dipodomys elator.* J. Mamm., 58:873–877.

Maxell, M. H., and L. N. Brown. 1968. Ecological distribution of rodents on the High Plains of eastern Wyoming. Southwestern Nat., 13:143–158.

Mead, R. A. 1968. Reproduction in western forms of the spotted skunk (genus *Spilogale*). J. Mamm., 49:373–390.

Mech, L. D. 1974. Canis lupus. Mamm. Species, 37:1–6.

Merritt, J. F. 1981. Clethrionomys gapperi. Mamm. Species, 146:1–9.

Michener, G. R. 1979. The circannual cycle of Richardson's ground squirrel in southern Alberta. J. Mamm., 60:760–768.

_____. 1980. Estrous and gestation periods in Richardson's ground squirrels. J. Mamm., 61:531–534.

Michener, G. R., and D. R. Michener. 1977. Population structure and dispersal in Richardson's ground squirrels. Ecology, 58:359–368.

Miller, D. F., and L. L. Getz. 1969. Botfly infections in a population of Peromyscus leucopus. J. Mamm., 50:277–283.

Moncrief, N. D., J. R. Choate, and H. H. Genoways. 1982. Morphometric and geographic relationships of short-tailed shrews (genus Blarina) in Kansas, Iowa, and Missouri. Ann. Carnegie Mus., 51:157–180.

Moore, J. C. 1957. The natural history of the fox squirrel, Sciurus niger shermani. Bull. Amer. Mus. Nat. Hist., 113:1–72.

Moulton, M. P., J. R. Choate, and S. J. Bissell. 1983. Biogeographic relationships of pocket gophers in southeastern Colorado. Southwestern Nat., 28:53–60.

Moulton, M. P., J. R. Choate, S. J. Bissell, and R. A. Nicholson. 1981. Associations of small mammals on the central High Plains of eastern Colorado. Southwestern Nat., 26:53–57.

Mumford, R. E., and J. O. Whitaker, Jr. 1982. Mammals of Indiana. Univ. Indiana Press, Bloomington, xvii + 537 pp.

Murie, A. 1961. Some food habits of the marten. J. Mamm., 42:516–521.

Murie, J. O. 1973. Population characteristics and phenology of a Franklin ground squirrel (Spermophilus franklinii) colony in Alberta, Canada. Amer. Midland Nat., 90:334–340.

Murie, O. J. 1951. The elk of North America. The Stackpole Co., Harrisburg, Pennsylvania, and Wildlife Manag. Inst., Washington, D.C. (10) + 376 pp.

Myers, P., and L. L. Master. 1983. Reproduction by Peromyscus maniculatus: size and compromise. J. Mamm., 64:1–18.

Nadler, C. F., R. S. Hoffmann, J. H. Honacki, and D. Pozin. 1977. Chromosomal evolution of chipmunks, with special emphasis on A and B karyotypes of the subgenus Neotamias. Amer. Midland Nat., 98:343–353.

Nellis, C. H., S. P. Wetmore, and L. B. Keith. 1972. Lynx-prey interactions in central Alberta. J. Wildlife Manag., 36:320–329.

O'Farrell, M. J., and E. H. Studier. 1980. Myotis thysanodes. Mamm. Species, 137:1–5.

O'Gara, B. W. 1978. Antilocapra americana. Mamm. Species, 90:1–7.

Olsen, R. W. 1973. Shelter-site selection in the white-throated woodrat, Neotoma albigula. J. Mamm., 54:594–610.

Packard, R. L. 1956. The tree squirrels of Kansas. Misc. Publ. Mus. Nat. Hist., Univ. Kansas, 11:1–67.

_____. 1969. Taxonomic review of the golden mouse, Ochrotomys nuttalli. Misc. Publ. Mus. Nat. Hist., Univ. Kansas, 51:373–406.

Packard, R. L., and J. D. Roberts. 1973. Observations on the behavior of the Texas kangaroo rat, Dipodomys elator Merriam. Mammalia, 37:680–682.

Paradiso, J. L., and R. M. Nowak. 1972. Canis rufus. Mamm. Species, 22:1–4.

Pearson, O. P. 1944. Reproduction in the shrew (*Blarina brevicauda* Say). Amer. J. Anat. 75:39–93.

_____. 1945. Longevity of the short-tailed shrew. Amer. Midland Nat., 34:531–546.

Pefaur, J. E., and R. S. Hoffmann. 1974. Notes on the biology of the olive-backed pocket mouse *Perognathus fasciatus* on the Northern Great Plains. Prairie Nat., 6:7–15.

_____. 1975. Studies of small mammal populations at three sites on the Northern Great Plains. Occas. Papers Mus. Nat. Hist., Univ. Kansas, 37:1–27.

Pelton, M. R. 1982. Black bear. Pp. 504–514, *in* Wild mammals of North America: biology, management, and economics (J. A. Chapman and G. A. Feldhamer, eds.), Johns Hopkins Univ. Press, Baltimore, xiii + 1147 pp.

Phillips, G. L. 1966. Ecology of the big brown bat (Chiroptera: Vespertilionidae) in northeastern Kansas. Amer. Midland Nat., 75:168–198.

Pils, C. M., and M. A. Martin. 1978. Population dynamics, predator-prey relationships and management of the red fox in Wisconsin. Tech. Bull. Wisconsin Dept. Nat. Res., 105:1–56.

Powell, R. A. 1981. Martes pennanti. Mamm. Species, 156:1–6.

_____. 1982. The fisher: life history, ecology, and behavior. Univ. Minnesota Press, Minneapolis, xvi + 219 pp.

Randall, J. A. 1978. Behavioral mechanisms of habitat segregation between sympatric species of *Microtus:* habitat preference and interspecific dominance. Behav. Ecol. Sociobiol., 3:187–202.

Rausch, R., and A. M. Pearson. 1972. Notes on the wolverine in Alaska and the Yukon Territory. J. Wildlife Manag., 36:249–268.

Reich, L. M. 1981. Microtus pennsylvanicus. Mamm. Species, 159:1–8.

Rideout, C. B. 1978. Mountain goat. Pp. 149–159, *in* Big game of North America (J. L. Schmidt and D. L. Gilbert, eds.), Stackpole Books, Harrisburg, Pennsylvania, xv + 494 pp.

Rideout, C. B., and R. S. Hoffmann. 1975. Oreamnos americanus. Mamm. Species, 63:1–6.

Robbins, L. W., M. D. Engstrom, R. B. Wilhelm, and J. R. Choate. 1977. Ecogeographic status of *Myotis leibii* in Kansas. Mammalia, 41:365–367.

Roberts, J. D., and R. L. Packard. 1973. Comments on movement, home range and ecology of the Texas kangaroo rat, *Dipodomys elator* Merriam. J. Mamm., 54:957–962.

Roe, F. G. 1970. The North American buffalo, a critical study of the species in its wild state. Univ. Toronto Press, xi + 991 pp.

Rusch, D. A., and W. G. Reeder. 1978. Population ecology of Alberta red squirrels. Ecology, 59:400–420.

Russell, R. J. 1968. Revision of pocket gophers of the genus Pappogeomys. Univ. Kansas Publ., Mus. Nat. Hist., 16:581–776.

Scheck, S. H., and E. D. Fleharty. 1979. Daily energy budgets and patterns of activity of the adult thirteen-lined ground squirrel, Spermophilus tridecemlineatus. Physiol. Zool., 52:390–397.

Schmidly, D. J. 1974a. Peromyscus attwateri. Mamm. Species, 48:1–3.

――――. 1974b. Peromyscus pectoralis. Mamm. Species, 49:1–3.

――――. 1977. The mammals of Trans-Pecos Texas. Texas A&M Univ. Press, College Station, xiv + 225 pp.

――――. 1983. Texas mammals east of the Balcones Fault Zone. Texas A&M Univ. Press, College Station, xviii + 400 pp.

Schmidt-Nielsen, K., and B. Schmidt-Nielsen. 1952. Water metabolism of desert mammals. Physiol. Rev., 32:135–166.

Schoonmaker, W. J. 1968. The world of the grizzly bear. J. B. Lippincott Co., Philadelphia, 190 pp.

Schwartz, C. W., and E. R. Schwartz. 1981. The wild mammals of Missouri. Univ. Missouri Press and Missouri Dept. Conserv., Columbia, revised ed., viii + 356 pp.

Sealander, J. A. 1979. A guide to Arkansas mammals. River Road Press, Conway, Arkansas, x + 313 pp.

Setzer, H. W. 1949. Subspeciation in the kangaroo rat, Dipodomys ordii. Univ. Kansas Publ., Mus. Nat. Hist., 1:473–573.

Severinghaus, W. D. 1977. Description of a new subspecies of prairie vole, Microtus ochrogaster. Proc. Biol. Soc. Washington, 90:49–54.

Sexson, M. L., and J. R. Choate. 1981. Historical biogeography of the pronghorn in Kansas. Trans. Kansas Acad. Sci., 84:128–133.

Sexson, M. L., J. R. Choate, and R. A. Nicholson. 1981. Diet of pronghorn in western Kansas. J. Range Manag., 34:489–493.

Sheppard, D. H. 1972. Home ranges of chipmunks (Eutamias) in Alberta. J. Mamm., 53:379–380.

Shump, K. A., Jr., and A. U. Shump. 1982a. Lasiurus borealis. Mamm. Species, 183:1–6.

――――. 1982b. Lasiurus cinereus. Mamm. Species, 185:1–5.

Skoog, R. O. 1968. Ecology of the caribou (Rangifer tarandus granti) in Alaska. Unpublished Ph.D. dissertation, Univ. California, Berkeley, 699 pp.

Skryja, D. D. 1974. Reproductive biology of the least chipmunk (Eutamias minimus operarius) in southeastern Wyoming. J. Mamm., 55:221–224.

Smith, C. C. 1968. The adaptive nature of social organization in the genus of tree squirrels Tamiasciurus. Ecol. Monogr., 38:31–63.

――――. 1970. The coevolution of pine squirrels (Tamiasciurus) and conifers. Ecol. Monogr., 40:349–371.

Smith, R. E. 1967. Natural history of the prairie dog in Kansas. Misc. Publ. Mus. Nat. Hist., Univ. Kansas, 49:1–39.

Smolen, M. J. 1981. Microtus pinetorum. Mamm. Species, 147:1–7.

Smolen, M. J., H. H. Genoways, and R. J. Baker. 1980. Demographic and reproductive parameters of the yellow-faced pocket gopher (Pappogeomys castanops). J. Mamm., 61:224–236.

Snyder, D. P. 1982. Tamias striatus. Mamm. Species, 168:1–8.

Soper, J. D. 1961. The mammals of Manitoba. Canadian Field-Nat., 75:171–219.

Sorenson, M. W. 1962. Some aspects of water shrew behavior. Amer. Midland Nat., 68:445–462.

Spencer, S. R., and G. N. Cameron. 1982. Reithrodontomys fulvescens. Mamm. Species, 174:1–7.

Stanley, W. C. 1963. Habits of the red fox in northeastern Kansas. Misc. Publ. Mus. Nat. Hist., Univ. Kansas, 34:1–31.

Steiner, A. L. 1975. Bedding and nesting material gathering in rock squirrels, *Spermophilus (Otospermophilus) variegatus grammurus* (Say) (Sciuridae) in the Chiricahua Mountains in Arizona. Southwestern Nat., 20:363–370.

Storm, G. L. 1972. Daytime retreats and movements of skunks on farmlands in Illinois. J. Wildlife Manag., 36:31–45.

Streeter, R. G., and C. E. Braun. 1968. Occurrence of pine marten, *Martes americana*, (Carnivora: Mustelidae) in Colorado alpine areas. Southwestern Nat., 13:449–451.

Streubel, D. P., and J. P. Fitzgerald. 1978a. Spermophilus spilosoma. Mamm. Species, 101:1–4.

———. 1978b. Spermophilus tridecemlineatus. Mamm. Species, 103:1–5.

Swenk, M. H. 1908. A preliminary review of the mammals of Nebraska, with synopses. Proc. Nebraska Acad. Sci., 8:61–144.

Taylor, W. P. (ed.). 1956. The deer of North America . . . . The Stackpole Co., Harrisburg, Pennsylvania, and Wildlife Manag. Inst., Washington, D.C., xvii + 922 pp.

Thomson, C. E. 1982. Myotis sodalis. Mamm. Species, 163:1–5.

Tiemeier, O. W., M. F. Hansen, M. H. Bartel, E. T. Lyon, B. M. El-Rawi, K. J. McMahon, and E. H. Herrick. 1965. The black-tailed jackrabbit in Kansas. Tech. Bull. Kansas Agric. Exper. Sta., 140:1–75.

Toll, J. E., T. S. Baskett, and C. H. Conaway. 1960. Home range, reproduction, and foods of the swamp rabbit in Missouri. Amer. Midland Nat., 63:398–412.

Trapp, G. R. 1972. Some anatomical and behavioral adaptations of ringtails, *Bassariscus astutus*. J. Mamm., 53:549–557.

Turner, B. N., S. L. Iverson, and K. L. Severson. 1976. Postnatal growth and development of captive Franklin's ground squirrels (Spermophilus franklinii). Amer. Midland Nat., 95:93–102.

Turner, R. W. 1974. Mammals of the Black Hills of South Dakota and Wyoming. Misc. Publ. Mus. Nat. Hist., Univ. Kansas, 60:1–178.

Turner, R. W., and J. B. Bowles. 1967. Comments on reproduction and food habits of the olive-backed pocket mouse in western North Dakota. Trans. Kansas Acad. Sci., 70:266–267.

Tuttle, M. D. 1975. Population ecology of the gray bat (*Myotis grisescens*): factors influencing early growth and development. Occas. Papers Mus. Nat. Hist., Univ. Kansas, 36:1–24.

———. 1976a. Population ecology of the gray bat (*Myotis grisescens*): philopatry, timing and patterns of movement, weight loss during migration, and seasonal adaptive strategies. Occas. Papers Mus. Nat. Hist., Univ. Kansas, 54:1–38.

———. 1976b. Population ecology of the gray bat (*Myotis grisescens*): factors influencing growth and survival of newly volant young. Ecology, 57:587–595.

———. 1979. Status, causes of decline, and management of endangered gray bats. J. Wildlife Manag., 43:1–17.

Tuttle, M. D., and D. E. Stevenson. 1977. An analysis of migration as a mortality factor in the gray bat based on public recoveries of banded bats. Amer. Midland Nat., 97:235–240.

Uhlig, H. G. 1955. The gray squirrel, its life history, ecology and population characteristics in West Virginia. West Virginia Conserv. Comm., P.-R. Proj. Rept., 31–R:1–175.

U.S. Forest Service. 1978. Ecosystems of the United States, RARE II, Map B, 1:7,500,000.

Van Gelder, R. G. 1959. A taxonomic revision of the spotted skunks (genus *Spilogale*). Bull. Amer. Mus. Nat. Hist., 117:229–392.

Van Wormer, J. 1966. The world of the black bear. J. B. Lippincott Co., Philadelphia, 163 pp.

van Zyll de Jong, C. G. 1972. A systematic review of the Nearctic and Neotropical river otters (genus *Lutra*, Mustelidae, Carnivora). Life Sci. Contrib., Royal Ontario Mus., 80:1–104.

———. 1976. A comparison between woodland and tundra forms of the common shrew (*Sorex cinereus*). Canadian J. Zool., 54:963–973.

———. 1980. Systematic relationships of woodland and prairie forms of the common shrew, *Sorex cinereus cinereus* Kerr and *S. c. haydeni* Baird, in the Canadian prairie provinces. J. Mamm., 61:66–75.

———. 1983. Handbook of Canadian mammals. 1. Marsupials and insectivores. Nat. Mus. Canada, Ottawa, 210 pp.

Varland, K. L., A. L. Lovaas, and R. B. Dahlgren. 1978. Herd organization and movements of elk in Wind Cave National Park, South Dakota. U.S. Natl. Park Serv. Res. Rep., 13:ii + 1–28.

Vaughan, T. A. 1967. Food habits of the northern pocket gopher on shortgrass prairie. Amer. Midland Nat., 77:176–189.

Vorhies, C. T., and W. P. Taylor. 1933. The life histories and ecology of the jack rabbits, *Lepus alleni* and *Lepus californicus* ssp. in relation to grazing in Arizona. Tech. Bull. Univ. Arizona Exper. Sta., 49:471–587.

Wade-Smith, J., and B. J. Verts. 1982. Mephitis mephitis. Mamm. Species, 173:1–7.

Wallmo, O. C. (ed.). 1981. Mule and black-tailed deer of North America. Wildlife Manag. Inst. and Univ. Nebraska Press, Lincoln, xvii + 605 pp.

Warner, R. M., and N. J. Czaplewski. 1984. Myotis volans. Mamm. Species, 224:1–4.

Watkins, L. C. 1972. Nycticeius humeralis. Mamm. Species, 23:1–4.

Webster, W. D., and J. K. Jones, Jr. 1982. Reithrodontomys megalotis. Mamm. Species, 167:1–5.

Weckwerth, R. P., and V. D. Hawley. 1962. Marten food habits and population fluctuations in Montana. J. Wildlife Manag., 26:55–74.

Weigl, P. D. 1978. Resource overlap, interspecific interactions, and the distribution of the flying squirrels, Glaucomys volans and G. sabrinus. Amer. Midland Nat., 100:83–96.

Wetzel, R. M. 1955. Speciation and dispersal of the southern bog lemming, *Synaptomys cooperi* (Baird). J. Mamm., 36:1–20.

Whitaker, J. O., Jr. 1972. Zapus hudsonius. Mamm. Species, 11:1–7.
———. 1974. Cryptotis parva. Mamm. Species, 43:1–8.
Wiehe, J. M., and J. F. Cassel. 1978. Checklist of North Dakota mammals (revised). Prairie Nat., 10:81–88.
Wiley, R. W. 1980. Neotoma floridana. Mamm. Species, 139:1–7.
Wilks, B. J. 1963. Some aspects of the ecology and population dynamics of the pocket gopher (Geomys bursarius) in southern Texas. Texas J. Sci., 15:241–283.
Willey, R. B., and R. E. Richards. 1981. Vocalizations of the ringtail (Bassariscus astutus). Southwestern Nat., 26:23–30.
Williams, D. F. 1978. Karyological affinities of the species groups of silky pocket mice (Rodentia, Heteromyidae). J. Mamm., 59:599–612.
Williams, D. F., and H. H. Genoways. 1979. A systematic review of the olive-backed pocket mouse, Perognathus fasciatus (Rodentia, Heteromyidae). Ann. Carnegie Mus., 48:73–102.
Willner, G. R., G. A. Feldhamer, E. E. Zucker, and J. A. Chapman. 1980. Ondatra zibethicus. Mamm. Species, 141:1–8.
Wilson, D. E. 1982. Wolverine. Pp. 644–652, in Wild Mammals of North America: biology, management, and economics (J. A. Chapman and G. A. Feldhamer, eds.), Johns Hopkins Univ. Press, Baltimore, xxii + 1147 pp.
Wishart, W. 1978. Bighorn sheep. Pp. 161–171, in Big game of North America (J. L. Schmidt and D. L. Gilbert, eds.), Stackpole Books, Harrisburg, Pennsylvania, xv + 494 pp.
Wolfe, J. L. 1982. Oryzomys palustris. Mamm. Species, 176:1–5.
Wolfe, J. L., and A. V. Linzey. 1977. Peromyscus gossypinus. Mamm. Species, 70:1–5.
Wood, J. E. 1949. Reproductive pattern of the pocket gopher (Geomys breviceps brazensis). J. Mamm., 30:36–44.
Woods, C. A. 1973. Erethizon dorsatum. Mamm. Species, 29:1–6.
Wright, P. L., and R. Rausch. 1955. Reproduction in the wolverine, Gulo gulo. J. Mamm., 36:346–355.
Yates, T. L., and D. J. Schmidly. 1978. Scalopus aquaticus. Mamm. Species, 105:1–4.
Young, S. P. 1944. Their history, habits, economic status, and control. Pp. 1–385, in S. P. Young and E. A. Goldman, The wolves of North America. Amer. Wildlife Inst., Washington, D.C., xx + 636 pp.
———. 1958. The bobcat of North America, its history, life habits, economic status, and control, with list of currently recognized subspecies. The Stackpole Co., Harrisburg, Pennsylvania, and Wildlife Manag. Inst., Washington, D.C., xi + 193 pp.
Young, S. P., and E. A. Goldman. 1946. The puma, mysterious American cat. Amer. Wildlife Inst., Washington, D.C., xiv + 358 pp.
Zegers, D. A. 1984. Spermophilus elegans. Mamm. Species, 214:1–7.

Index to Scientific and Vernacular Names